Colección Támesis

SERIE A: MONOGRAFÍAS, 207

A COMPANION TO LATIN AMERICAN FILM

Latin American cinema has seen major developments in the past half-century, to a level where some of the most exciting work in contemporary film now originates there – most recently *And your Mother Too* (2001) and *City of God* (2002). This *Companion* begins with a history of Latin American cinema from its beginnings in the mid-1890s to the present day, with particular attention to the early period when it was dominated by foreign film makers (or foreign models such as Hollywood) and to the 1960s when as a genre it found its feet – the New Latin American Cinema movement. Detailed analysis of the best twenty-five films of Latin America follows, each one covered in depth: cast and crew, awards, plots, themes and techniques. The Guide to Further Reading includes all the important books, articles and Internet sites.

STEPHEN M. HART is Professor of Hispanic Studies, University College London and Profesor Honoris Causa of The Universidad Nacional Mayor de San Marcos, Lima, Peru.

A COMPANION TO
LATIN AMERICAN FILM

Stephen M. Hart

TAMESIS

First published 2004
by Tamesis, Woodbridge
Paperback edition 2010

Transferred to digital printing

ISBN 978-1-85566-106-6 hardback
ISBN 978-1-85566-210-0 paperback

Tamesis is an imprint of Boydell & Brewer Ltd
PO Box 9, Woodbridge, Suffolk IP12 3DF, UK
and of Boydell & Brewer Inc.
668 Mt Hope Avenue, Rochester, NY 14620, USA
website: www.boydellandbrewer.com

A CiP catalogue record for this book is available
from the British Library

This publication is printed on acid-free paper

CONTENTS

PLATES

We are grateful to the following for permission to reproduce illustrations in this book: Sr. Jorge Sanjinés (plate 1), Bolivian Film Institute (plate 2); the Cuban Film Institute and Sr. Julio García Espinosa (plate 6), and Optimum Releasing (plate 9). Every attempt has been made to contact copyright holders and any acknowledgement not listed here will be rectified in subsequent editions. The author would also like to record his thanks to the British Film Institute for providing the original stills.

PROLOGUE: COMPANION TO LATIN AMERICAN FILM

This companion to Latin American film seeks to provide an introduction to the development of Latin American film over the last seventy years via an analysis of the most salient examples of the genre. For this reason, twenty-five films have been chosen, and in each case, some background information about the film – including cast and crew, as well as the basics of the plot – has been provided before the analysis of a discrete set of ideas, themes, and devices is provided. The pattern is similar in each case, although not uniformly so. Some essays focus more on camerawork than others, some treat literary sources while others do not; in each case it is hoped that the essay is tailored to cover the most significant aspects of the film under consideration.

The book is intended for all those interested in Latin American cinema but is particularly suitable for Spanish majors at U.S. universities taking introductory courses (300–400-level), and for first-year university students majoring in Spanish in the UK. A guide to further reading is provided as well as a glossary to explain some of the more technical terms which are used. The emphasis throughout has been on clarity of exposition and, for this reason, footnotes have not been introduced.

The list of films studied is, of course, not exhaustive and, for reasons of space, some important films have not been included. The idea behind the selection was to stress the varying genres that Latin American film has explored, ranging from the political-ethnographic (*Qué viva México*, *Los olvidados*), to the documentary (*El chacal de Nahueltoro*, *La batalla de Chile*), and the serious social commentary film (*Pixote*). Latin American film has produced playful, light-hearted blockbusters (*Como agua para chocolate*, *Y tu mamá también*) and serious social-commentary type blockbusters (*Cidade de Deus*). It has produced films which treat issues such as slave rights (*La última cena*) women's rights (*Lucía*, *Camila*), gay rights (*Fresa y chocolate*) and lesbian rights (*Yo, la peor de todas*). Lastly, in order to stress the osmotic nature of Latin American film – which is not as reducible as Hollywood film to a list of the greats – some account has been taken of films which were born from that interplay between film and other media, in this case, the film industry and TV (*Cartas del parque*, *La tarea*).

This book has benefited from conversations with a number of experts, including Jorge Sanjinés, Beatriz Palacios, Julio García Espinosa, Octavio Cortázar, Paul Julian Smith, John Beverley, John King, Robert Stam, Efraín Kristal, Jason Wilson, Robin Fiddian, Andrea Noble, John Kraniauskas, Ann Cross, Gwynne Edwards, Peter Evans, and Vladimir Smith. I express my gratitude to them and also to David Henn for all the press cuttings. The above cannot be blamed, of course, for any errors in the manuscript which I claim as my own.

Half of the proceeds of the royalties from this book will be donated to the Hogar Clínica San Juan de Dios in Lima Peru.

For Natasha, Matthew, Christian and Jordan

INTRODUCTION TO LATIN AMERICAN FILM

Latin American film has developed in a unique way over the past one hundred years. The *cinématographe* – an early moving image projector to which we owe the word 'cinema' itself – was given its first commercial demonstration by two brothers, Auguste and Louis Lumière in the Grand Café, Paris, on 28 December 1895. Given its portability – it weighed less than 20 pounds – the Lumière brothers sent their cameramen around the world to give demonstrations of their new invention. In Rio de Janeiro, Brazil, the first screening of what was then called the 'Omnigrapho' took place on 8 July 1896 (Johnson and Stam, p. 19); the address was listed as 57, rua do Ouvidor (Hennebelle and Gumucio-Dagrón, p. 94). On 28 July 1896, the Lumière brothers' film, *L'arrivée d'un train* (Train Arriving at the Station) was screened in the Odeon Theatre in Buenos Aires (Hennebelle and Gumucio-Dagrón, p. 84). In Mexico City in August 1896 audiences were thrilled to see the first moving images projected onto a screen by the *cinématographe*; the cameraman was Gabriel Vayre, and the showing took place at the Cinematógrafo Lumière, no. 9, Plateros Avenue (Mora, p. 6). For many years the film industry developed in Latin America along the lines suggested by this mould – it was an offshoot of cultural and technological developments happening off-screen in Europe and – gradually more and more – in the United States. Film developed along two rather different tracks since its early inception in Europe; the Lumière brothers emphasised the need to capture the ordinary and the everyday, as suggested by their first reportage piece, *L'arrivée d'un train* (1895), while Georges Méliès strove to give filmic expression to the fantastic in his 30-scene, 15-minute narrative film *Le Voyage dans la lune* (Trip to the Moon, 1902) which was based on a novel by Jules Vernes, and was the first film to achieve international distribution. These two distinct film styles were at the heart of the language of film as it developed in the early twentieth century (although account must be taken of Jean-Luc Godard's important observation that these two poles were not as far apart as might at first be thought; see Lehman and Luhr, p. 249).

The earliest films produced in Latin America aspired to what might be called the Lumière blueprint. Yet, even though they focused on the discourse of the quotidian, this proved in some cases to be rather more gripping than a film about a train entering a station packed full of commuters. At precisely the time that cinematographers were going to Mexico to record live footage, for example, the country was racked with the trauma of the Revolution (1911–1919). One of the revolutionaries involved in the struggle, Pancho Villa, sensing that some money as well as fame could be made, signed a contract with Mutual Film Corporation for $25,000, giving in exchange permission for the battles he waged to be filmed and broadcast back in the United States (King, *Magical Reels*, p. 17). He even agreed – rather grotesquely – to have the ritual of his dawn executions filmed. As he promised the cameraman: 'Don't worry Don Raul. If you say the light at four in the morning is not right for your little machine, well, no problem. The executions will take place at six. But no later. Afterwards we march and fight. Understand?' (quoted in King, *Magical Reels*, p. 15).

Despite colourful exceptions such as Villa's brief foray into the world of celluloid, the films seen in Latin American movie theatres during the first two decades of the twentieth century – and they were restricted, in the main, to the large urban centres such as Mexico City, Buenos Aires, Rio de Janeiro and São Paolo – typically came from abroad. From the beginning, given the huge investment that a film industry requires in order to get off the ground, the countries of Latin America found it difficult to develop a national film industry. Up until World War I the film industry was dominated by French and Italian cinema. Charles Pathé, a phonograph importer, acquired the Lumière patent in 1902, set up a large production plant in Vincennes, and began to expand abroad, opening up production companies in Spain (Hispano Film, 1906), Russia, Italy, Britain and the United States. Thus, in 1914, Argentina imported ten times more European films than North-American films (King, *Magical Reels*, p. 10). But there were a number of factors which eventually provided decisive in giving the United States the competitive edge. The first was the viewing population. While there were only a handful of film theatres across the United States in 1904, by 1908, there were between 8,000 and 10,000, and, by 1910, the number of people going to the movies had risen to the staggering figure of 26,000,000 a week. The second reason was the creation of Hollywood. The film studio was set up on the outskirts of Los Angeles in 1911, and offered the perfect environment for the film industry to grow. Within a fifty-mile radius there were natural film sets featuring deserts, mountains, forest, sea coasts and islands; what is more, taxes were low, and there was a plentiful supply of cheap land and low-cost labour. By 1915 Hollywood employed 15,000 workers and was producing more than half of all the films released in the United States.

The third reason for the gradual dominance of the American film industry – and perhaps the main reason – was D.W. Griffiths, the Hollywood film director who, almost single-handedly, was instrumental in the creation of a new and instantly recognisable film style – classical Hollywood narrative style. Beginning his career as an actor in 1907, Griffiths graduated to film direction in which he excelled as the 'father of film technique'. An obsessive experimentalist, he exploited the dynamic combination of the three standard film shots – long shot, medium shot, and close-up – and he devised a new concept – parallel editing – as well as inventing what is now known as the tracking shot. His films – despite these innovations – did not appeal just to the connoisseur; his major epic, *The Birth of a Nation* (1915), for example, was seen by 3,000,000 viewers. Though classic Hollywood cinema grew out of Griffiths' techniques, it gradually evolved into a tried and tested formula for producing films. A few features of the Hollywood narrative style are worth noting here. First of all, in the typical Hollywood film the narrative is built around the triad of 'order/disorder/order restored' whereby the film begins with an event which disrupts a harmonious order which in turns leads to a series of events after which order is once more restored; the ending must be happy, or – if not – there must be closure, i.e. no unresolved subplots or loose ends. The typical Hollywood film encapsulates the notion of the 'American dream'; it separates the goodies from the baddies, and its underlying ideology – when not made explicit – is capitalist and Americanocentric. The filmic style should be invisible (i.e. not draw attention to itself) and will follow the code of continuity editing; match cuts and eyeline cuts are scrupulously observed. Given the high level of editorial – and indeed budgetary – control needed in order to create the illusion of seamless continuity, it was typical for Hollywood film directors to favour using studio sets whenever possible rather than on-location filming. Futhermore, since, in the typical Hollywood feature film, the plot is character-led, it also feeds off the star system which, from very early on, was part and parcel of the Hollywood formula: 'By the mid-1910s, the star system was taking hold and actors like Charlie Chaplin were making over a million dollars a year' (Lehman and Luhr, p. 150).

Another important early player in the evolution of film language was Soviet cinema. After the Russian Revolution, the VGIK (All Union State Institute of Cinematography) was set up, the first of its kind; in Lenin's often-quoted words, 'the cinema is for us the most important of the arts' (Leyda, pp. 121–54). The primary aim of the VGIK was to train people to produce *agitki* (agitprop), namely, the re-creation of existing newsreels for the purposes of propaganda (Leyda, pp. 134–7). These *agitki* were transplanted to the furthest reaches of the Soviet Union on trains and steamers, and the Cuban Film Institute – some forty years later – used some of these same ideas to propagandise its revolutionary message. Soviet cinema during its early phases was arguably one of the most innovative in the world; Sergei Eisenstein's *Strike* (1924), *Battleship Potemkin* (1925) and *October* (1928) were landmarks of silent film, and were forceful illustrations of Eisenstein's dynamic and revolutionary theories about montage, which he saw as conflictual and dialectical rather than seamless, as the contemporary Hollywood model required (Leyda, pp. 180–5; 194–200; 210–12). Eisenstein's cinema also had a specific impact on Latin American cinema via his classic – though unfinished – film about the Mexican Revolution (see chapter 1). Another Soviet film director, Dziga Vertov, evolved a theory of *kinoglaz* (cinema-eye) which he implemented in an extraordinarily vivid way in his documentary *Man with a Movie Camera* (1929), which showcases Moscow from dawn to dusk (Leyda, pp. 250–2), and which is acknowledged as the main inspiration of the *cinéma-vérité* of the 1960s and 1970s. This period of creativity, however, came to an abrupt end in the 1930s when Stalin forced Soviet film directors to toe the Party line; individual creativity was claimed to be subservient to the will of the People and the State, and the filmic language imposed by diktat was Socialist Realism, the so-called 'art of the people' which set out to glorify representative Soviet heroes in a naturalistic, 'real' setting. Eisenstein, for example, was brought into line, and the so-called errors of his early work were highlighted (Leyda, p. 299; see also pp. 318–40). A number of Latin American film directors looked back to the Soviet experience as an absorbing example of the thrills and perils of creating art with a political purpose – not only in Cuba (Gutiérrez Alea, Solás; chapters 5–6) but also in Bolivia (Sanjinés; chapter 8) and Chile (Guzmán; chapter 9).

The evolution of the U.S. film industry during the same period could not have been more different. From its shaky beginnings, it evolved into the most powerful player in world cinema by World War II. Thus, whereas the American film industry lagged behind European cinema up until World War I (1914–1918), it had caught up by the conclusion of the war. During World War I, the European film industry virtually closed down, not least because the same chemicals – that is, nitrates – used to produce film celluloid were also used to manufacture explosives and gun powder. A year after the conclusion of the war 90 per cent of all films screened in Europe were American, and the preeminence of the American film was not seriously challenged for the following forty years. In Latin America the figure was even higher; by 1920, about '95 per cent of screen time in South America was taken up by U.S. films' (King, *Magical Reels*, p. 11). The story had not changed a decade later; thus, in Argentina in 1930 there were about 1,000 small movie houses, with mainly North American films being shown (King, *Magical Reels*, p. 9). Such films as saw the light of day in Latin America were often poorly made, and looked inferior compared to European or North-American films of the same era, even though there were some successes, such as Enrique García Velloso's 1914 adaption of José Mármol's Romantic novel, *Amalia* (1851).

The dilemma faced by Latin American exhibitors often boiled down to finance. Robert Stam and Randall Johnson outline the contours of the problem in Brazil in the 1920s:

> Since local distributors lacked the infrastructural organization possessed by foreign distributors, the internal market began to function for the benefit of the industrial products from abroad. From that point on, when forced to choose between the guaranteed profit of inexpensive foreign films that covered costs easily in their home market, and the risks involved in dealing with the national product, exhibitors tended to opt for the foreign film. The Brazilian market became a tropical appendage of the North American market.
>
> (Stam and Johnson, p. 22)

While there were examples of home-spun films in various parts of Latin America, the Brazilian experience as described above was the typical pattern. As Jorge Schnitman points out: 'While the U.S. had the technical, financial and market size conditions to allow for innovation in its production, distribution and exhibition aspects, Latin American dependent capitalism could only develop its distribution and exhibition aspects on the basis of foreign films, to the detriment of local production' (Schnitman, p. 19).

Furthermore, if home-grown films were to be made, the only safe route – it appeared – was to make a film which echoed a foreign model – which meant it could achieve a larger audience eventually – and then add some home-grown ingredients. One of the best examples of this import-driven formula was the genre of the Mexican melodrama which dominated the scene from the mid-1930s until the early 1950s (see Mora, pp. 28–88); the Mexican film industry used the Hollywood notion of building a film around a star and a show and focused very much on the entertainment value of the film. The Hollywood musical, for example, which itself 'typically features musical and dance numbers woven around a backstage plot' (Johnson and Stam, p. 27), is characteristic of an era which was still focused on the movie as a record of a cultural event – such as a Broadway show – which could be presented to a still larger audience. The film was, in effect, still using the language of theatre in order to present its product to the larger world. The Mexican melodramas of the time followed the patent, simply substituting American songs with Mexican *rancheras*, popular songs about how good life was back on the ranch (see Ramírez Berg, pp. 98–100). *Allá en el Rancho Grande* (Back Home on the Big Ranch, 1936), for example, itself the prototype of the *comedia ranchera*, was seen at the time as a vehicle of the unique 'national colour' of Mexico (quoted in Mora, p. 45; see also pp. 46–8). During this period a number of stars were born, such as the beautiful Dolores del Río and the equally ravishing María Félix (see King, *Magical Reels*, pp. 48–50). Mexico began to assert its dominance in the internal Latin American market; whereas in 1939 it had only managed 39 films compared to Argentina's 50, by 1950 Mexico produced 125 films, more than twice more than Argentina's 56 (Hennebelle and Gumucio-Dagrón, p. 33). A typical example of this trend was *Dos tipos de cuidado* which is analysed in chapter 3 of this study.

In Brazil a similar phenomenon emerged, that of the *chanchada*, which was partially based on the Hollywood musical, dominating Brazilian film production from the 1930s until the 1950s (Hennebelle and Gumucio-Dagrón, pp. 130–1). Both the *comedia ranchera* and the *chanchada* can be seen as symptoms of a culture struggling to find its voice beneath the pressure of acculturation from without. It is clear that the Mexican melodramas and the Brazilian *chanchadas* – in that they were essentially re-vampings of the Hollywood idiom – led to commercial success but also to an artistic cul-de-sac. There were always going to be the poor cousins, and Mexican melodramas dried up, or rather they went underground in order to re-surface in a new mass medium, the TV, and specifically the *telenovelas* (soap operas) which captivated audiences around the world in the 1980s and 1990s, in the same way that the Brazilian *chanchada* re-emerged years later in the form of the rather racy *pornochanchada* (Hennebelle and Gumucio-Dagrón, pp. 156–7).

By the 1940s and 1950s, however, commercial film directors were attempting to develop a new language for film, seeking to present it as a new, unique art form. The roots of this artistic search can be traced back at least to the *cinéastes* of the 1920s, Soviet directors such as Sergei Eisenstein who wanted to create a new language for the moving image (and for this reason, Eisenstein was quite hostile to the advent of sound, since he saw it as a step backwards to the dependence on the language of the theatre), but it was only in the 1940s and 1950s that a critical mass of film directors all around the world emerged with the commonly felt desire to express a new social vision. Films began during this period to be taken seriously as an art form which could say something significant about the world, rather than being simply adjuncts to the world of popular entertainment. Unfortunately, by the time cinema became available as a new vehicle with which to express an artistic vision (and one, it should be added, which was proving to be tailor-made for the modern world), the means by which it could come into being – film studios, actors, film production, trained camera teams, and even in some cases a developed TV culture which could act as a safety-net, *inter alia* – was already being controlled from elsewhere. By the time the desire to use film as a way of earning a living (the bourgeoisie), or offering a new vision (the new artistic classes) emerged, it came with so many strings attached that it was almost impossible for Latin Americans to get on the band wagon. This is why the first stirrings of a national focus in Latin American cinema, or the emergence of a *cinéaste* tradition – paradoxically enough – came via foreigners, sympathetic foreigners it is true (such as Sergei Eisenstein the Russian, or Luis Buñuel the Spaniard, or Marcel Camus the Frenchman), but still foreigners. Despite the fact that they were not Latin American (in effect they were cultural ventriloquists), these film directors brought a breath of fresh air to the evolving tradition of Latin American cinema, and set down the foundation on which later *cinéastes* would build. That is why it is important to study their work; there are separate chapters in this book on Eisenstein's *¡Qué viva México!* (Long Live Mexico, 1932; chapter 1), Luis Buñuel's *Los olvidados* (The Young and the Damned, 1950; chapter 2) and Marcel Camus's *Orfeu negro* (Black Orpheus, 1959; chapter 4). These were, however, isolated examples of the eruption of European talent into the discourse of Latin American cinema, and they had little long-lasting impact. The lesson offered by Mexico is paradigmatic. Hennebelle and Gumucio-Dagrón put the point bluntly: 'le cinéma mexicain ne sut pas assimiler les vertus cardinales de l'oeuvre de Buñuel' (Hennebelle and Gumucio-Dagrón, p. 381). What was still needed was a critical mass, and this came in the form of two experimental film movements which would leave an indelible impact on Latin American film: Italian Neo-Realism and French New Wave.

After World War II Italian cinema developed a new cinematic style, Neo-Realism, which focused on the everyday reality of a country which had been decimated by the war (the Italian nation was one of the Axis power which lost the war, of course). Films were shot on location, and they therefore had a documentary feel about them, and were characterised by gritty realism, but – more importantly – non-professional actors were used. Important films of the movement were Roberto Rossellini's *Roma, città aperta* (Open City, 1945), Luchino Visconti's *La terra trema* (The Earth Trembles, 1945) and Vittorio De Sica's *Ladri di biciclette* (Bicycle Thieves, 1948). Following hard on the heels of Italian Neo-Realism was the French New Wave Movement. André Bazin crystallised the key concept of the movement when he coined, in 1948, the term *caméra-stylo* (camera-pen) to describe the role of the film director, who was seen more as a creative writer rather than a camera technician. Centred around the influential film review, *Cahiers du Cinéma*, founded in 1951, a new concept of the film director was born, christened *la politique des auteurs* (the policy of authors), according to which film was seen as a medium bearing the personal imprint, or signature, of the film director's worldview (Armes, pp. 175–82). 1959 was an important year for the movement; François Truffaut's *Les Quatre cents coups* (The Four Hundred Blows) and Alain Resnais's *Hiroshima, mon amour* (Hiroshima, my Love) came out, and Jean-Luc Godard's *À bout de souffle* (Breathless) was released the following year. Seemingly overnight, a new cinematic style had come into being; relying on location shooting with hand-held cameras, as well as elliptical editing favouring the long take and composition-in-depth, the French New Wave constituted a radical departure from contemporary Hollywood style.

Both Italian Neo-Realism and the French New Wave played a crucial role in the formulation of a new cinematic style in the work of Latin American film directors in the 1960s, for that was the decade in which Latin American film finally established its uniqueness and identity. It is arguable, though, whether these artistic experiments would have led to the formulation of a new cinematic movement were it not for the arrival in Latin America of a new political language, specifically that new political horizon which was provided by the Cuban Revolution. Régis Debray argued that the Cuban Revolution was, in effect, a 'revolution in the revolution' (Debray); as Robert Young has suggested, it brought about 'a fundamental break with the increasingly bankrupt role of bureaucratic communist parties controlled by Moscow and the achievement of a new form of socialism founded on the revolutionary agency of local people, in the first instance the peasantry rather than the urban proletariat (. . .) The Cuban Revolution showed that a different sort of revolution was possible' (Young, p. 209). As one of the ideologues of the Cuban Revolution, Che Guevara, suggested, Marxism was now to be seen as a political philosophy based on the human: 'It was love of man, of humanity, the desire to combat the distress of the proletariat, the desire to fight poverty, injustice, suffering, and all the exploitation of the proletariat, that gave rise to Marxism' (Guevara, p. 194).

The Cuban Revolution was, indeed, to have a far-reaching effect on the evolution of cinema in Latin America. Fidel Castro followed Lenin's line that cinema is 'the most important of the arts' (see above), and established the Instituto Cubano de Arte e Industria Cinematográficas. As a state-funded cultural institution it helped to formulate a new image of Latin American reality, one which was specifically not constrained by the ideological baggage of colonialism. The Cuban Film Institute brought together a number of key cultural figures, including Tomás Gutiérrez Alea, Humberto Solás and Julio García Espinosa. Following the Soviet model, it used documentaries to educate the masses, producing what was in effect transculturated agitprop, but it was also involved in promoting the Cuban film industry. Octavio Cortázar remembers how, in Imías, a small town in the South East of Cuba, in 1966, he saw a group of farm labourers, many of them on horseback, watching a Charlie Chaplin film in the 'transportable cinema' ('unidad de cine móvil') set up there, an event which persuaded him to make his own documentary, *Por primera vez* (Cortázar). García Espinosa, for his part, has described what the situation was like in pre-Revolutionary Cuba; the Hollywood film industry called the shots: 'If we wanted one of their hits they would force us to take nine other films of lower quality. The glossy-produced films with big budgets were always put in the best cinemas, so Latin films screened in the less well-kept theatres. The public therefore assumed their own films were inherently inferior' (Payne, p. 10). After the Revolution, however, García Espinosa and his colleagues informed the Hollywood studios that they would be showing more Latin American and Cuban films than previously: 'The studios said that we were forcing films on the public that they didn't want to see and that cinema attendance would fall. This didn't happen. Attendances stayed the same. We broke the myth' (Payne, p. 10).

The 1960s, indeed, were characterised by a radical cultural transfusion which took place all over Latin America and not just in Cuba. The Argentine Fernando Birri – as well as the Cubans Gutiérrez Alea and García Espinosa – went to study at the Centre for Experimental Cinematography in Rome, where they received an ideological drenching in Neo-Realism. In Brazil a group of young film directors and theorists coalesced around a journal, *Metropolitano*, which was modelled on Bazin's *Cahiers du Cinéma*. Indeed, one of the first signs of the dawn of a truly independent Latin American cinema emerged in Brazil in the early 1960s in the form of its so-called *cinema novo* (New Cinema). Brazilian 'New Cinema' drew inspiration from Italian Neo-Realism and the French New Wave. Low-budget, independent films were shot on location with non-professional actors in an attempt to encapsulate a new authentically Brazilian *politique des auteurs* which pointedly flew in the face of the *chanchada*, memorably dismissed by Glauber Rocha as 'Public Enemy No. 1' (Hennebelle and Gumucio-Dagrón, p. 145). Films such as *Ganga Zumba* (1963) by Carlos Diegues, *Deus e o Diabo na Terra do Sol* (Black God, White Devil, 1964) and *Terra em Transe* (Land in Anguish, 1967) by Glauber Rocha, *Os Fuzis* (The Guns, 1964) by Rui Guerra, and *Vidas Secas* (Barren Lives, 1963) and *Fome de Amor* (Hunger for Love, 1968) by Nelson Pereira dos Santos, were recognised as independent, autochthonous versions of Latin American reality. Though initially inspired by contemporary European films, *cinema novo* had more of a political edge for, as Diegues scornfully observed: 'We were making political films when the New Wave was still talking about unrequited love' (quoted in Johnson and Stam, p. 33). Perhaps just as important the film directors were keen to theorise about what they were doing; Diegues, Rocha, and Pereira dos Santos were, in effect, producing metafilm just as much as film (for a good selection of their theoretical writings, see Johnson and Stam, pp. 58–103). Rocha's famous phrase – 'uma idéia na cabeça e uma câmera na mão' (an idea in your head and a camera in your hand) – became almost a leitmotif of the times.

With hindsight it is now clear that the various film festivals organised in the late 1960s were crucial to a sense of Latin American cultural identity being formed, beginning with the Viña del Mar, Chile, festival held in 1967, followed by the festival in Mérida, Venezuela, in 1968, and then back again in Viña del Mar in 1969. At the time these were new venues for Latin American film directors to present their work, and they encouraged other budding film directors to try their luck. It soon became clear that Latin American film directors had something new to say, something which was intrinsic to their culture, which was recognised as different by Europeans, and – much more importantly – was understood by Latin Americans as expressing something intrinsically different about the way life was lived in the southern continent of the Americas. In Cuba both Gutiérrez Alea's *Memorias del subdesarrollo* (Memories of Underdevelopment; see below chapter 5) and Humberto Solás's film, *Lucía* (chapter 6), which came out in the same year (1968), moulded a new revolutionary language which turned against Hollywood, drew inspiration from Italian Neo-Realism and French New Wave, but in the event produced a more politicised, ideologically-laden version of reality. Pointing in a similar political direction was Jorge Sanjinés's *Yawar Mallku* (Blood of the Condor, 1969; chapter 8). During the 1970s the vogue of the documentary grew in intensity, and it came to be identified with an unmistakable left-wing message. Patricio Guzmán's *La batalla de Chile* (The Battle of Chile, 1973; chapter 9) was a landmark of the fresh documentary style of its decade, and was an international hit at European film festivals and the non-commercial film circuits.

It was during the 1960s that a new radical theory of film emerged in Latin America, one which we would nowadays call postcolonial. In his essay, 'Cinema and Underdevelopment', Fernando Birri, the Argentine film maker, argued that underdevelopment is an intrinsic part of the fabric of Latin American culture, that it is caused by colonialism and that – up until then, namely, the 1960s – cinema inevitably shared the characteristics of this superstructure ('it presents us with a false image of both society, and our people'; Birri, p. 12). Birri therefore called for a new type of documentary which would reverse this representational paradigm: 'it shows matters as they irrefutably are, and not as we would like them to be (or as, in good or bad faith, others would like to make us believe them to be)' (Birri, p. 12). The Brazilian film director, Glauber Rocha, in a powerful essay, 'The Aesthetics of Hunger', argued from a similar postcolonial viewpoint ('Latin America remains a colony'; Rocha, p. 13) to propose that Latin America is therefore characterised by 'philosophical undernourishment' and 'impotence'. As Rocha went on to suggest:

> It is for this reason that hunger is Latin America is not simply an alarming symptom; it is the essence of our society. Herein lies the tragic originality of Cinema Novo is relation to world cinema. Our originality is our hunger and our greatest misery is that this hunger is felt but not intellectually understood.
> (Rocha, p. 13)

For their part, Fernando Solanas and Octavio Getino, in an important manifesto, 'Towards a Third Cinema', advocated a new cinema which threw off the shackles of colonial oppression in ideological as well as industrial terms and, in the process, they became important spokesmen for anti-colonialist film directors all around the world and not just in Latin America: 'The anti-imperialist struggle of the peoples of the Third World and of their equivalents inside the imperialist countries constitutes today the axis of the world revolution. *Third cinema* is, in our opinion, the cinema that *recognises in that struggle the most gigantic cultural, scientific, and artistic manifestation of our time*, the great possibility of constructing a liberated personality with each people as the starting point – in a word, the *decolonisation of culture*' (authors' emphasis; Solanas and Getino, p. 18).

A more vivid catchword, perhaps, than 'third cinema' was 'imperfect cinema', a term coined by the Cuban film director, Julio García Espinosa. In a wide-ranging essay, 'For an Imperfect Cinema', García Espinosa contrasted the gritty, more realist cinema emerging from Cuba with the slick, commercially effective but ideologically barren film coming out of Hollywood:

> Imperfect cinema is no longer interested in quality or technique. It can be created equally well with a Mitchell or with an 8 mm camera, in a studio or in a guerrilla camp in the middle of the jungle. Imperfect cinema is no longer interested in predetermined taste, and much less in 'good taste'. It is not quality which it seeks in an artist's work. The only thing it is interested in is how an artist responds to the following question: What are you doing in order to overcome the barrier of the 'cultured' elite audience which up to now has conditioned the form of your work? (García Espinosa, p. 33)

Just as radical was the theoretical position taken up by Jorge Sanjinés. In a concise and punchy essay, 'Problems of Form and Content in Revolutionary Cinema', the Bolivian film director rejected the ideology and content of imperialism and advocated a cinema which was revolutionary, collective and people-centred: 'revolutionary cinema, as it reaches maturity, can only be collective, just as the Revolution itself is collective' (p. 34). Latin American Film gradually began to play a central role in the evolution of a new concept of Third World Film during the 1960s and 1970s (Mestman).

But there were drawbacks in the single-minded search for an ideology-laden language with which to record reality in which Latin American film directors were involved. It was clear, for example, that – in creating a politicised image – Latin American cinema was typecasting itself into a ghetto of Third World cinema, an image which it would with some difficulty cast off. Indeed, part of the strength of their vision was grounded in their direct connection to concrete political realities. It was still – it seemed – gritty realism that the audience wanted from Latin American cinema. But this audience was European and (often) middle-class. In other words, the Latin American film directors of the 1960s and 1970s – *cinéastes* such as Jorge Sanjinés, Fernando Birri and Patricio Guzmán – were producing films which were making waves in European film festivals but – in direct contradistinction to the Hollywood blockbuster – were not 'popular' in the sense of attracting large audiences in Latin America. They had a cultural role which was similar to that played by poetry rather than the best seller Boom novel. The cultural transfusion of the 1950s (via Italian Neo-Realism and French New Wave) which had led to a series of independent, anti-Hollywood and artsy-style films in Latin America from the 1960s until the 1980s had led to a rather curious situation in which film directors in Latin America were producing intellectually innovative films imbued with a postcolonial ideology which were making waves, but not necessarily at home. John King has drawn attention to the paradox underlying viewer response to Latin American cinema during this period:

> Third cinema was taken from its historical moment, the revolutionary optimism of the late 1960s and early 1970s, and began to act as a template against which other films should be judged, and also serve as a definition of what Latin American cinema should be. The fact that 99 per cent of cinema production in Latin American did not adhere to the strict tenets of third cinema did not seem to be of great critical concern.
>
> (King, 'Stars: Mapping the Firmament', pp. 143–4)

For throughout this period – indeed right up until the early 1990s – cinema audiences in Latin America, apart from a specialised minority, were still regularly going to the movies to see the latest Hollywood blockbuster (as I discovered when visiting Mexico City in the summer of 1992). Beatriz Sarlo has alluded to the catch-22 nature of the situation in her important 1997 essay, 'Cultural Studies and Literary Criticism at the Cross-Roads of Value':

> Whenever I was on committees, along with European and American colleagues, judging videos and films, we had difficulties in establishing a common ground for making decisions: the non-Latin-American judges looked at the Latin American videos with sociological eyes, pointing to their social or political merits and ignoring their discursive problems. I personally was inclined to judge the videos from an aesthetic point of view, relegating their social and political impact to a secondary position. The non-Latin Americans behaved like cultural analysts (and occasionally like anthropologists) while I took on the role of art critic. It was difficult to reach a conclusion because we were talking different languages. A young Argentine film director had a similar experience during a European film festival. He showed his film (which was a highly sophisticated version of one of Cortázar's short stories) but the critics at the festival told him that this type of film was European territory, and that they expected something more political from a Latin American film. Everything seems to suggest that we Latin Americans should produce works which are suitable for cultural analysis whereas Others (basically Europeans) have the right to create works which are suitable for art criticism.   (Sarlo, p. 33)

According to the panel, Latin American films should be 'sociological' and 'political' rather than 'artistic' (which was seen to be the exclusive remit of European cinema). For many budding Latin American film directors of the 1970s and 1980s this manicheistic situation was an artistic and ideological cul-de-sac from which there seemed to be no escape. In the 1980s Latin American cinema seemed to be stuck in the mould of consistently achieving second best, namely, being nominated for – and even winning – Best Foreign Film at the Oscars in Hollywood. María Luisa Bemberg's *Camila* (1984; chapter 13) was nominated for an Oscar as Best Foreign Film and Luis Puenzo's *La historia oficial* (The Official Version, 1984; chapter 14) was not only nominated but also won precisely this distinction in 1985 ('Awards Database'). Even those films which were a little more adventurous in political and expressive terms – such as Babenco's rather acerbic *Pixote* (1981; chapter 11) – were still caught in the trap of offering to their respective audiences a politicised, anti-establishment message.

This picture was irrevocably changed during the 1990s, the 'era of de-nationalisation of the [large] screen', as Erica Segre has it (see Segre, passim). In Brazil in 1990, the President, Collor de Melho, stopped all funding of the national Brazilan film industry and, as a result, Embrafilme, the national film body, was forced to close its doors (Shaw, p. 161). At the same time private investment was encouraged and, indeed, grew apace as the decade progressed. The picture was a similar one in Mexico. At an international film conference held in Cancun in 1993, a new law was promulgated (the so-called Nueva Ley Federal de Cinematografía) whereby the National Film Institute (the IMCINE) would 'now only subsidize 60% of the costs of production', with the other 40% to be raised by the director through private funding (Segre, p. 43). The release of *Como agua para chocolate* (Like Water for Chocolate; chapter 21) in Mexico City in February 1993 was a test-case of just how much the cinematic landscape had changed. Following the new law to the letter, Alfonso Arau's film had split public/private funding, which consisted of a state grant from IMCINE, along with private funds from Aviasco, a Mexican airline, the Mexican Ministry of Tourism, and the State Government of Coahuila where the film is set (Shaw, p. 39). It was an unprecedented success. *Como agua para chocolate* first became a hit with Latin American audiences (it was screened continuously in Mexico in six movie theatres for six months) before being exported abroad; it went on to be a Hollywood blockbuster. The secret of its success – apart from its heady mixture of exoticism, sex, and magical realism – was that, from the outset, it was a film which had its eyes firmly on its audience. *Como agua para chocolate* owed as much to the financial jolt that the Mexican economy received in the early 1990s as to the determination and perseverance of its director (Alfonso Arau) and author (Laura Esquivel). While a number of critics have pointed out that *Como agua para chocolate* offers up rather stereotypical images of men, women, Mexico and the United States – thereby pandering to some of the easy clichés of Hollywood's filmic idiom – there is no escaping the fact that it allowed Latin American cinema a new lease of life, a passport to being taken seriously as an artistic product on its own merits. That the success of *Como agua para chocolate* was not dependent on the Hollywood machine is suggested by the fact it was not even nominated for Best Foreign Film. It had transcended the category ('Awards Database'). There were many, particularly those of the old school such as Arturo Ripstein, who disagreed with the new policy – Ripstein famously went to see President Zedillo in 1997 on behalf of IMCINE to complain about the lack of state funding: 'A country without film is a sad country' were his words (de la Mora, p. 2) – but the paradigm-shift was leading to irreversible changes in the film industry in Latin America.

If *Como agua para chocolate* was the harbinger, Salles's *Central do Brasil* (Central Station, 1998; chapter 22) was the breakthrough, and was the final, irrevocable proof that Latin American cinema no longer needed the accolade of 'best foreign film' in order to achieve the accolade of international acceptance. The fact that the lead actress, Fernanda Montenegro, was nominated for Actress in a Leading Role category at the 71st Oscar Awards Ceremony ('Awards Database') – a bold gesture since these are routinely reserved for English-language films (in fact Judi Dench won it for her performance in *Shakespeare in Love*) – shows the extent to which Latin American film has transcended its category as a token player in the field of world cinema. *Central Station*, indeed, was a tremendous box-office hit in Brazil before smashing box-office records in the U.S. and Europe. This success was followed – almost, it seemed, year on year – by the successes of *Amores perros* (Love's a Bitch, 2000; chapter 23), *Y tu mamá también* (And Your Mother Too, 2001; chapter 24) and *Cidade de Deus* (City of God, 2002; chapter 25). These four films demonstrated to the world that Latin American cinema had finally come into its own. One important feature of these films that marked them off from their predecessors was that they were financed by private capital rather than state funds. Alejandro González Iñárritu, the director of *Amores perros*, epitomises this paradigm-shift. In an interview for *Sight and Sound*, he stated that he and his co-producer, Guillermo Arriaga, 'loathe the government-financed movie-making that seems to operate by the maxim: "If nobody understands or nobody goes to see a movie, that it must mean it's a masterpiece" ' (Pérez Soler, p. 29). *Y tu mamá también* was funded by a nutritional supplements corporation and *Cidade de Deus* had a budget of $3,500,000, and for this reason, perhaps, had an audience-centred focus.

What these films managed to do was to present a vision of the world which rejected the picture-postcard version of Latin America, and in the process express a message which was, of course, intrinsically Latin American but also addressed wider, supranational issues, themes and problems. But, perhaps, just as important, the filmic idiom employed in each of these films was not recognisably 'Third World' or 'provincial' or 'cute'. *Amores perros* addresses the theme of violence and the animal roots of human behaviour in such a way as to speak to a wider audience. *Y tu mamá también* raises issues about the meaning of life as a journey, about sexual mores and human bonding, which go beyond the Mexican context. *Cidade de Deus* addresses issues such as the role of children in society, poverty and its intimate connection with corruption within the state, which are as relevant to a viewer in London as in New York or Rio de Janeiro. The important point is that these new films were addressing issues which stretched beyond their local context. But perhaps just as significant, these films used a filmic idiom which was as sophisticated as anything found in Paris or Hollywood. *Amores perros* and *Cidade de Deus* have recourse to breathtakingly innovative filmic techniques which astounded even juries and audiences in Hollywood and Paris. It was when Latin American films made audiences round the world sit up and say 'how did they do that?', rather than 'authentic, but the special effects aren't that good' that Latin American film had come of age, seemingly overnight.

It is difficult to predict where Latin American film will go in the future. In some ways it is still governed by the either/or dialectic of the choice between pro-Hollywood or anti-Hollywood films. Two students currently at the Escuela Internacional de Cine y Televisión in San Antonio de Baños, Cuba, sum up the dilemma:

> 'There's no way I'm leaving here just to make more films like they do in Europe or Hollywood', says Marina from São Paolo, Brazil. 'Most of them are just escapism.' Her boyfriend, Victor, from Cartagena in Colombia, shakes his head. 'South America is full of all these messianic directors preaching this and that to audiences that are not interested any more. I think Hollywood sometimes gets it right. If you want to reach people, you must entertain. I think I'm going to make comedies. But dark ones of course.'   (Payne, p. 10)

It is clear that this new explosion of interest in Latin American cinema has been accompanied by a rise in new Latin American film stars. Stars are, naturally, the most visible aspect of any film and it is a tried and tested formula that audiences will pay to see their favourite stars act on the big screen. The Mexican actor, Gael García Bernal, is a case in point. Playing leading roles in films such as *Amores perros* (2000), *Y tu mamá también* (2001), and *El crimen del Padre Amaro* (Father Amaro's Crime, 2002), he has – almost single-handedly, it appears – produced box-office hits. This has been the case even when his casting (as in *El crimen del Padre Amaro*) has not been at its best; his performance in *Amores perros*, it must be said, though, was stunningly good. This is a new phenomenon in Latin American cinema, which repays further study (see King, 'Stars: Mapping the Firmament'), but it cannot be ignored that Bernal's good looks are enough to bring women flocking to the cinema, especially if there is a hint that he will be strutting his stuff on screen. Gael García Bernal has, in effect, become the David Beckham of the Spanish-speaking filmic world, and his star status linked with the boom of interest in Latin American cinema augurs well for the future of an independent-minded as well as an independently-run film industry in Latin America.

Works Cited

Armes, Roy, *French Cinema*, 3rd ed. (London: Secker and Warburg, 1985).

'Awards Database [Academy of Motion Picture Arts and Sciences, Hollywood]', www.awardsdatabase.oscars.org (consulted on 18 December 2003).

Birri, Fernando, 'Cinema and Underdevelopment', in *Twenty-Five Years of the New Latin American Cinema*, ed. Michael Chanan (London: BFI, 1983), pp. 9–12.

Che Guevara, Ernesto, *Che Guevara and the Cuban Revolution: Writings and Speeches of Ernesto Che Guevara,* ed. David Deutschman (Sydney: Pathfinder, 1987).

Cortázar, Octavio, 'Email to author', 3 January 2004.

De la Mora, Sergio, 'A Career in Perspective: An Interview with Arturo Ripstein', *Film Quarterly,* 52.4 (Summer 1999), 2–11.

Debray, Régis, *Revolution in the Revolution? Armed Struggle and Political Struggle in Latin America,* trans. Bobbye Ortiz (New York: Monthly Review Press, 1967).

García Espinosa, Julio, 'For an Imperfect Cinema', in *Twenty-Five Years of the New Latin American Cinema,* ed. Michael Chanan (London: BFI, 1983), pp. 28–33.

Hennebelle, Guy, and Alfonso Gumucio-Dagrón, *Les Cinémas de l'Amérique latine* (Paris: Pierre L'Herminier, 1981).

King, John, *Magical Reels: A History of Cinema in Latin America* (London: Verso, 1990).

——, 'Stars: Mapping the Firmament', in *Contemporary Latin American Cultural Studies,* eds Stephen Hart and Richard Young (London: Arnold, 2003), pp. 140–50.

Johnson, Randal, and Robert Stam, *Brazilian Cinema* (East Brunswick, NJ: Associated University Presses, 1982).

Lehman, Peter, and William Luhr, *Thinking about Movies: Watching, Questioning, Enjoying* (Oxford: Blackwell, 2003).

Leyda, Jan, *Kino: A History of the Russian and Soviet Cinema,* 3rd ed. (Princeton, NJ: Princeton University Press, 1983).

Mestman, Mario, 'From Algiers to Buenos Aires: The Third World Cinema Committee (1973–74)', *New Cinemas: Journal of Contemporary Film,* 1.1 (2001), 40–53.

Mora, Carl J., *Mexican Cinema: Reflections of a Society 1896–1980* (Berkeley: University of California Press, 1982).

Payne, Chris, 'A Vatican for Film-Makers', *The Guardian* (28 November 2003), pp. 10–11.

Pérez Soler, Bernardo, 'Pup Fiction', *Sight and Sound* (May 2001), pp. 29–30.

Ramírez Berg, Charles, *Cinema of Solitude: A Critical Study of Mexican Film, 1967–1983* (Austin: Texas, 1992).

Rocha, Glauber, 'The Aesthetics of Hunger', in *Twenty-Five Years of the New Latin American Cinema,* ed. Michael Chanan (London: BFI, 1983), pp. 13–14.

Sarlo, Beatriz, 'Cultural Studies Literary Criticism at the Cross-Roads of Values', in *Contemporary Latin American Cultural Studies,* eds Stephen Hart and Richard Young (London: Arnold, 2003), pp. 24–36.

Sanjinés, Jorge, 'Problems of Form and Content in Revolutionary Cinema', in *Twenty-Five Years of the New Latin American Cinema,* ed. Michael Chanan (London: BFI, 1983), pp. 34–8.

Schnitman, Jorge A., *Film Industries in Latin America: Dependency and Development* (Norwood, NJ: ABLEX, 1984).

Segre, Erica, ' "La desnacionalización de la pantalla": Mexican Cinema in the 1990s', in *Changing Reels: Latin American Cinema Againsts the Odds,* eds Rob Rix and Roberto Rodríguez-Saona (Leeds: Trinity and All Saints' College, 1997), pp. 33–57.

Shaw, Deborah, *Contemporary Cinema of Latin America: 10 Key Films* (London: Continuum, 2003).

Solanas, Fernando and Octavio Getino, 'Towards a Third Cinema', in *Twenty-Five Years of the New Latin American Cinema*, ed. Michael Chanan (London: BFI, 1983), pp. 17–27.

Young, Robert J.C., *Postcolonialism: An Historical Introduction* (Oxford: Blackwell, 2003).

1

¡QUÉ VIVA MÉXICO! (LONG LIVE MEXICO, 1931), DIRECTED BY SERGEI EISENSTEIN

Crew

Director: Sergei Eisenstein
Co-director/producer: Grigory Alexandrov
Director of photography: Edouard Tissé

Reconstructions

Qué viva México, 1979: Grigory Alexandrov and Nikita Orlov
Mexican Fantasy, 1998: Oleg Kovalov
The following film analysis is mainly based on the 1979 reconstruction of the original film by Grigory Alexandrov, the co-director of the film in 1931 (see Seton, p. 228) and Nikita Orlov, based on the original print materials now owned by Mosfilm Studios. Alexandrov had worked with Eisenstein on earlier films such as *October* (Leyda, p. 223). Also included is a brief discussion of Oleg Kovalov's creative re-writing of the film footage entitled *Mexican Fantasy* and released in 1998.

Plot

The film – though never completed by Eisenstein – was to consist of six separate sections, which are described below. **I: Prologue:** Images of Mayan pyramids, followed by a funeral. **II: Tehuantepec:** This first novella is set in the isthmus of Tehuantepec, a region in southern Mexico and home to a matriarchal society. Concepción finally obtains the last gold coin necessary to marry the man of her dreams, Abundio. We see the marriage preparations and the ceremony. **III: The Fiesta:** This novella focuses on the drama of the colonisation of the Aztecs by the Spanish, as recorded in various dance ceremonies and, subsequently, the pilgrimage. This sequence was based on footage taken of the Corpus Christi festival in Tetlapayac in 1931 (Seton, p. 205). Next we focus on a different type of fiesta, the bullfight, and in particular David Lisiaga, the Mexican bullfighter, and the Picador, Baronito. The bullfighters are much admired by the women during the bullfight, and, afterwards, take their young ladies out on boats, heavily festooned with flowers, and bearing the title '¡Qué viva México!' inscribed on them. **IV: The Maguey Cactus:** This novella is set in the State of Hidalgo at the beginning of the twentieth century during the dictatorship of Porfirio Díaz. It was filmed in the Tetlapayac ranch, part of an old Spanish plantation belonging to don Julio Saldívar, eighty miles or so to the south-east of Mexico City (Seton, p. 195). María and Sebastián are soon to marry, but there is a rule that every girl about to marry must be introduced to the landowner. While visiting the ranch, Sebastián is pushed to one side, and María ends up getting raped. Sebastián challenges the rapist, but he is thrown down the stairs, and María is imprisoned. Sebastián swears to get even, and with some accomplices – including his brother, Feliciano – they attack the ranch. Outnumbered, they are beaten back and retreat to the maguey cactus plantation. In the pistol exchange, they kill the landowner's daughter. Eventually Sebastián and his two accomplices are captured, though Feliciano lies undetected nearby. As punishment, Sebastián and his two accomplices are forced to dig a hole in which they are buried with just their torsos revealed, at which point the horses are forced to stampede them to death. A violent, cruel death. María is released from her cell and, coming across Sebastián's corpse, she collapses in grief. **V: Soldadera:** This novella only exists as an early draft, and was not shot by Eisenstein. The main idea was going to be that the female soldier was a symbol of the revolutionary Mexico which was going to sweep aside the past. Contains some rudimentary battle scenes, showing the forces of reaction being routed. **VI: The Day of the Dead:** The film's epilogue centres on the Day of the Dead, celebrated in Mexico on 1 November. Scenes of Mexicans eating on the gravestones of their departed loved ones are followed by scenes of a carnival in which masked dancers accompany the merry-go-round in the background. Finally the masks are cast off, and the film concludes with the close-up of the face of a smiling young boy, the son of a 'soldadera', as the voice-over suggests, and a symbol of the future of Mexico when it is truly free.

Analytical Overview

The most important point to mention about *¡Qué viva México!* (1931; reconstructed by Grigory Alexandrov in 1979) is that it was not completed by Eisenstein, and therefore we can only speculate about what form it might finally have taken had Eisenstein been given the opportunity to edit the film. Ed González has made this point effectively: 'No version of the film can ever capture exactly how Eisenstein would have assembled the footage he shot in Mexico from 1931 to 1932, and as such Alexandrov's interpretation of the director's *¡Qué viva México!* ("as Eisenstein conceived it and as we planned it") becomes rather slippery when analysed using an *auteurist* model' (Gonzalez). The film was funded in 1931 by the distinguished socialist writer, Upton Sinclair, and his wife, who were keen to encourage the famous Soviet film director to produce a revolutionary film about Mexico. But after the initial three months ran out, and Eisenstein was clearly not close to producing a finished product, Sinclair decided to pull the funding on the project. As he later explained: 'What first led us to distrust him [Eisenstein] was that when the money was spent he wrote us that we'd have to send more or we'd have no picture . . . He kept that up, over and over, and we realised that he was simply staying in Mexico at our expense in order to avoid having to go back to Russia' (Seton, p. 231). As a result Eisenstein and Sinclair fell out with each other, and Sinclair kept the raw footage Eisenstein had been sending him, and subsequently refused to allow Eisenstein to edit the film. Some of the negatives were sold by Sinclair – who was trying to recoup some of the capital he had raised for the venture – and released piece-meal as *Thunder over Mexico* (1933; based on the 'Maguey sequence'), *Eisenstein in Mexico* (1934), *Death Day* (1934; based on the Epilogue), and *Time in the Sun* (1939). Eisenstein was extremely upset by what he saw as an act of personal betrayal. When asked years later by Jan Leyda why he had not directed any major film since *¡Qué viva México!*, 'he gave me the most genuinely anguished look I ever saw on his face and shouted at me: "What do you expect me to do? How can there be a new film when I haven't given birth to the last one?" And he clutched his belly with an equally painful gesture' (Leyda, p. 302).

Finally, in the 1970s, the raw footage found its way to Moscow and, in 1979, Grigory Alexandrov – who had worked with Eisenstein on the original project in Mexico in 1931 as his co-director – produced a new reconstruction of the whole project – calling it by the original title – which was released in that year by Mosfilm Studios. While not definitive, Alexandrov's reconstruction is probably as near as we are going to get to the final version of Eisenstein's project, *¡Qué viva México!* It is important to point out, however, that Alexandrov and Eisenstein grew apart as the project was maturing in Mexico in 1931, and also that Alexandrov left the film team as soon as the film was completed (Seton, p. 229).

It is clear that Eisenstein went to Mexico since, like a number of artists and intellectuals of the time – such as D.H. Lawrence, Aldous Huxley, and Graham Greene – he felt drawn to Mexico as an image of an alternative to Europe (Podalsky, p. 27). As such *¡Qué viva México!* is emblematic of the early phase of Latin American cinema – continuing up until the 1950s – when the most significant films were directed – or funded – by foreigners, or foreign corporations. This phase continued with films such as *Los olvidados* (1950), directed by a Spaniard, and *Orfeu negro* (1959), directed by a Frenchman. Despite its truncated status *¡Qué viva México!* is an absorbing film which proved to be highly influential for the way in which the language of film was to develop in Latin America. Eisenstein, indeed, was hostile to the advent of sound in the cinema and, in 1928, he, Grigory Alexandrov and Vsevolod Pudovkin co-signed a manifesto which expressed hostility to 'sound cinema'; sound, they argued, would 'degrade' cinema and make it too similar to the theatre (Aumont, p. 34, and p. 131). Eisenstein was much more interested in the artistry of the image, and his film is, as we shall see, extremely sophisticated in a visual sense. As Ismael Xavier pointed out, 'the montage principle typical of modernist prose provided the ground for Eisenstein's intellectual cinema, which refused a more conventional political pedagogy based on classical narrative and proposed instead a rich variety of experiments in film language that triggered a level of conceptualization rejected by the Soviet bureaucracy and by film industries everywhere' (Xavier, p. 347).

Similar to Alexander Dovzhenko's film *Earth*, *¡Qué viva México!* addresses a theme almost too big for a movie, namely, the interplay between life and death. As Leyda puts it: 'How strange that on opposite sides of the planet the two greatest Soviet artists should be filming the same theme: death as part of life – Dovzhenko in the utter simplicity of *Earth* and Eisenstein in the complex structure and grand range of *¡Qué viva México!*' (Leyda, p. 275).

Montage

Eisenstein's work is closely identified with montage, so much so, in fact, that French critic Christian Metz linked Eisenstein to the 'montage or bust' group. Classical film theory typically acknowledges the existence of three distinct though overlapping types of montage – narrative, graphic and ideational – and *¡Qué viva México!* has recourse to all three in differing degrees. In narrative montage, for example, various images and scenes focus on a single subject followed from point to point. This is the type of montage we find in the opening sequences of the film in which we gradually build up a picture of the Mayan pyramids at Chichen-Itza when viewed from different angles; in some ways this establishing sequence gives the impression of being a highly choreographed succession of postcards of an exotic location. We find a similar device used when the tropical landscape of Tehuantepec is introduced later on in the prologue, and when the maguey plantation is introduced at the beginning of the 'Maguey Cactus' novella (IV). Graphic montage, for its part, is normally reserved for describing those shots which are juxtaposed on the basis of their physical similarity. A good example of graphic montage occurs in the Tehuantepec sequence which describes the means whereby Concepción will be able to marry. She is first shown combing her hair and, subsequently, a voice-over explains to us that she is saving up for her dowry, which is a necklace made of gold coins. This still image of the necklace – shown in a crescent shape – then dissolves to reveal a man in a hammock, the focus of her desire. This graphic montage – also called visual rhyming – underlines the strict complementarity between the necklace and Abundio. Once the crescent shape is complete, Concepción will be able to exchange it for her husband. Though it appears dated to modern eyes – precisely because modern-day directors avoid its stagey feel – this type of graphic montage was an important resource for Eisenstein as he explored the different depths available in the semiosis of the film image.

But it was the third type of montage in which Eisenstein excelled, the so-called ideational montage, an innovation of which the Soviet film director can be called the inventor. In ideational montage two separate images are brought together and their juxtaposition gives rise to an idea which shows how they are linked, rather like the tenor and vehicle in a vivid metaphor. In his film *Strike* (1924), for example, Eisenstein had managed to convey the sense of the brutality of slaughter when he juxtaposed images of cattle being butchered with shots of workers being cut to pieces by the cavalry. He uses a similar technique most notably in the 'Maguey Cactus' section. Just after Sebastián learns that María has been raped (and here the rape is, as Podalsky points out, a 'trope of societal breakdown', p. 34), the novella cuts to the landowner who – from the balcony – orders the celebrations to continue, and instructs the musicians to carry on playing. At the same time we hear – via a voice-over – that Sebastián is determined to get his revenge, and his brother and the three men say they will help him. Shots of the drunk party revellers drinking pulque and having it drip from their lips are interspersed with images of pigs eating off the floor, and flies buzzing around the drink, a juxtaposition which underlines the piggish brutishness of the people at the fiesta. The viewer is thereby predisposed to see with great sympathy Sebastián's desire for revenge. The same novella has another example of ideational montage which is perhaps more subtle in symbolic terms. During the exchange of pistol shots in the maguey plantation to which Sebastián and his men have been forced to retreat, we find a highly choreographed sequence of shots comparing the sap from the maguey cactus with the workers' blood. Exchange of fire is cross-cut with images of the cactus being destroyed and its sap dripping out. The landowner's daughter's death is prefaced by the shot of an exploding cactus leaf. Later on, when Sebastián leaves his brother hidden under a maguey bush, the image of his distress is followed by the shot of sap weeping from a broken cactus leaf. Given the importance of the opening sequences of the film in which the maguey cactus is shown to be the life-blood of the region, especially for the farm labourers epitomised by Sebastián's family, it is clear that, via a process of ideational montage, Eisenstein is creating an analogy between the workers' blood and the maguey cactus sap, which includes not only the obvious visual similarities between the two liquids but is also used to expose the notion of exploitation. Eisenstein shows his Marxist credentials by focusing on the cruel exploitation of the peasants by the landowners – here associated with the authoritarian regime of Porfirio Díaz, whose portrait adorns the walls of the ranch – in the era which preceded the Mexican Revolution. The notion of exploitation is imaged very clearly via the sap which the peasants have to suck laboriously from the cactus plants, in order for it to be fermented and then drunk by the rich – a classic case of the workers' produce being used as an agent of their own oppression. The image of sap/pulque thereby also has the added ideational resonance of fermentation. This was clearly an image that Eisenstein wished to explore; in his introduction to the following novella, 'The Maguey Cactus', speaks of the Revolution which is about to explode onto the front stage of history in terms of the 'fermenting Mexico', and this indicates how resonant the image of the maguey cactus became in Eisenstein's hands.

Comparison of the Novellas

It is, of course, frustrating to have to content ourselves with the raw film footage rather than the edited version of the film, but, even with what we have, it is possible to get a sense of Eisenstein's aim in filming *¡Qué viva México!* The most successful of the novellas – the one which most obviously hangs together – is clearly the 'Maguey Cactus' sequence, while the least successful – because of its radical incompleteness – is the 'Soldadera' sequence. The plot of the 'Maguey Cactus' novella is well worked-out, and combines a political story of oppression

with a story of young love, bound together with a powerful image drawn from
the landscape, the maguey cactus, whose sap (as we have seen above) brings
together – in an orthodox Marxist way – the sense of exploitation with the idea
of the life-blood of the people. The opening sequence is visually impressive and
has been noted by a number of critics, although the film as it stands does not successfully integrate the sequence describing the burial. The Tehuantepec novella,
though lush and evocative, is at times rather emotionally cloying, and rather surprising as the opening novella for a political committed *cinéaste* like Eisenstein.
The film's epilogue, though truncated, is masterful, in that it overlays a religious,
cultural ceremony – the Day of the Dead – with a political significance. Rather
than simply rehearsing the Aztec notion of the continuity of life and death,
Eisenstein uses the masks which characterise the celebrations of the Day of the
Dead to make a political point. When the masks are cast off, some reveal the face
of smiling young boys, while others show the skull of a socially doomed class,
the military, the gendarmes. It is not insignificant that one of the people chosen
to represent this class is wearing spurs, namely, the social class which, in the pre-
Revolutionary era, had raped humble women such as María and murdered men
such as Sebastián if they dared to rebel. Given the particularly brutal way in
which Sebastián and his accomplices were murdered, it is unlikely that the
viewer will shed a tear on account of the demise of the landowner class. The
epilogue concludes with the shot of a face of a smiling young boy, a symbol of
the future of Mexico in the post-Revolutionary era.

The Tapestry

Eisenstein referred to *¡Qué viva México!* in terms of the Mexican sarape: 'A
sarape is the striped blanket that . . . every Mexican wears. So striped and violently contrasting are the cultures in Mexico running next to each other and at
the same time being centuries away . . . we took the contrasting independent
adjacence of its violent colors as the motif for constructing our film: 6 episodes
following each other' (quoted in Seton, p. 197). Though the four novellas are distinct in many ways – in turn they focus on a pre-historical matriarchal society,
the Spanish influence in Mexican culture (specifically Catholicism and bullfighting), the oppression of the Mexican working class by the landowners in the
pre-Revolutionary era, and female agency within the Mexican Revolution – there
are a number of common strands which suggest that Eisenstein was attempting
to produce a unified artistic vision of Mexico. Leyda has drawn attention to the
subtle overlay in Eisenstein's film: '*¡Qué viva México!* employed both the great
solid blocks of contrasting sections and the intricate lacy geometry of a growth
that can be found in plant-life as well as in mathematics. The separate stones of
cells of this elaborate structure were sometimes as minimal in movement or
drama as shots in *Arsenal* or *Earth*, Eisenstein's movement being planned as
successive impacts of these lightly breathing compositions' (Leyda, p. 276).

   The soothingly edenic culture portrayed in Tehuantepec (Part II) offers a necessary counterpoint to the aggressively violent eddies characterising Catholicism

and bullfighting (Part III). The notion of feminine agency underlies the culture of Tehuantepec (Part II) as much as the unfinished section on the role of the female soldier in the Revolution (Part V). Other visual twinnings are more subtle. The Christological resonance of the final scene of the 'Maguey Cactus' sequence – in which the three men are trampled to death – is enhanced via the visual similarity of this scene with the depiction of the re-enactment of Christ's passion in Part III (as in the later scene, there are three Christ figures, and the ropes used in each sequence mutually reinforce their interconnectiveness). Eisenstein's notes suggest that he intended to splice the depiction of Sebastián's death with images of the Corpus Christi, but, because he was unable to edit, it remained an intention rather than an accomplishment (Seton, p. 205).

Mexican Fantasy

Mexican Fantasy (1998), written and directed by Oleg Kovalov, is a new version of Eisenstein's *¡Qué viva México!*, described in the blurb as a 'thoughtful and contemplative interpretation of the film that might have been' ('Blurb'). Unlike Alexandrov's version – which combines a selection of the first-cut with a running commentary provided by Alexandrov explaining the gestation of the film – Kovalov's version attempts to recreate Eisenstein's original vision. This he does by cross-cutting between the separate novellas, using 'The Maguey Cactus', which is the fourth section in Alexandrov's edition, as the central narrative around which all the other stories are woven. Although it is, of course, impossible in an empirical sense to reconstruct what Eisenstein would have created, it is clear that Kovalov's version draws inspiration from Eisenstein's theory of montage in order to achieve its various cinematic effects. Whereas the raw footage, for example, in Alexandrov's section III, entitled 'The Fiesta', simply shows us the Corpus Christi festival in Tetlapayac and, subsequently, the bullfight, Kovalov cross-cuts between the two festivals, attempting to show the similarities between the two. Perhaps more interesting than this, though, is the way in which Kovalov attempts to build sequences from the two festivals as well as the preparations for the marriage between Concepción and Abundio (which appears in Alexandrov's version as Section II) into the 'Maguey Cactus' section. This leads to some interesting montage effects. For example, the tragedy visited upon Sebastián and María as a result of their desire to marry (María is raped, and Sebastián murdered in a savage manner because he rebelled) is rendered all the more acute by being spliced with the happy outcome of Concepción and Abundio's love which takes place against the idyllic backdrop of Tehuantepec, a contrast which is absent from Alexandrov's version. Likewise María's suffering at the hands of the landowner's friend is enhanced by being directly compared to Christ's Passion; after a scene depicting the three men walking painfully up the hill to the Church during the Corpus Christi ceremony we cut immediately to a long shot of María, accompanied by Sebastián, riding her donkey (like Christ perhaps) to the ranch.

Some of the contrasts in the 1998 version are inventive. Thus, whereas in the first-cut version, María is raped and then summarily ejected from the room – producing a rather bathetic effect which ill suits the circumstances – Kovalov's version intensifies the suspense by cross-cutting to a number of other sequences while the rape is 'in process' (in particular, the real bullfight sequence followed by the mock bullfight performed in the ranch-yard). Perhaps just as important, these sequences, particularly those showing the fireworks burning in the model bull's torso – since we know that María is being raped off-screen – allude suggestively to the pyrotechnics of passion. Kovalov's editing brings to the fore some metaphorical resonances which are merely hinted at in Alexandrov's version. Whereas the rather protracted scenes depicting the extraction of the sap from the maguey cactus appear in Alexandrov's version to be related to the life-blood of the people, in Kovalov's version they take on a sexual depth since the sucking of the cactus sap is spliced with a scene in which Abundio is portrayed as about to kiss Concepción's exposed nipple on the hammock – just before the palm tree leaf discreetly blocks our view. In Alexandrov's version though Concepción does appear with her breasts exposed when frolicking with Abundio on the hammocks the effect is less sexual. Although Kovalov clearly did not follow Eisenstein's notes to the letter (thus he does not splice Sebastián's death with images of the Corpus Christi ceremony, as Eisenstein's notes suggest was the latter's original intention, which is a pity; see Seton, p. 205), it is clear that his version offers some thoughtful analyses of the raw footage.

Works Cited

Aumont, Jacques, *et al.*, *Aesthetics of Film* (Austin: University of Texas Press, 1992).

'Blurb', *Mexican Fantasy*, written and directed by Oleg Kovalov, produced by Sergei Selianov, 1998. (Russian with English subtitles.)

Geduld, Harry M., and Ronald Gottesman (eds), *Sergei Eisenstein and Upton Sinclair: The Making and Unmaking of* ¡Qué viva México! (Bloomington, IN: Indiana University Press, 1970).

Gonzalez, Ed, '¡Qué viva México!', www.rottentomatoes.com/m/QueVivaMexico-1036049/reviews.php (consulted on 18 December 2003).

Leyda, Jan, *Kino: A History of the Russian and Soviet Cinema*, 3rd ed. (Princeton, NJ: Princeton University Press, 1983).

Podalsky, Laura, 'Patterns of the Primitive: Sergei Eisenstein's *¡Qué viva México!*', in *Mediating Two Worlds: Cinematic Encounters in the Americas*, eds John King, Ana M. Lopez and Manuel Alvarado (London: BFI, 1993), pp. 25–39.

Seton, Marie, *Sergei M. Eisenstein* (London: Dennis Dobson, 1978).

Xavier, Ismail, 'Historical Allegory', in *A Companion to Film Theory*, eds Toby Miller and Robert Stam (Oxford: Blackwell, 2004), pp. 333–62.

2

LOS OLVIDADOS (THE YOUNG AND THE DAMNED, 1950), DIRECTED BY LUIS BUÑUEL

Cast

Jaibo, played by Roberto Cobo
Pedro, played by Alfonso Mejía
Carmelo (the Blind Man), played by Miguel Inclán
Marta (Pedro's mother), played by Estella India
Meche, played by Alma Delia Fuentes
Julián, played by Javier Amézcua
Judge, played by Héctor López Portillo
Poxy, played by Efraín Arauz
Ojitos (Little-eyes), played by Mario Ramírez
Reform School Director, played by Francisco Jambrina

Crew

Editor: Carlos Savage
Art Directors: Edward Fizgerald, W.W. Claridge
Music: Rodolfo Halfter; themes by Gustavo Pittalunga
Sound: José B. Carles
Production: Ultramar Films, Oscar Dancingers
Photography: Gabriel Figueroa
Script: Luis Buñuel, Luis Alcoriza
Assistant Director: Ignacio Villareal
Director: Luis Buñuel

Award

Winner, mise-en-scène, Cannes International Film Festival, 1951

Plot Summary

Pedro and Jaibo belong to a gang of thieves who live in Mexico City; their gang is the 'young and the damned' of the English translation of the title. Jaibo has just escaped from prison. They steal some money from a blind old man,

Carmelo, and break up his instruments. They also steal from a helpless cripple. Jaibo goes to see Julián at his place of work, and accuses him of ratting on him. Julián goes to meet him in a deserted place, and is hit on the head from behind with a rock by Jaibo. Julian dies, and Jaibo – and Pedro who is the only witness – flee. Pedro goes to see his mother but she refuses to show him any affection. When Pedro is accused of stealing a knife that Jaibo in fact stole, he goes to a reform school, and his mother is happy for this to happen. Jaibo seduces Pedro's mother, Marta. Pedro is entrusted with some money by the reform school director, but he is pounced on by Jaibo who steals the money. Pedro confronts Jaibo later on, and spills the beans about how he murdered Julián. Jaibo kills Pedro in revenge. Carmelo finds out where Jaibo is hiding, tips off the police, and Jaibo – much to Carmelo's delight – is shot dead by the police as he is trying to escape.

Analytical Overview

The first point that needs to be made is that it may seem a little strange including a film by a Spanish director in a book about Latin American cinema. To an extent this is an important consideration. Buñuel was born in Spain, he grew up there, and began to make his first films in Spain. It was there, after all, that he made his name. But the fact is that, in the 1940s, Buñuel decided to try his luck elsewhere; his experience in Hollywood was not a good one, and he then tried Mexico. The point about the films he made in Mexico is that they do not appear to be those of a Spanish film director trying to make a fast buck abroad. At that point in time he was committed to working in the Mexican film industry, he was dependent for funding on national film agencies, he was using Mexican actors and Mexican studios, and his films addressed recognisably Mexican themes. Last but not least, the films Buñuel produced during this period are acknowledged as important landmarks in the history of Mexican cinema. They emerged in a period when the Mexican film industry was caught in the rut of producing complacent cinema for a middle-class audience; even the heyday of the Mexican melodrama was coming to an end. Buñuel, his credentials already well established in Europe, set out to do something different, and it was something of a shock for Mexican, and indeed Latin American, cinema. His vision was one not of love but of hate, not of reconciliation but of conflict – a cinema which focused on the blind force of revenge. Given that, at the time, the Mexican film industry was still producing feel-good melodramas about the rural idyll – the so-called *comedias rancheras* – Buñuel was, at the time, very much a 'voice crying in the wilderness' (King, p. 131). As Mora suggests, for Mexican audiences, 'accustomed to the sentimentalized poor of Rodríguez's *Nosotros los pobres, Los olvidados* was an unsettling experience and the film initially was not a commercial success' (Mora, p. 91). Not surprisingly, therefore, the film did not garner any Mexican awards, though it won first prize for mise-en-scène at the Cannes International Film Festival in 1951 ('Cannes 1951').

Revenge

The film begins and ends with the theme of revenge. In the opening scenes we meet Jaibo who is boasting about how much he learned while in prison during the last year and who then swears that he will get even with Julián who, he believes, shopped him, and whom he therefore holds to blame for his prison sentence. Julián is clearly part of the same set of friends as Jaibo, but he is revealed in the opening scenes of the film to be a clean-living, upstanding member of society. He does not smoke, and refuses to bend to peer pressure when he is called a 'mariquita' (pansy) for refusing a drag. He does not drink, as is suggested very plainly by the scene early on in the film when he is seen dragging his drunk father home from the local bar. The suggestion – as the script makes clear – is that he has to do this every night. But perhaps most important is the fact that he works for a living; and he does so not only to sustain himself but also his father, as his father rather weepily acknowledges when he is being escorted home by Julián. His conduct therefore flies in the face of that of the more hardened members of the gang for whom working is a mug's game ('sólo los burros trabajan' – only donkeys work). Julián is muscular and fit, and – given Jaibo's slim physique – he would seem to be more than a match for Jaibo. Yet Jaibo tricks him by pretending that he has broken his arm; in his sling he is hiding the stone that he will use to crush Julián's skull from behind. He carries on hitting Julián once he has fallen to the ground, but Julián's sickening moan uttered as he is hit suggests he may already be dead. The pathos of this murder is made all the more vivid by the scenes later on in which Julián's hapless father is seen wandering around the town – as usual drunk – screaming revenge against the man who killed his son. Buñuel's point in emphasising the pathetic depths of degradation to which the father falls is that murder not only destroys one life but also blights countless others.

At this point the viewer may begin to suspect that Buñuel is about to create a moral fable showing how evil vanquishes good and, as the plot gradually unfolds, his suspicions are gradually confirmed. As a number of commentators have pointed out, Buñuel has suggested that there is no escape from moral and social degradation. Unlike Cernuda, for whom Mexico was heaven, Mexico for Buñuel was the very picture of hell (Faber). Harvey O'Brien has argued that the film 'convincingly sustains an atmosphere of social deprivation' (O'Brien) while, for Gabe Leibowitz, the film is a 'blend of surrealism and horrific Neo-Realism which implants itself on the viewer's mind for days' (Leibowitz). Pedro is, of course, the litmus test. His first step along the 'path to hell' is the point at which he accepts part of the money Jaibo has stolen from Julián's wallet as he lies dead on the floor; he is in effect a partner in crime. This despite the fact that he attempted to stop Jaibo from beating Julián with a stick when he lay helpless on the ground. His second 'flaw' occurs when he allows Jaibo into the Knife Sharpener's Shop where he has recently been taken on as an apprentice. Jaibo steals the knife and is quite happy to allow Pedro to take the blame for his actions. To cap it all, Jaibo is even present in his mother's house when the police arrive with a warrant for Pedro's arrest, and feigns ignorance of the whole drama. The irony could not be more sharply etched. But Pedro's final flaw occurs when he is given the fateful errand by the supervisor of the reform school where he has been sent by his heartless mother (she simply wants to get rid of him). The supervisor in an act of genuine if ingenuous trust gives Pedro a 50-peso bill and asks him to buy him some cigarettes from the shop on the corner just outside the borstall. Jaibo is outside, sees the money, wrestles Pedro to the ground and, by taking the money, in effect strips Pedro of his last hope of 'social redemption'. It is at this point that a change occurs in Pedro and he decides – foolishly perhaps – to attempt to destroy Jaibo. He avails himself of a knife – which he keeps hidden – and then challenges Jaibo to a fight, which he loses, but – no doubt in order to avenge himself – he then publicly reveals that Jaibo killed Julián. Carmelo, the blind man, who has been wronged by Jaibo – he beat him up and destroyed his livelihood by puncturing his drum with a rock – overhears the conversation and also decides to get his own back. Carmelo tells the police where they can capture Jaibo. Pedro, for his part, goes to Meche's barn, evidently in order to lie in wait for Jaibo, but he is beaten to it, and Jaibo kills him. In the final scene which concludes this fast-moving drama, Carmelo is shown exultantly gloating over Jaibo's death, wishing that all of the ragamuffins of Mexico's streets could be destroyed before the advent of a new day. While Pedro's desire for revenge was not requited, Carmelo's has. By ratting on Jaibo he has avenged himself of the attack that Jaibo carried out on him with the help of his gang. *Los olvidados* begins and ends with scenes of revenge.

Symbolism and Repetition

The film essentially tells a story and does so in a linear fashion, ending in a standard way with the death of the villain. As Gwynne Edwards points out, the film 'moves from beginning to end in a simple, direct and incisive manner, with all the speed and clarity of the better Spanish picaresque novels' (Edwards, p. 107). There are a number of points in the film, though, when the story-line becomes more jagged; these are what Marsha Kindley has called the 'hot spots' in Buñuel's films (Kinder, p. 8). Firstly there are scenes in which certain actions are repeated and/or re-interpreted such that the overlay and semantic accretion points to the existence of a deeper level of significance beyond the strictly visible. A good example is the first murder scene in which Julián is hit repeatedly by a branch; the victim is off-screen, and the mise-en-scène focuses on the aggressor dealing out the blows. As Pedro attempts to stop him, he shouts the words: 'no lo pegues, no lo pegues más' (don't hit him, don't hit him any more). This scene is re-enacted when Pedro's mother hits the black cockerel which has been causing strife in the barn with a broom; once more the victim is out of camera shot, while the camera focuses on the aggressor hitting the cockerel; Pedro's pained expression as he repeats the words 'no lo pegues, no lo pegues más' (don't hit it, don't hit it any more) makes it quite clear that he has re-experienced the vision of Julián's murder. Pedro re-creates this scene of primal aggression when he attacks the two white hens in the borstall after he is told off for eating the eggs; his anger is so brutal that it is clear that the hens are a substitute victim for his aggression towards society, authority, and perhaps his mother. As the supervisor rather smugly points out to Pedro after he has killed the hens, Pedro was releasing his aggression against the Reform School. The final re-enactment of this scene occurs when Pedro himself now becomes the victim. Once more the camera focuses on Jaibo as he beats Pedro to death; now the same words are used but the object has changed: 'no me pegues, no me pegues' (don't hit me, don't hit me). In all four cases Buñuel is careful to combine a similar mise-en-scène with a similar script in order to underline the overwhelmingly repetitive nature of the primal aggression being enacted on screen. Investing the film with an internal dramatic coherence, the re-enactment of a violent act in four crucial scenes serves to indicate how Pedro has changed from unwilling observer to helpless witness, and then from perpetrator to victim.

The theme of violence is, indeed, enhanced by the preponderance of dark and semi-lit scenes in the film, producing very much a nocturnal vision of the human psyche which 'defetishizes' the spectacle of that violence (Kantaris, pp. 181–2). In this Buñuel was expressing an interesting departure from contemporary filmic mores. Geoffrey Nowell-Smith has drawn attention to a distinction between two identifiable genres of city film. On the one hand, he argues, there is 'the kind of film which is mostly studio-shot (. . .) and often offers a generally dystopian vision of an undifferentiated "city" which is either unidentifiable with any actual place or only loosely so' (Nowell-Smith, p. 101), and he mentions *films noirs* as falling broadly into this category. On the other hand, there are films which are mostly 'location-shot and happen in a place which is identifiable, very often named, and where the name may even form part of the title'; the example he cites here is Val Guest's *Hell Is a City* (1959). The overwhelming nocturnal atmosphere of *Los olvidados* has striking parallels with those *films noirs* of the late 1940s – precisely the years when Buñuel was in Hollywood before he went to Mexico – in which the city is a 'place of crime, corruption, and darkness' (Nowell-Smith, p. 102), *The Big Sleep* (1946), *The Killers* (1946) and *Out of the Past* (1947) being classics of the genre. What is so original about Buñuel's re-writing of the *film noir* trope is that he took its vocabulary of darkness and violence, but at the same time avoided the urban *anomie* of the prototype, instead tying his vision specifically to Mexico City, which is recognisable in all of the location shots. As Michael Wood suggests, 'like Godard's Paris, Buñuel's Mexico City is permanently being built' (Wood, pp. 49–50).

Dreams and the Subconscious

With hindsight it would have been unthinkable for a film director such as Buñuel not to insert at least some scenes into his film in which the subconscious is given some outlet. Indeed the dream sequence which occurs immediately after Pedro returns home and gets into bed has confounded viewers. Given the rather rudimentary conditions under which *Los olvidados* was filmed the sequence is nothing short of remarkable. The dream sequence is split into two halves, the first being a projection of Pedro's wish fulfilment and the second being a nightmare in which all his worse fears are confirmed. In the first part his mother comes to his bedside and comforts him, showing herself to be the mother she has never been in real life (she hates him, we may surmise, because he was the product of rape when she was a defenceless, fourteen-year-old girl). In the second half of the dream sequence, she floats towards him – her white dress billowing unnaturally in the wind, with lightning sounding off-screen – and she offers him a large piece of raw meat (the meat she never offered him during the day), which Jaibo grabs as he emerges from beneath the bed. As Peter Evans has suggested, the raw meat symbolises the mother's 'torn vagina' (Evans, p. 86). The underside of the bed from which Jaibo appears is associated explicitly with death; under the bed Pedro had seen the bloodied face of Julián who had been beaten to death by Jaibo. The significance of this scene is not altogether clear but a few points may be made. Firstly it is clear that Pedro and Jaibo are fighting over the same thing and are in a sense bitter rivals; the meat appears to stand in more obvious fashion for daily sustenance (which Pedro's mother is refusing him), and also for her love and, indeed, her sexuality. It should be noted that in all of these different contests, Jaibo wins while Pedro loses, since he is able to persuade Pedro's mother to have sex with him (the door which Jaibo pushes shut signals what will follow), and his persuasion is based on the need for a mother-figure. By empirical standards a rather unusual chat-up line, it serves to remind the viewer that Jaibo is supplanting Pedro from the family unit. An extraordinarily powerful sequence, Pedro's dream underlines the drama of rejection which is going round his mind, and explains why he goes to such extreme measures in order to attempt to destroy Jaibo: he is attempting to win back his mother's love, a tragic mission in which he finally fails.

Meche and 'leche'

The only brief ray of light in this rather gloomy pessimistic film is provided by Meche. She is a pretty girl with long hair, and presented throughout as innocent and untouched. Her mother is suffering from extreme back pain, to relieve which she has recourse to the quackery of a white dove which is rubbed along her spine by Carmelo in return for a jug of donkey's milk. Her father is a suspicious man, as witnessed whenever he finds anyone in the barn, while her brother colludes with Jaibo, finding him a hiding place, and unconcerned at the thought of Jaibo attacking her; as he remarks to Ojitos, Jaibo is simply 'playing'. Meche is associated with milk (with which her name rhymes in Spanish 'Meche-leche') since she tends the donkey which produces the milk for the family. The association is deepened when Ojitos tells her that his mother used to wash brides in milk in order to soften and beautify their skin, and Meche bathes her arms and then splashes her legs in milk as an experiment. The sexual nature of this act is underlined by the fact that the word 'leche' in Spanish is a colloquial term for 'semen'. Jaibo had been spying on her, this sight is too much for me, and he drops out of the rafters to confront her. Meche fights him off – in the same way that she is later to fight off Carmelo – and it is important to underline that she is the only individual in the film who is able to remain uncorrupted by Jaibo's influence. (It is true, of course, that she helps her father dispose of Pedro's dead body, but, in her defence, it should be added that she is following her father's instructions rather than committing a crime.)

In conclusion: Buñuel's *Los olvidados* is a masterpiece which offers an unremittingly pessimistic view of the young and the damned in Mexico City of the 1950s. Focusing on the trials and tribulations of a young boy called Pedro, it shows that, despite his various attempts to escape a life of vice, he is inevitably drawn into its web, until he meets his seemingly inevitable demise when finally murdered by his older 'mentor', Jaibo. In filmographic terms, *Los olvidados* is notable for its ruthlessly efficient plot, its subtle re-enactment of primal scenes of violence, and its innovative use of the dream sequence in Pedro's famous dream about his mother; it manages to capture the mystery operating within the mind of the subaltern (Hart).

Works Cited

Aub, Max, *Conversaciones con Buñuel* (Madrid: Aguilera, 1985).

Buñuel, Luis, *My Last Sigh: The Autobiography of Luis Buñuel* (London: Faber and Faber, 1978), pp. 197–216.

'Cannes 1951', www.festival-cannes.fr/archives/fichedition.php?langue=60002& edition=1951 (consulted on 18 December 2003).

Faber, Sebastian, 'Between Cernuda's Paradise and Buñuel's Hell: Mexico Through Spanish Exiles' Eyes', *BSS*, LXXX.2 (2003), 219–39.

Edwards, Gwynne, *The Discreet Art of Luis Buñuel: A Reading of his Films* (London: Marion Boyars, 1983).

Evans, Peter, '*Los olvidados* and the "Uncanny"', in *The Films of Luis Buñuel: Subjectivity and Desire* (Oxford: OUP, 1995), pp. 72–89.

Hart, Stephen, 'Luis Buñuel's Box of Subaltern Tricks: Technique in *Los olvidados*', in *Luis Buñuel: New Readings*, ed. Peter Evans (London: BFI, 2004), pp. 65–79.

Kantaris, Geoffrey, 'The Young and the Damned: Street Visions in Latin American Cinema', in *Contemporary Latin American Cultural Studies*, eds Stephen Hart and Richard Young (London: Arnold, 2003), pp. 177–89.

Kinder, Marsha, 'Hot Spots, Avatars, and Narrative Fields Forever: Buñuel's Legacy for New Digital Media and Interactive Database Narrative', *Film Quarterly*, 55.4 (Summer 2002), 2–15.

King, John, *Magical Reels: A History of Cinema in Latin America* (London: Verso, 1990).

Leibowitz, Gabe, 'Review', www.rottentomatoes.com/m/LosOlvidados-1954295 (consulted on 18 December 2003).

Mora, Carl J., *Mexican Cinema: Reflections of a Society 1896–1980* (Berkeley: University of California Press, 1982).

Nowell-Smith, Geoffrey, 'Cities: Real and Imagined', in *Cinema and the City: Film and Urban Societies in a Global Context*, eds Mark Shiel and Tony Fitzmaurice (Oxford: Blackwell, 2001), pp. 98–108.

O'Brien, Harvey, 'Review', www.rottentomatoes.com/m/LosOlvidados-1954295 (consulted on 18 December 2003).

Wood, Michael, 'Buñuel in Mexico', in *Mediating Two Worlds: Cinematic Encounters in the Americas*, eds John King, Ana M. López and Manuel Alvarado (London: BFI, 1993), pp. 40–51.

3

DOS TIPOS DE CUIDADO (TWO TYPES OF CARE, 1952), DIRECTED BY ISMAEL RODRÍGUEZ

Cast

Jorge Bueno, played by Jorge Negrete
Pedro Infante, played by Pedro Infante
Rosario, played by Carmen González
María (Jorge's sister), played by Yolanda Varela
General, played by José Elías Moreno
Don Elías, played by Carlos Orellana
Genoveva, played by Queta Levant
Doctor, played by Arturo Soto Rangel
Josefa (Pedro's mother), played by Mimí Derba

Crew

Cinematography: Ismael Carlos Rodríguez
Photography: Nacho Torres, Humberto Daniel López
Photography assistants: Ignacio Romero, Pablo Ríos
Sound: James L. Fields
Dialogue recording: José B. Carlos
Editing: Gloria Schoemann
Editing assistant: Pedro Velázquez
Scenography: José Rodríguez G.
Special Effects: Jorge Benavides
Producer: Antonio Guillermo Tello
Assistant Director: Mario Llorca
Annotator: Pedro López
Make-up: Rosa Guerrero
Hair stylist: Juana Lepe
Music: Manuel Esperón
Executive Producer: David Negrete
Director: Ismael Rodríguez
Produced by: Estudios y Laboratorios Churubasco Azteca

Songs

'La Mujer'	Federico Curiel
'Canción Mexicana'	M. Esperón
'Serenata Tapatia'	M. Esperón and E. Cortázar
'Copla'	M. Esperón and P. Urdimalas
'Dos almas'	M. Esperón and F. Bermejo
'La tertulia'	Salvador Flores R.
'Serenata Mexicana'	Manuel M. Ponce
'Ojos Tapatios'	J. Elizondo Méndez Velázquez
'La Gloria eres tú'	José Antonio Méndez

Plot

The film opens with a 'Prólogo', which offers a preview in miniature of the film which is to follow. The two main men – Pedro and Jorge – discuss their strategies of seduction; while Jorge favours asking the woman for a Platonic relationship and thereby forcing the woman to play her hand, Pedro favours a more direct, flirtatious approach. We see both men wandering into the countryside with their girlfriends, singing popular Mexican songs as they go. Jorge, as expected, gets the girl as a result of his clean-cut approach. But Pedro, as a result of snatching a kiss, gets whacked over the head by María. She calls out, and her brother, Jorge, comes to the rescue. At first angry, Jorge then becomes amused, and Pedro is told to be a good boy. The prologue ends, and the film proper then begins. Jorge Bueno brings his car to be repaired at a garage. He says he is interested in buying some cattle, and is persuaded by a friend to look at a ranch to see if he is able to purchase it. Jorge's partner mentions Pedro's name, and Jorge scowls in disgust, saying he is no longer his friend. We cut to Pedro whose wife, Rosario, has just given birth to a baby girl. After saying the baby is ugly, he goes off to a bar to celebrate. His father-in-law complains that Pedro is a womaniser and a good-for-nothing. At the bar Pedro starts dancing with other women, and plays the violin. Jorge appears in the same bar, demands to talk to Pedro, calls him a 'desgraciado' since he stole his 'novia', Rosario, and then slaps him in the face. Pedro does not respond. Jorge returns to his friend's table and agrees to buy the ranch. We cut to the father-in-law asking Jorge why he didn't marry his daughter, Rosario. In flashback we witness what happened that night. Rosario, Jorge's 'novia' at the time, becomes jealous that Jorge is sitting with a girl called Victoria. She asks him to leave, he refuses, and she breaks off their engagement. Seeing his chance, Pedro befriends Rosario, and they elope to Mexico City where they get married. Back to the present. Jorge picks up his car which is now repaired. We cut to a new scene in which Jorge is playing cards with his friends. Pedro arrives and Jorge is rude to him; Pedro then asks how much Jorge will charge for water now that he owns the ranch. Jorge says it will cost 5,000 pesos a month (the previous rent was 200 pesos a year). Pedro borrows 1,000 pesos against his land, and then joins in the card game. He beats Jorge's three aces with four fours. Pedro is invited by the General to his daughter's betrothal party (she happens to be Jorge's new 'novia'). Pedro meets his father-in-law in the street and is criticised for his wanton behaviour. We see Jorge with his new 'novia', although the latter knows that Jorge is still in love with Rosario. Jorge goes to meet Rosario, and he shouts at her angrily that she has betrayed him. At Jorge's betrothal party, Pedro and Jorge – who are both excellent singers – begin insulting each other in clever songs full of innuendo. Pedro tries to win over María – Jorge's sister – who was once in love with him. Jorge threatens Pedro, saying he will kill him if he doesn't leave town by the next day. Jorge catches Pedro playing cards; he challenges him to a duel, gives him a pistol. They disappear into an adjoining room; both emerge unharmed, as if they have decided something important, though the audience is left in the dark about what was decided. Jorge begins serenading outside Rosario's window, and Pedro begins serenading outside María's window. Both women cry since it is an impossible love. Jorge and Pedro come to blows in the countryside, but then agree to leave it. The General accosts Pedro in the street and says that, since he has been dishonoured by Jorge's behaviour, he must kill him. The General hands Pedro a pistol. We cut to Jorge writing a letter to the General's daughter, saying he is suffering from an incurable illness (his love for Rosario) and must break off their relationship. Pedro tells the General that Jorge cannot marry his daughter since he is suffering from a genetic infirmity that will produce deformed children. They meet Jorge, and the General demands to read the letter written to his daughter. Since it mentions the 'illness' Jorge is suffering from, he accepts Pedro's fabricated story. At the party that evening, Jorge begins dancing with Rosario, and Pedro with María (Jorge's sister). Jorge and Pedro explain to Rosario and María that they should all elope to Mexico City. The father-in-law arrives and is about to spill the beans so they lock him in a room. The doctor arrives and they make him leave with a cock-and-bull story about the 'mayordomo' falling ill and requiring urgent medical treatment. The General's daughter arrives, sees Jorge dancing with Rosario, and calls off the engagement. The doctor comes back, says that the whole thing has been a lie to the General who swears revenge. Jorge's mother arrives, and tells him to calm down, and that everything will work out if Jorge marries Rosario and Pedro marries María. The film ends with a set of 'ranchera' songs. All's well that ends well.

Analytical Overview

Listed as coming in at 34th place out of the top best 100 Mexican films (Maza), *Dos tipos de cuidado* is typical of the hundreds of Mexican melodramas which were produced during the heyday of their popularity in the 1930s, 1940s and the early 1950s. It is a prime, though late, example of the *comedia ranchera* which, during this period, in Carlos Monsiváis's words, 'proliferated, generating two idols with a huge popular following, Jorge Negrete and Pedro Infante, and produced comedies and dramas that revolved around the idea of a paradise lost located in an indefinite time where men were strictly male and women definitely female' (Monsiváis,

p. 118). The Mexican film industry during this period – in a gesture recalling the idiom of Hollywood – created films which catered to a popular Mexican and Latin American audience, and which focused on the star quality of its actors and actresses at the expense of plot, social commentary or artistic filmmaking. *Dos tipos de cuidado* was produced when the popularity of the *comedia ranchera* was waning, and, for this reason, the film included both of the two main attraction *charros* of the time, Jorge Negrete and Pedro Infante (Medina de la Serna, pp. 164–5; de la Vega Alfaro, p. 171). The plot of the film, though complicated (in the sense of being replete with tension-building reverses, especially in the last quarter of an hour or so), is superficial, and weaves its way around a set sequence of *ranchera* songs, sung mainly by the main male singers, Jorge Negrete and Pedro Infante, though – in the concluding sequence – the women join in.

The film – again following the formula – indulges in some flashes of situational as well as verbal humour. The situational humour mainly occurs at the end of the film when the two protagonists, Jorge and Pedro, are intent on pulling the wool over everyone's eyes in order to lay plans for their escape to Mexico City. (Mexico City is, itself, a convenient off-stage space where events occur – the elopement of lovers, extramarital sex, non-socially condoned marriage, as well as divorce – which would not occur in the controlled and safe space of the rural community where the Mexican melodrama is conventionally set.) First of all they push the father-in-law into one of the rooms of the house, and lock the door – the slapstick continues when he gets covered in flour, and then finally emerges to the bewilderment of guests when the 'fiesta' is in full swing. Another occurs when the doctor is sent packing with a cock-and-bull story of the 'mayordomo' being in need of medical attention, but actually bumps into him in the street. Verbal humour occurs in the deliberately comical misspellings of the advertisements in the garage in the early scenes of the film, as well as the Asian speech of the father-in-law; the latter humour comes to a climax in the latter's comment: 'me engañaron como a un chino'. Some of the situational humour verges on the gratuitously slapstick, such as when – during the final fiesta – Pedro stands under a deer's antlers hung on the adjoining wall and the party-goers as well as the audience see the antlers on his head, thereby providing a visual expression of the pun to the effect that Pedro is 'cornudo' (literally 'with horns on his head', but metaphorically, 'cuckolded'). Perhaps the most subtle example of humour – which is at once situational and verbal – occurs when Pedro is attempting to pull the wool over the General's eyes and makes up the story about Jorge's genetic illness which means it is not advisable for him to marry. Jorge's letter – which refers in metaphorical terms to his love for Rosario as an 'incurable illness' – and which is read out loud to the General confirms him in his initial misapprehension. It is a joke that continues throughout the film until its conclusion, getting a great deal of mileage.

Ideology

There is no escaping the conservative, bourgeois and *machista* ideology of the film. This comes as no surprise given its self-appointed audience. Jorge, the hero of the piece with whom the audience is encouraged to identify, is a rich man who owns an impressive car – he is the only person we know for definite to be a car-owner – who becomes a landowner early on – specifically the point at which he buys the ranch from a friend in the opening sequences of the film. It ought to be underlined, as well, that he does not need to organise a loan in order to buy the land – he simply agrees to buy it. When a landowner he decides to use his newly-acquired social power to turn the screw on his rival, Pedro, by charging an exorbitant amount for water. During the first few decades of the twentieth century – mainly as a result of the Mexican Revolution (1911–1919) in which the landless attempted to seize more control of social space – land ownership and water rights were extremely fraught social issues throughout Mexico. *Dos tipos de cuidado*, however, simply presents Jorge's decision to capitalise on his newly-acquired land as an example of a personal grudge, carefully avoiding to make the struggle transparent on contemporary social issues. By avoiding the issue, and focusing instead on a game of cards (the idea being 'you win some, you lose some') Ismael Rodríguez's film shows its bourgeois ideological credentials. Pointing in the same conservative direction, the lower classes – when they appear, which is rare – are figures of fun, rather like Falstaff in Shakespeare's plays: the garage mechanics cannot spell ('le preztamos cavallo' instead of 'le prestamos caballo'), and the young boy, who tries to borrow a horse when he brings his bike in to be repaired, is simply laughed off the stage.

Machismo is passed off in the film in a similar way as a naturalised ideology. The women in the movie – despite or, indeed, as a result of their beauty – are totally at the whim and mercy of the men. Both Rosario and María are like putty in their men's hands when they hear their men serenading them while in bed. The women, it seems, either sigh or cry. When we first meet Pedro he is given the baby to look at and, after making some rude comments about it, suddenly notices his wife – a little surprising since she has just given birth. He comments: 'Oh, I didn't notice you were there.' The comment is an ideological rather than a naturalistic one. Despite overwhelming evidence that her husband is a womaniser, Rosario ignores it, and argues with her father, defending Pedro's behaviour. When Pedro and Jorge need to talk, the women are simply dismissed off the set, and disappear routinely without a comment. Any action of rebellion by the women leads to their coming unstuck. When Rosario – one would think justifiably – complains that Jorge is at a 'fiesta' with another woman even though he is betrothed to her, and asks him to leave, Jorge takes offence, claiming that her request means that he is the 'offended party'. He simply leaves, and Rosario is left to pick up the pieces. *Machismo* becomes the wellspring of the plot during the second half of the film especially. Thus the General forces Pedro to agree to kill Jorge, since his family honour has been besmirched. Pedro's comment that he will seek legal redress – he will bring about his rival's 'muerte civil' as he says – is treated with derision by the General, who says that only death will do. Though the scene is gently humorous – especially as Pedro tries to hold up the proceedings by saying he wants to drink some lemonade – there is little within the scene which would suggest that the ideology of *machismo* is being either questioned or undermined. But it could be argued that there is more to this *comedia ranchera* than meets the eye. The fact that it has two rather than one *charro* upsets the gender balance of the traditional *comedia ranchera*. Indeed, as Jorge Ayala Blanco has pointed out, *Dos tipos de cuidado* is a comedy of errors with a latent homosexual sub-plot (Ayala Blanco, pp. 77–83).

Hollywood, Melodrama and the Ranch

Hollywood is clearly the template for this type of movie, mainly as a result of its use of the star, the musical, and the use of a number of motifs common in the western movie. Jorge comes over in this film as a kind of Clark Gable of the Mexican hinterland, the good-looking tough man who never backs down, has a high sense of personal honour, and always gets the girl. Melodrama is often seen as an unsophisticated genre, which presents the difference between good and evil in unproblematic terms. Up to a point this is true in *Dos tipos de cuidado*, since Jorge is the good guy – loyal, a man of his world, and tough –while Pedro is the bad guy – treacherous (prepared to steal his best friend's girl), a coward (he backs down when taunted by Jorge), a womaniser (as we see in the first bar scene), and a drunkard (in a clearly choreographed sequence, Jorge is shown sitting at a table high up in the restaurant with Victoria drinking discreetly, while Pedro is shown down below forcing a young girl to drink tequila neat out of a bottle). But this manichean distinction becomes undermined as the film progresses until – as mentioned above – during the simultaneous serenade scenes, Jorge and Pedro become fused. It is striking that Jorge is now the one who is drinking heavily and it is not coincidental that, during the next scene, the two men have in a sense changed places, since Pedro now has Jorge's white hat (which he is wearing in the opening scene of the film proper), while Jorge has Pedro's black one.

The Ranch fulfils an important function in this as in countless other Mexican melodramas. It is the home to which the film always finally gravitates. Inevitably re-working Fernando de Fuentes's *Allá en el Rancho Grande* (1936), *Dos tipos de cuidado* tends to idealise, in Monsiváis's words, 'the purity of the maidens, the character of the peasant farmer, the kindness of the hacienda-owners, the perpetual jollity of the fiestas, the advantages of living on the margins of modernity' (Monsiváis, p. 118). Bought at the beginning, it becomes the setting for the final reconciliation of everyone during the fiesta in which Pedro and Jorge share the lead in singing popular *ranchera* songs. In one significant shot taken mid-way through the Rancho sequence, we see the Doctor, the General and Jorge's mother all drinking merrily as they watch the show unfold before their eyes. Though there is little to differentiate the style of the entertainment provided in the Rancho with that provided in the bar early on, the film implicitly draws a distinction between them. Dancing with various women in the bar early on, Pedro was depicted as the bad man, the womaniser, the depraved, lustful Mexican; in a word used on many occasions during the film, he was the archetypal 'desgraciado'. But now the dancing and drinking and fraternising has been 'cleaned up', in effect, 'redeemed', since it is now taking place within the bourgeois space of the

Ranch. Once a social outcast, Pedro has now been re-integrated into the space of Mexican bourgeois identity. The middle classes – after a bit of piquant entertainment – are now free to breathe a sigh of relief.

Camerawork

The camerawork is conventional enough during the film, as one might expect. During the simultaneous serenades the screen is split to show both women in reaction shots to the serenade, and to emphasise the similarity of their respective plights (both of the loves are impossible, and therefore highly romantic, hence the tears). The serenades themselves are also shown in split screen to emphasise how – in reality – the two main protagonists have now grown much closer. The important point here is that the musical sequences are designed to undermine the individuality of the characters as actants within a defined plot. The viewer is thereby encouraged to project into the film's portrayal of love in 'universalist' terms. The characters, though, are not simply wallpaper on which the musical performances are hung. After this particular scene, Jorge Bueno is no longer as good as he was at the beginning of the film, while Pedro is able to elicit the audience's sympathy much more effectively. It is for this reason that the immediately following sequence shows Jorge with a black hat and Pedro wearing a white one, and – perhaps more important – shows Jorge as the aggressor (he strikes Pedro first, and Pedro retaliates, but refuses to kill him, thereby echoing the reaction of the good guy in the classic western). One other feature deserves mentioning. The two protagonists, when depicted singing, are often caught in low angle shots, thereby enhancing the grandiose nature of their singing abilities: the film, after all, is not so much a narrative as a sequence of stage props via which the 'ranchera' songs are showcased.

Works Cited

De la Vega Alfaro, Eduardo, 'The Decline of the Golden Age and the Making of the Crisis', in *Mexico's Cinema: A Century of Film and Filmmakers*, eds Joanne Hershfield and David R. Maciel (Wilmington, Delaware: Scholarly Resources, 1999), pp. 165–91.

King, John, *Magical Reels: A History of Cinema in Latin America* (London: Verso, 1990).

Hart, Stephen, 'Cinema in Mexico', in *An Encyclopedia of Latin American Culture*, ed. Peter Standish (Detroit: Manley Publishers, 1995–6), pp. 78–81.

Maza, Maximiliano, 'Las 100 mejores películas mexicanas' www.cinemexicano. mty.itesm.mx/peliculas/dostipos.html (consulted on 18 December 2003).

Medina de la Serna, Rafael, 'Sorrows and Glories of Comedy', in *Mexican Cinema*, ed. Paulo Antonio Paranaguá, trans. Ana M. López (London: BFI, 1995), pp. 163–70.

Monsiváis, Carlos, 'Mythologies', in *Mexican Cinema*, ed. Paulo Antonio Paranaguá, trans. Ana M. López (London: BFI, 1995), pp. 117–27.

4

ORFEU NEGRO (BLACK ORPHEUS, 1959), DIRECTED BY MARCEL CAMUS

Cast

Orfeu, played by Breno Mello
Eurydice, played by Marpessa Dawn
Death, played by Adhemar da Silva
Mira, played by Lourdes de Oliveira
Serafina, played by Lèa Garcia
Hermes, played by Alexandro Constantino
Chico Boto, played by Waldetar de Souza
Benedito, played by Jorge dos Santos
Zeca, played by Aurino Cassanio

Crew

Director: Marcel Camus
Production Companies: Dispat Film / Gemma / Cinematografica / Tupan Filmes
Producer: Sacha Gordine
Production Manager: Jacques Gibault
Music: Luis Bonfá, Antonio Carlos Jobim
Screenplay: Vinitius de Morães, based on his play
Photography: Jean Bourgoin
Editor: Andrée Feix

Awards

Oscar for Best Foreign Language Film, Academy of Motion Picture Arts and Sciences, Hollywood, 1959
Best Film (Palme d'Or), Cannes International Film Festival, 1959
Best Film, Venice Film Festival, 1959

Plot

Establishing scenes show excited preparation for the Rio de Janeiro Carnival taking place in the shanty town of the 'Morros' on the steep cliffs above Rio. Eurydice arrives on the ship coming into the harbour, and she is invited onto a tram by the driver, Orfeu. When they arrive at the terminal, Eurydice is directed by Orfeu's boss, Hermes, to the house of her cousin, Serafina. Orfeu is met by his girlfriend, Mira, who persuades him to go along to the marriage ceremonies office to arrange their marriage. Afterwards he refuses to buy her a ring, choosing instead to get his guitar back from the pawn shop. Eurydice arrives at Serafina's house and tells her that she has run away because a man is after her to kill her. Meanwhile Orfeu is asked by the two young boys, Benedito and Zeca, if it is true that his songs make the sun rise; he sings for them and Eurydice, who is next door, hears his song and is charmed. Orfeu introduces himself to Eurydice and tells her the story of the Greek myth of Orpheus's love for Eurydice. Serafina takes Mira off, thereby allowing Orfeu to dance with Eurydice; a dionysian-erotic frenzy ensues. While Eurydice is having her dress prepared, Death appears at the window, and she takes fright and runs off. Death finally catches up with her, and is about to kill her when Orfeu frightens him off. Serafina decides to let Eurydice go to the Carnival so she can spend time with her boyfriend, Chico, who has arrived from Montevideo. During the Carnival, Mira suddenly realises she has been tricked, pulls off Serafina's veil, and discovers she is Eurydice; she then tries to kill her. Eurydice runs off, and death chases her to the Tram Terminal. To escape Death, Eurydice hangs onto the overhead electrified lines; Orfeu arrives and turns on the electricity, unwittingly electrocuting Eurydice. Orfeu is then knocked unconscious by Death and, when he awakes, he goes looking for her. He first of all goes to the Department of Lost People, but just finds a man sweeping paper in empty rooms. He then goes to a Brazilian 'santería' religious ceremony; and a medium speaks to him in Eurydice's voice, but he loses her by turning around. Orfeu then goes to the morgue, collects her body, and returns to the 'Morros'. Mira throws a stone at Orfeu, hitting him on the head, and knocks him off the cliff, killing him. The final scene of the film shows a young girl dancing to music played by the two young boys, Benedito and Zeca.

Analytical Overview

Orfeu negro, as Peter Rist points out, 'is not, strictly speaking, a Brazilian film' (Rist, p. 123), since the director was French and most of the production team French or Italian. It may seem a little stagey to audiences nowadays, but it is a classic of its time. It scooped the Palme d'Or at Cannes, first prize at Venice, and first prize for Best Foreign Film at the Oscars in Hollywood ('Cannes 1959'; 'Academy Awards'). In terms of its production history it has similarities with Buñuel's *Los olvidados* (1950; see chapter 2), for, like Buñuel, the director of *Orfeu negro* was a foreigner (Marcel Camus was French and, indeed, this may well have helped the film achieve some international awards; see below). Like his Spanish counterpart, Camus spent a great deal of time walking the streets of the big Latin American city, getting his story, as it were, from the streets. 'For weeks I had to walk around the streets of Rio, since I couldn't even afford to take taxis. At least this gave me the chance to get to know the city better, to feel

I really understood something of its character and people' (Video Cassette Cover, BFI). There was one other similarity. Like Buñuel, Camus chose to use non-professional actors for his film. Camus used his wife, Marpessa Dawn, a former actress, for the lead role of Eurydice, but the starring role of Orfeu was played by Breno Mello, a part-time professional football player and lawyer. It will not come as a surprise, therefore, to learn that Marcel Camus had worked briefly with Buñuel after the Second World War.

The fact that Camus was a foreigner probably explains the choice of location for the major scenes of the film, the spectacular, rather exotic view of Rio as seen from the steep cliffs of 'Os Morros' overlooking the bay. Pointing in a similar direction, there are long sequences focusing specifically on the dance routines, processions and general merrymaking of the Carnival which appear to have been included for their entertainment value rather than their filmic strength. However, when the film harmonises the cityscape environment with its plot – as, for example, in the scenes when Orfeu and Eurydice first dance together, or when Eurydice is chased by Death through the 'hell' of deep, dark valleys outside Rio – the effect achieved is often impressive.

Orfeu negro re-works the Greek myth of Orpheus and Eurydice. The story is a familiar one. Orpheus married Eurydice, and make heartbroken when she died from a snake bite. With his singing and playing he managed to make his way back to the netherworld, charming Charon, the ferryman on the river Styx, Cerberus, the dead, and even Hades, the king of the underworld. He was allowed to bring her back to the world of the living, but with the condition that he should never look back. Emerging from the underworld and seeing the sun, he feels the need to share his experience with Eurydice; turning back, he sees her briefly, but then she disappears.

Camus's film is essentially a re-writing of Jean Cocteau's *Orphée* (1950). Cocteau focused on the myth of Orpheus in a number of works, including his 1950 masterpiece but also in two other films he directed – *Le Sang d'un poète* (1932) and *Le Testament d'Orphée* (1959), as well as the script which he wrote for Jean Delannoy's *L'Éternel retour* (1943). As Roy Armes has suggested, Cocteau 'regarded the myth of Orpheus as *his* myth, for he felt himself to be a man with one foot in life and the other in death' (author's emphasis; Armes, p. 144). Camus's *Orfeu negro* shares with Cocteau's *Orphée* the sense of re-creation of a classical myth within a contemporary setting. Cocteau's film, for example, 'makes full use of the trappings of the real world: black-clad motorcyclists, machine guns, Rolls-Royces and mysterious messages which echo wartime Resistance codes' (Armes, p. 143). Camus, for his part, re-enacts the Orpheus myth within the fraught atmosphere of the Rio de Janeiro carnival. For both Camus and Cocteau, the Orpheus theme allows death to be presented as if it had 'lost its sting'. As Armes suggests: 'For a work dealing so largely with death, *Orphée* is remarkably idyllic in tone. There is no sense of terror here, for death is a beautiful woman. There is no sense of physical decline or decay and death is totally lacking in irrevocability or awesomeness' (Armes, p. 144). A very simi-lar structure of feeling, as we shall see, permeates Camus's *Orfeu negro*, though

Camus's main aim is produce an endogenous version of the Orpheus myth which is more in tune with Brazil's cultural and ethnic identity.

In his racialising gesture Camus was in certain key respects taking a leaf out of Jean-Paul Sartre's book. The French philosopher had published an influential essay in 1948 entitled 'Orphée noir' which acted as a prologue to Léopold Sédar Senghor's influential anthology of black francophone poetry published in that year. In his rather dramatic essay Sartre envisaged a scene in which the blacks of the world, who had for so long accepted their subaltern status, were now beginning to turn the tables. It was the whites now who came under the gaze of the blacks:

> Voici des hommes noirs debout que nous regardent et je vous souhaite de ressentir comme moi le saisissement d'être vus. Car le blanc a joui trois mille ans du privilège de voir sans qu'on le voie; il était regard pur, la lumière de ses yeux tirait toute chose de l'ombre natale, la blancheur de sa peau c'était un regard encore, de la lumière condensée. L'homme blanc, blanc parce qu'il était homme, blanc comme le jour, blanc comme la vérité, blanc comme la vertu, éclairait la création comme une torche, dévoilait l'essence secrète et blanche des êtres. Aujourd'hui ces hommes nous regardent et notre regard rentre dans nos yeux.   (p. ix)

From a situation of cultural inferiority now the black in Sartre's eyes was able to speak of his and her own experience; the black slave had regained subject-ivity. Sartre's essay was also important in that it stressed the creativity of the French Caribbean subject. Orpheus – the iconic singer of ancient Greece – is now black. Perhaps more important than the original inspiration, though, was the use that Camus made of the idea. Like Sartre, Camus appears in *Orfeu negro* to advocate a new Brazilian mythology, and intends to achieve that by inflecting Western myths with a new ethnic coding. Nowadays we would see this as an example of transposition rather than transculturation or synthesis, and in what follows we will look at the strengths and weaknesses of such an approach.

Greek Mythology

The film is replete with classical cultural references. Not only are the lovers – as mentioned above – a reasonably faithful rendering of the story of Orpheus and Eurydice but there are a number of other characters and events which are lifted from Greek mythology. The blind man who bumps into Eurydice at the begin-ning of the film as she gets off the boat – given that he seems very knowledge-able – appears to allude to the blind seer, Tiresias. Hermes – Orfeu's boss at the Tramway Terminal – recalls the Greek God of the same name who is famed for his abilities as a messenger. To all intents and purposes, this is his role in the film – first when Eurydice arrives and he tells her how to get to Serafina's house, and, secondly, when he instructs her to go to the Tramway Terminal. Like his Greek counterpart, his messages come from the Gods, and they are not always positive. By instructing Eurydice to go back to the Terminal he is sending her to her death. The dog protecting the house where the 'santería' session is going on is called Cerberus, a reference to the dog protecting hell in classical literature, and, particularly, in the Sixth Book of Virgil's *Aeneid*. Though more subtle, the kite which appears at the beginning of the film – and which appears to be dragged earthwards – alludes to the ill-fated plight of Icarus, who flew too close to the sun. Other references to European literature are characterised by a similar type of transposition; the stairs down which Orfeu descends after visiting the Disappeared People Department are redolent of the seven circles of hell in Dante's *Inferno*. Some critics have criticised the film for this over-elaborate use of Greek tragedy. As one critic points out: 'The central conceit of *Orfeu Negro*, the overarching structure of Greek tragedy, is one of the reasons for its world-wide success. One could criticise such imposition of an outside culture as being emblematic of the film's non-Brazilian, European nature, and this would be jus-tified' (Rist, p. 125).

Perhaps more interesting than the examples of straight transposition are those cases when the original myth has been transmuted and thereby given a life of its own. An obvious example of this is the music with which Orpheus is intrinsic-ally associated. Whereas in classical accounts it is the lyre, in Camus's film it is the guitar, which allows for some simple yet charming love-songs sung to Eurydice by Orfeu; Bonfá's guitar sound-track, in particular featuring 'Manhã de Carnaval' and 'Samba de Orfeu', was subsequently released and became a worldwide hit ('Orfeu Negro'). Other transpositions are effective. The terminal is an effective and realistic modern-day image of hell, and electricity – especially the high voltage of overhead power cables – is an effective transformation of the snakebite of the original Greek myth.

The Search

Camus's film also changes the nature of the search that Orfeu conducts for Eurydice when she dies. Whereas in the Greek myth, Orpheus goes back to hell, in Camus's version he looks for Eurydice in three separate locations. Firstly he goes to the 'Departamento de Desaparecidos' (The Department of Disappeared People) where a man is seen simply sweeping up paper in large, empty rooms. It is a remarkably effective image of the 'lostness' of the dead – a clearly symbolic space lacking any sense of empiric realism – possessing a grotesque Kafkian air about it. Secondly, Orfeu goes to a 'santería' session. Many of the strands of clas-sical mythology are in evidence here – the dog is called Cerberus, for example, as mentioned above – but they are integrated effectively into a new set of cultural references. The Orphic movement in ancient Greece – with which Orpheus's name is associated – involved shamanistic rites in which an individual represent-ing the God Dionysus is thought to have been symbolically or actually dismem-bered, and then reborn. Camus evokes the notion of life after bodily death central to the Hellenistic Orphic movement in his re-enactment of an Afro-Brazilian shamanistic rite in which a medium is possessed by the dead lover's soul. At this point the Greek mythological story is tucked neatly into a Brazilian context. In a striking and, in some degree shocking, re-creation of the Greek myth – Orfeu turns around and 'sees' that he has now lost Eurydice for ever. (The shocking element is that the medium is the opposite of the beautiful, young Eurydice; she is fat and ugly.) The third – more realistic – stage of the search involves Orfeu returning to the Rio Morgue and picking up her body. He expresses his gratitude for a new day, despite holding Eurydice's lifeless corpse in his arms, and then returns to the shanty town where he lives. In a sequence that not all would find artistically satisfactory, Mira throws a stone at Orfeu's head and he falls off the cliff. Thus the film ends, except for the epilogue in which a young girl – dressed in a white dress and therefore to be understood as a reincarnation of Eurydice – dances seductively in time to the music of the new Orpheus, Zeca. In this sense the film concludes on a positive note; not all has been lost. Eurydice and Orfeu have died, but they have been reincarnated in the form of two young 'lovers'. The Eternal Cycle has started up again.

Flaws and Flashes of Brilliance: A Balance Sheet

There are a few points in the film where the modern viewer may become a little impatient with Camus's vision and mise-en-scène. Most of these are a result of the difficult circumstances under which the film was produced, and the extremely ambitious scale on which it was created. They do not detract from the overall positive impression derived from this film. Some of the 'flaws' of the film concern those points at which the mythic elements jar with the depiction of a contemporary Brazilian cultural reality. Despite the fact that the characters live in the shanty town in the high cliffs overlooking Rio, they look remarkably clean and free of economic problems. In the only sequence when poverty is mentioned, it is overridden by the suggestion that giving the local grocer a kiss is enough to solve the problem of scarcity. Most would agree that this is an unrealistic, if charming, view of life in the shanty towns of Rio. In some ways, Os Morros looks like a paradise; it is a vision which contrasts very sharply with the gritty view of life in a shanty town that we find in Fernando Meirelles's more recent film, *Cidade de Deus* (see chapter 25). The use of a character called simply Death – and recognised in a matter-of-fact way as such by the younger characters in the film, Benedito and Zeca – has a dramatic force about it but, as the film progresses, its effectiveness seems to wane. Eurydice's death is depicted in a rather wooden way. While the use of the electricity wires is an effective modern-urban image of death, the manner in which Eurydice seems to be 'hanging' on the wire is not realistic, and the reason why Orfeu should simply turn the electricity on is not explained. The way in which Orfeu dies – is it an accidental throw to the head by Mira, or did she mean it? if she did, why the sadness afterwards? – is not verisimilous, and does not provide a satisfactory sense of completion to the film.

There are a number of flashes of brilliance in this film. The acting provided by all actors is excellent, which is quite remarkable given that the majority were not professional actors. Breno Mello, Marpessa Dawn and Lourdes de Oliveira all provide subtly choreographed performances. The establishing scenes of the film are vibrant, and combine various sequences of dancing in various parts of the cliffs which appear 'natural'. It is difficult to think of how even a Hollywood blockbuster would manage to give a sense of the Carnival affecting all elements of the population. The fact that the very first shot of the film shows a dancer in mid-air gives a clear indication of the pulsating atmosphere of what is to come; the sounds and rhythms of the Carnival are never far away. The sequences in which Eurydice is surrounded by dancers in a dance of entrapment – once at the beginning of the film soon after she gets off the boat, and once near the end when she is attempting to escape Death who is hot on her trail – are delightful. Likewise the playful love-scenes between Serafina and Chico, which act as an earthy, humorous counterpoint to the transcendent love occurring between Orfeu and Eurydice upstairs, are masterfully done.

Works Cited

'Academy Awards', Academy of Modern Pictures Arts and Sciences, Hollywood, www.awardsdatabase.oscars.org (consulted on 18 December 2003).

'Cannes 1959', www.festival-cannes.fr/archives/fichedition.php?langue=60002& edition=1959 (consulted on 18 December 2003).

Armes, Roy, *French Cinema*, 3rd ed. (London: Secker and Warburg, 1985).

King, John, *Magical Reels: A History of Cinema in Latin America* (London: Verso, 1990).

'Orfeo Negro', www.kanzi.zinbun.kyota-u.ac.ip/~yasuoka/Bonfa/Orfeu.html (consulted on 18 December 2003).

Rist, Peter, 'Orfeu Negro', in *South American Cinema: A Critical Filmography 1915–1994*, eds Timothy Barnard and Peter Rist (Austin: University of Texas Press, 1996), pp. 123–5.

Sartre, Jean-Paul, 'Orphée Noir', in *Anthologie de la nouvelle poésie nègre et malgache de langue française*, ed. Léopold Sédar Senghor (Paris: Presses Universitaires de France, 1969), pp. ix–xliv.

5

MEMORIAS DEL SUBDESARROLLO
(MEMORIES OF UNDERDEVELOPMENT, 1968),
DIRECTED BY TOMÁS GUTIÉRREZ ALEA

Cast

Sergio, played by Sergio Corrieri
Elena, played by Daisy Granados
Pablo, played by Omar Valdés
Noemí, played by Eslinda Núñez
Laura, played by Beatriz Ponchera
Elena's brother, played by René de la Cruz

With

Yolanda Far
Ofelia González
José Gil Abada
Daniel Jordán
Luis López
Rafael Sosa

Crew

Screenplay: Tomás Gutiérrez Alea, based on novel *Inconsolable Memories* by
Edmundo Desnoes
Photography: Ramón F. Suárez
Editor: Nelson Rodríguez
Music: Leo Brouwer
Conductor: Manuel Duchesne Cuzán
Director: Tomás Gutiérrez Alea
Produced by: the Cuban Film Institute

Awards

Winner, Best Foreign Language Film, XVI International Film Festival, Karlovy
Vary, Czechoslovakia, 1968
Winner, Sirena Prize, Critics' Club, Varsovia, Poland, 1970

Jury Selection, London Film Festival, 1971
Nominee, Rosenthal Prize, U.S. National Society of Film Critics (Alea was refused
a visa by U.S. State Department to attend the award ceremony)
Selected by the *New York Times* as one of the best ten films of 1973 (the year in
which it opened commercially in New York)

Plot

Film opens with a street scene in which someone is shot and then led off – a scene
which reappears later on in the consciousness of the main character and narrator,
Sergio Camona. Set in Havana in 1961, we see footage of people leaving Havana
for Miami at passport control. Sergio says good-bye to his wife, Laura, and his parents who are leaving for the United States. Throughout the film we hear his thoughts
in voice-over. We follow Sergio as he returns to his luxurious apartment. We see
him surveying the city through his telescope, trying to work out if it has changed or
not as a result of the Revolution. He is writing a diary, and spends his time listening to a recorded conversation he had with his wife shortly before she left. He goes
to a book shop and muses that Havana, once considered the Paris of the Caribbean,
is now no better than Guatemala. He meets his well-to-do friend, Pablo, and they
exchange notes on how everything has gone downhill since the Revolution. Sergio
meets a pretty young girl called Elena, whom he introduces to one of his contacts
in the Film Institute, since she says she wants to be an actress. He takes her to his
apartment and they make love. As he gets to know Elena, he begins to think that
she is 'underdeveloped', 'inconsistent', and therefore an epitome of Cuba. Pablo
decides he can remain no longer and emigrates to the United States. Sergio remembers his school days and how he used to visit brothels as a young man. He goes with
Elena to the Hemingway museum, and then they both attend a lecture about cultural underdevelopment. He meets a new girl, who is blond and from Germany,
Hannah, and he has a passionate affair with her. He doesn't answer the door when
Elena calls. He has an interview with an unidentified individual who writes down
a description of his apartment; his property is subsequently seized by the Castro
government. Elena's brother bursts into the apartment and angrily demands that he
marry Elena. An ugly street scene in which Elena's father attempts to attack Sergio.
They charge him with rape. The judge, however, dismisses the case. The Cold War
is hotting up, and we see press coverage of the war of words between the Soviet
Union and President Kennedy. Fidel Castro gives a speech and mobilises the population ready for the Yankee attack. Sergio cannot comprehend what is going on, and
he sits around in his apartment idly flicking his lighter, or watching the water go
down the sink. We see Sergio once more surveying the city. The film ends on a note
of indecision as the suspense mounts as to where the Cold War is leading.

Analytical Overview

The fact that it is easy to mis-interpret this film on a first take is suggested by
the controversy that surrounded its U.S. release in 1973. Some critics – such as

Andrew Sarris of the U.S. National Society of Film Critics – saw it as an anti-Castro, anti-Revolution film (for more information see Chanan, 'Lessons of Experience', pp. 12–14). Others, however, saw it as a rejection of all those bourgeois values which Fidel Castro himself saw as holding Cuba back from its future. Oil was added to an already incandescent situation when the U.S. State Department denied Alea a visa in January 1974 to attend a ceremony in which he was to be honoured by the National Society of Film Critics, because of his alleged anti-American activities (Fornet, pp. 143–9). The reason for the confusion is that the protagonist of *Memorias del subdesarrollo*, in direct contra-distinction to the Hollywood model, is used deliberately as the butt of political satire. Our assumption is that – as viewers – we will identify and sympathise with the protagonist of a film. This will almost certainly be the frame of mind of the viewer during the opening scenes of the film. But as *Memorias del subdesarrollo* develops it becomes more and more difficult to sympathise with Sergio, especially when we see how he treats the various women in the film. Starting out as a kind of Cuban version of James Bond, the image cracks as the film develops, and we end up with an image of him as 'old', 'rotten' (like a fruit), aloof and disconnected from the world in which he lives.

From Book to Film

Memories of Underdevelopment follows the plot of Edmundo Desnoes's novel *Inconsolable Memories* quite closely, but – as one might expect – it develops some new themes and introduces some new scenes, including 'Sergio and Pablo's conversation in the automobile, the scene at Hemingway's home, the tape-recorded arguments between Sergio and Laura, Sergio's erotic fantasies about Noemí, and the speeches by Kennedy and Castro' (*Memories of Underdevelopment*, ed. Chanan, p. 113). It is important to note that these particular sequences grow naturally from the plot – i.e. they are consistent with what comes before – but, perhaps more importantly, in filmic terms they are extremely successful sequences, powerful and moving. Alea, not surprisingly, regarded *Memories of Underdevelopment* as one of his two best films (the other was *La última cena*) (Évora, p. 65).

Sergio's Blindness

Despite the fact that we are seeing the world through Sergio's eyes from beginning to end of the film, it is soon quite apparent that he is blind to the reality of Cuba. He is, in the words of Michael Chanan, 'suspended between the old and the new' ('Lessons of Experience', p. 4). As Deborah Shaw has pointed out: 'Alea revealed that Sergio's self-perception is flawed and that the accusations of underdevelopment which Sergio levels at the Cuban people are more appropriately directed toward himself' (Shaw, p. 15). He is guilty, we might say, of misrecognition. He misunderstands the reasons why his wife leaves him, refusing to analyse the reasons for her discontent with him. He miscalculates in his seduction of Elena; by treating her as a mere plaything for his lust, he underestimates the virulence that his actions will elicit from Elena's family. Being so naïve leaves him very vulnerable (he refuses to do the honourable thing and marry Elena now that he has taken her virginity), such that he is accused of rape, and perhaps, in retrospect, lucky to have been exonerated. He sees himself as very different from all the people who are leaving Cuba; he compares them to parts of himself that he is vomiting out – and yet there is no immediately recognisable way of distinguishing him from those who are fleeing Cuba for the United States. He speaks very disparagingly of his 'friend' Pablo, whom he accompanies to the airport, calling him an 'idiot', and seeing his departure as a means whereby he can take revenge on all the idiots of Cuba. He mis-interprets the interview he has with the two government officials, failing to realise that they are able to impound his property. Finally, he sees Ernest Hemingway as an 'insufferable' person, but given the similarities between the two of them – they are not part of Cuba, they simply see it as a haven from the world, they exploit their environment for their own enjoyment – the viewer, on reflection, is more likely to see them as kindred souls. The greatest irony of all, of course, is the way in which he sees Cuba as characterised in terms of 'underdevelopment'. The women stare too much, they have no interest in culture or art, and they are therefore underdeveloped (and here Elena carries the brunt of his dismissive attitude). Thus he prefers Hannah simply because she is blond. He takes the side of the North-American individual who attends the seminar on underdevelopment, who argues that the round-table discussion on 'underdevelopment' is itself a symptom of cultural underdevelopment. Yet, as the film progresses, we become gradually more critical of Sergio's attitude. His reaction to Castro's speech – when he calls on Cuban citizens to repel the impending invasion by Yankee forces – is seen indifferently by Sergio who simply says he is unable to understand what is going on. The closing section of the film, as Michael Chanan suggests, 'shows Sergio's ultimate self-paralysis as the city around him engages in defence preparations during the unfolding of the so-called Cuban missile crisis' (*The Cuban Image*, p. 245). The viewer is persuaded that his blindness is quite deliberate. He often simply turns the TV off, for example, when it becomes too political. The TV footage on various issues confronting Cuba simply washes over Sergio, though they have the effect of persuading the viewer to look beneath the surface. The fact that the narrator is blind suggests that Gutiérrez Alea is doing for the medium of film what Machado de Assis (in *Dom Casmurro*) and André Gide (in *La Porte étroite*) did for the novel. Sergio is an unreliable narrator. By letting us see everything through Sergio's eyes – but also gradually undercutting that vision – Gutiérrez Alea makes sure that our final appreciation of reality is a pro-Revolutionary one.

The Dialectic and History

As Ismail Xavier has pointed out, cinema in the 1960s in the developing world often focused on national politics and culture, and Cuba was no exception: 'In Latin America, Brazilian *cinema novo*, "Third Cinema" from Argentina, and the Cuban post-Revolutionary cinema from the 1960s took national destiny as a central theme. A concern with social issues such as poverty, labor exploitation, oligarchy, and foreign domination brought a new point of view on modern history, in opposition to the Eurocentric perspective usually expressed by North-American and European cinema' (Xavier, p. 355). Gutiérrez Alea has argued, indeed, that one of the aims of Cuban film is – following Marxist theory – to offer a dialectical view of Cuban history. One technique that Alea uses in order to do this is to splice the film narrative itself with live footage of actual events. In this sense the film narrative becomes a commentary on actual historical events. As Alea has pointed out: 'For cinema it was almost sufficient just to record events, to capture directly some fragment of reality, and simply reflect the goings-on in the streets. These images projected on the screen turned out to be interesting, revealing and spectacular' ('The Viewer's Dialectic', p. 108). There are a number of examples of *cinéma-vérité* in *Memorias del subdesarrollo*, beginning with scenes of people leaving Cuba at the port, footage of the war which propelled Fidel Castro to power and Batista into exile, footage on Calviño, a convicted murderer, footage of a public discussion between intellectuals about cultural underdevelopment, and – most important of all – footage of the stand-off between Kennedy and Kruschev during the Missile Crisis, and Castro's speeches urging Cuban citizens to join up. In Alea's words: 'The feature film is usually fiction (. . .) On the other hand, in Cuba, we have extensively developed a type of feature-length documentary in which real-life events are recreated or shown exactly as they are captured by the camera at the moment of their occurrence' ('The Viewer's Dialectic', p. 117). Yet *Memorias del subdesarrollo* is not simply a documentary since it is based also on a fictional plot – Desnoes's *Inconsolable Memories* – and both elements are necessary for the type of film Alea was interested in creating. As Alea has pointed out: 'Film has always moved between these two poles: documentary and fiction' ('The Viewer's Dialectic', p. 111). By having the montage oscillate between the recreation of real-life events and the fictional plot, Alea aimed to provoke a more active and less passive response in the viewer. This is essentially what Alea means by the viewer's dialectic, this oscillation between the real and the fictional: 'Film will be more fruitful to the extent that it pushes spectators toward a more profound understanding of reality and, consequently, to the extent that it helps viewers live more actively and incites them to stop being mere spectators in the face of reality. To do this, film ought to appeal not only to emotion and feeling but also to reason and intellect' ('The Viewer's Dialectic', p. 120). At times, therefore, Alea will use the repertoire of film language in a novel way which makes strange what is commonplace (what the Russian formalists called 'ostrananie'). Such is the case with the use of voice-over. Since the film uses voice-over to relay to the viewer Sergio's thoughts (which are highly subjective and individualist) as well as the newspeaker's statements (which are cast as objective and 'true'), the viewer at times hesitates when seeing both presented in the same code. For many viewers this is initially a disorientating experience, though it should be said that Alea is attempting to draw attention to the contradiction between the subjective and objective levels. Does the subjective really even exist? Alea seems to be saying.

Self-reflexivity

Memorias del subdesarollo is self-reflexive on a number of levels. More obviously, Alea uses reflections in mirrors and glass at points in the narrative when Sergio is reflecting on his life, and, of course, the Cuban *cinéaste* is not the first first director to do this. The use of the mirror image is something of a film director's stock-in-trade, and some film directors – such as Joseph Losey in *The Servant* (1963) and *Secret Ceremony* (1968) – have specialised in its use (see Aumont, p. 203), but Alea uses the mirror image in a consistently individual way to indicate – specifically in a political sense – self-reflexivity shot through with self-blindness (namely, we can see the truth but Sergio cannot). The film not only uses everyday reportage, there are sections within the film in which it reflects upon its own genesis. In the round-table discussion about underdevelopment, for example, which Sergio attends with Elena, one of the round-table participants is Edmundo Desnoes, the author of the novel (*Inconsolable Memories*) on which the film is based. In effect, the film is playing with the difference between the real and the fictional, allowing one to feed into another in a way which is redolent of Pirandello's *Six Actors in Search of an Author*. Sergio is totally unconvinced by Desnoes's interventions, which shows a character 'standing up' to the individual who created him. It is a scene which is at once ironic and humorous. The North American who stands up during the round-table debate, and questions its effectiveness, is none other than Jack Gelber, the author of the foreword to the English edition of the novel. Gelber is, thus, criticising the book he helped to bring into being in English. This Unamunesque play of creator against the created is further complicated by the scene in which Sergio and Elena watch a series of risqué film clips with a film director at the Cuban Film Institute. The director concerned is none other than Gutiérrez Alea himself. His subsequent comment to Sergio that he may well use the scenes in some concocted film later on is supremely ironic, since this is, after all, the film we – as viewers – are actually watching. These different scenes could all be interpreted as 'insider jokes' in which Alea is cocking a private snoop at the audience, but they can also be seen as scenes in which Alea is drawing attention to the osmotic nature of reality and fiction (for further discussion of this scene see Schroeder, pp. 34–5). *Memories of Underdevelopment* raises interesting questions about who is creating the reality that we take for granted. The idea behind all these postmodern games is that Alea is attempting to make his audience more attentive.

Acting and Camerawork

The acting within the film is excellent. Sergio Corrieri (Sergio) and Daisy Granados (Elena) in particular provide compelling performances. Even the highly-fraught scenes in which Sergio is attacked by various members of Elena's family are believable and well-constructed. It was a superb idea to have Sergio looking at various parts of Havana through his telescope, since these sequences thereby function simultaneously as Sergio's POV and general footage of everyday life in

Havana. They also avoid pointing to the director's POV, which could suggest that the viewer's ideology is being manufactured. (It **is**, of course, but the aim of the film is to make sure that it does not appear to be so.) The filming of the playful love scenes between Sergio and Elena – especially those featuring POV close-ups of Elena from Sergio's (lustful) perspective – are delicately done.

Works Cited

Aumont, Jacques, *et al.*, *Aesthetics of Film* (Austin: University of Austin Press, 1992).

Chanan, Michael, 'Lessons of Experience', in *'Memories of Underdevelopment', Tomás Gutiérrez Alea, Director, and 'Inconsolable Memories', Edmundo Desnoes, Author*, ed. Michael Chanan (New Brunswick: Rutgers University Press, 1990), pp. 3–14.

——, *The Cuban Image* (London: BFI, 1985).

Évora, José Antonio, *Tomás Gutiérrez Alea* (Madrid: Cátedra, 1996).

Fornet, Ambrosio (ed.), *Alea: una retrospectiva crítica* (Havana: Letras Cubanas, 1987).

Gutiérrez Alea, Tomás, 'The Viewer's Dialectic', in *New Latin American Cinema: Volume One: Theory, Practices and Transcontinental Articulations*, ed. Michael T. Martin (Detroit: Wayne State University, 1997), pp. 108–31.

King, John, *Magical Reels: A History of Cinema in Latin America* (London: Verso, 1990).

Shaw, Deborah, *Contemporary Cinema of Latin America: 10 Key Films* (London: Continuum, 2003).

Schroeder, Paul A., *Tomás Gutiérrez Alea: The Dialectics of a Filmmaker* (London: Routledge, 2002).

Xavier, Ismail, 'Historical Allegory', in *A Companion to Film Theory*, eds Toby Miller and Robert Stam (Oxford: Blackwell, 1999), pp. 333–62.

6

LUCÍA (1968), DIRECTED BY HUMBERTO SOLÁS

Cast

1895:   Raquel Revuelta, Eduardo Mouré
1932:   Eslinda Núñez
196..:   Adela Legra, Adolfo Llaurado, Idalia Andreus (playing Fernandina), Hermina Sánchez, Silvia Planas, Flora Lauten, María Elena Molinet, Rogelio Blain, Tete Vergara, Flavo Claderín, Aramais Delgado

Also Featuring

Ingrid González, Fernando González, Isabel Moreno, Piedad Zurbanán, Carmelina García, Antonio Cruz, Rafael González, Nancy Rodríguez, Julio Prieto, Farida Hernández, Eulalia Falcón, Aída Busto, Raul Eguren, Amelita Pita, Jesús Hernández, Alicia Agramonte, Olga González, Marta Llovío, Celia Quiñones, Elsa Cárdenas, Eva Pedroso, Aída Conde, Elisa Valdés, Mireyra Bello, Marta Valdés

Crew

Scenography: Pedro García Espinosa, Roberto Miqueli
Construction Manager: Eduardo Lawrence
Dress Designer: María Elena Molinet
Clothes: Carmelina García
Make-up: Magaly Pompa
Set: Pedro Horta
Sound: Eugenio Vesa, Carlos Fernández, Ricardo Istueta
Musical Composer: Leo Brouwer, Joseíto Fernández
Musical Director: Manuel Duchesne Cuzán
Musical recording: Adalberto Jiménez, Egrem Studios
Producers: Raúl Canosa, Camilo Vives
Script: Humberto Solás, Julio García Espinosa, Nelson Rodríguez
Editing: Nelson Rodríguez
Camera: Pablo Martínez, Alberto Menéndez
Effects: Ricardo Suárez
Lights: Rafael González

Photography: Jorge Herrera
Director's Assistants: Inger Seeland, María Ramírez, José G. Aguilar
Director: Humberto Solás

Awards

First Prize, Golden Medal, International Film Festival, Moscow, 1968
Critics' Prize, Havana Film Festival, 1968
Selected for Directors' Fortnight, Cannes International Film Festival, 1969
Honourable Mention, III Meeting of Iberoamerican Film, Barcelona, 1968

Plot

The film consists of three parts, each featuring the trials and tribulations of a woman called Lucía, the first set in 1895, the second in 1932, and the third sometime in the 1960s. Part I opens with a nineteenth-century street scene in which the well-to-do are out walking in their finery. Lucía arrives with her mother in a coach. As they go into church, Lucía brushes shoulders with a handsome man. The women are seen at home, embroidering and sewing in support of the War of Independence currently being waged. A Spanish general arrives – bringing his spoils of war with him – and insults the Cuban people. A mad woman, La Fernandina, starts laughing madly as she sees the dead bodies arrive. Rafaela, Lucía's sister, tells the story of La Fernandina, who used to be a nun until she went mad when raped by some soldiers on the battlefield. Rafael talks to Lucía, expresses his love for her, and is then seen at lunch with Lucía's family, explaining that he is half-Spanish half-Cuban. Lucía's brother, Felipe, who is fighting against the Spanish, arrives for a brief visit. The truth comes out that Rafael is already married, but Lucía agrees to meet him at the sugar mill; they make love and decide to elope. While eloping, however, Lucía is thrown from Rafael's horse when some soldiers fly past, and he leaves her there. In subsequent scenes we see the battles between the Spanish and the Cubans. Lucía comes across her brother, Felipe, dead on the battlefield. In revenge she stabs Rafael to death in the main square. Part II opens with Lucía shown working in a cigar factory. She then recalls how she and her mother were sent to live in a house in the country by their father far from the disturbances in Havana. A rumour soon emerges that the father is having an affair now his wife is out of the way. Lucía meets Aldo, a revolutionary, who is fighting against the Machado dictatorship, and they fall in love. To help him she gets a job in the cigar factory, and – along with Flora – the wife of Antonio, Aldo's fellow revolutionary – they write 'Abajo Machado' (Down with Machado!) in the bathroom. The women later take part in a political demonstration against Machado, which is brutally repressed. Aldo and Antonio shoot and kill some policemen who are watching some dancers in a local theatre house. News comes that Machado's regime has fallen. Aldo goes to Havana but he does not get the kind of job he is looking for; he sees Havana as a den of vice. While drinking with his friends, Aldo and Lucía accuse Antonio

and Flora of betraying the ideals of the revolution for which they all fought. Flora
bursts into tears. Aldo is assassinated, and Lucía identifies him at the morgue. Part
II concludes with an image of Lucía's loneliness. Part III opens with an image
of rural bliss; a truck trundles down the road, all the passengers are singing, and
they pick up 'compañeros' as they go along. Finally they pick up Lucía, who has
just got married to Tomás, and she tells Angelina, the boss on the collective, that
her husband does not want her to work anymore. Tomás sees Lucía talking to a
man at a party and he attacks the man, and decides to keep his wife locked up in
the house from now on. A teacher arrives from Havana to teach Lucía how to
read and write. Reluctant at first, Tomás finally accepts the situation. While he
teaches her to read, the teacher also advises Lucía to leave. Tomás attacks the
teacher, at which point Lucía runs off, and Angelina takes her under her wing.
Lucía begins work at the salt mines, and refuses to return with Tomás when confronted by him. He runs after her. In the final scene of the film Lucía says she
wants to come back, but he has to let her work. The final (happy) image of the
film is provided by a young goat girl laughing at their antics on the beach.

Analytical Overview

Voted second best Cuban film ever by the Parti Cuba/Cine Cubano (Agramonte),
and awarded the Golden Prize at the 1968 Moscow International Film Festival
(MIFF), *Lucía* offers a painful X-ray of the development of Cuban culture in the
twentieth culture. For Solás indeed culture and film are two closely related concepts. As he pointed out in an interview:

> I believe that the second half of this century has been dominated by audiovi-
> sual media. Even if the United States had little or no international presence and
> if Hollywood did not exist, I don't believe that any Latin American country
> would have developed a mature concept of itself as a nation unless it produced
> its own films. Artistic culture is an essential element in the configuration of
> nationhood.   (Martin and Paddington, p. 11)

It is in this sense that we can interpret *Lucía* as not only reflecting but creating
Cuban culture, often, as we shall see, in contradistinction to a hostile power. Part I
occurs against the backdrop of the war for independence in Cuba, a struggle
which was unsuccessful. Spain managed to cling on to its colony for three more
years (in 1898 Spain was drawn into a war with the United States which it lost,
and as a result of which it lost its remaining overseas colonies, including Cuba,
Puerto Rico and the Philippines). The film follows the historical account in the
sense that it shows the Spanish troops winning the war. Part I is arguably the
most inventive of the three parts, in terms of the subtlety of its message as well
as its filmic techniques. The main idea behind Part I concerns the betrayal of Cuba
by Spain in 1895, and this act of political repression is expressed natural-
istically as well as symbolically. Thus we see footage of the actual battle scenes,
in which the Spanish attack the coffee plantation where the Cuban independence

fighters are centred, as well as the scenes in which black Cubans – naked on their horses – attack the Spanish with machetes. The symbolic level – the more interesting – concerns the depiction of the betrayal of a beautiful Cuban woman (Lucía) by a Machievellian Spaniard (Rafael). He has no intention of marrying her and, once he has taken her virginity, he abandons her in a cowardly fashion. While on a naturalistic level the film stays loyal to the historical account, symbolically it expresses the desire for revenge, which takes place in the final scene of Part I in which Lucía stabs Rafael to death. There are other symbolic levels in Part I; La Fernandina acts as a foil to Lucía in that her fate prefigures Lucía's descent into madness. Like La Fernandina, Lucía is betrayed by a man. La Fernandina, indeed, appears to have an inkling about what will happen to Lucía if she runs off with Rafael and advises her not to go – advice which is ignored and which leads to Lucía's downfall. When Lucía is being led off by the crowd after stabbing Rafael, it is La Fernandina who strokes her face, comforting her. This act confirms that, in more than a symbolic sense, Lucía has turned into the mad woman of the village. Patriarchy drives women mad, the film appears to be telling us. Part II is set against the backdrop of the fall from power of the Cuban dictator, Machado, in 1932, while Part III occurs sometime in the 1960s, that is, after the Revolution (1959) has already taken root in Cuba. Parts II and III of the film are much less symbolic and much more realistic than Part I; they are more recognisable as stories about the everyday lives of a number of ordinary, representative individuals and differ drastically from the melodramatic tenseness of Part I.

Politics and Ideology

It is clear that the story of the three Lucías is meant to be understood in a political sense. As Ismail Xavier suggests, *Lucía* 'presents a very original structure based on the allegorical juxtaposition of three stories made in different moments of Cuban history: the time of the struggle for political independence from Spain in the nineteenth century, the time of a frustrated attempt to radically change the country by liberating it from a right-wing dictatorship in the 1930s, and the time of ideological change and new proposals on gender relationships that opposed the *macho* tradition in the post-revolutionary 1960s' (Xavier, p. 356). In each case the audience is provided with a story about a woman who is betrayed, and – given that Lucía is a transparent symbol of Cuba – the film is clearly attempting to voice an awareness of the ways in which Cuba has been exploited and colonised since the fifteenth century. As Solás himself pointed out: '*Lucía* is not a film about women; it's a film about society. But within that society, I chose the most vulnerable character, the one who is most transparently affected at any given moment by contradictions and changes' (quoted in Chanan, pp. 225–6). By implication the film has a message for the present (i.e. for the 1960s) in that it advocates the necessity of the struggle against Yankee imperialism. Each of the three historical junctures have been carefully chosen to make a point about Cuba's gradual transition to the Revolution. As Michael Chanan has pointed

out: 'A love story provides the basic plot for each episode: the first is tragic, the
second melodramatic, the third a comedy' (Chanan, p. 225). Part I portrays the
failed revolution (the enemy is Spain the imperialist country); thus the Cuban
troops lose their battle against the Spanish, although the desire to be free is
expressed in Lucía's destruction of her oppressor in love (Rafael). Part II, as
Solás has revealed, is based on his father's life: 'I'm reflecting a family experience, particularly the story of my father – a man who participated in the insurrection against the dictatorship of Gerardo Machado. He didn't die a violent
death then, as the character Aldo does, but he "died" as a vital human being – a
sort of death by frustration. When I was born, I was surrounded by all these
ghosts, by a failed revolution, by a man whose course in life was interrupted by
this collective failure' (quoted in Chanan, p. 231). The second part expresses precisely the sense of a betrayed revolution (the enemy is Machado and, concretely,
the police who oppress the people); Machado's demise is a positive event but the
new era that is ushered in is soon devalued. As Aldo sees when he gets to Havana
people there seem to have descended into state of lasciviousness and drunken-
ness. Even Antonio and his wife, Flora, as Lucía pointedly points out, seem to
have prostituted the ideals of the Revolution for a few lousy bucks. Part III portrays the Revolution as an authentic lived reality. The enemy is Batista and the
imperialistic power which backed him (U.S.); both are vanquished by Fidel
Castro's coup. It does not, however, offer a rosy-eyed view of the Revolution
since it also focuses – rather obsessively for the modern taste – on those retro-
grade ideological elements which still persist after the coming of the Revolution,
and which are typified by Tomás's *machismo*. The latter is indicated by a
number of telling details – his willingness to resort to violence when anyone
approaches his woman, his decision to keep her locked up in the house, and –
more stereotypically – the enormous Cuban cigar which he is always smoking.
Lucía's shortcoming in Part III is explained by Flavio, the Head of the Collective:
since she is illiterate, Lucía is a victim of 'Yankee imperialism'. The moral of
the film is that, by clinging to his old-fashioned beliefs – as Flavio points out to
Angelina, his wife, Tomás is like he is because he inherited his views about
women from his father – Tomás is in effect stopping the progress of the Cuban
Revolution and thereby aiding and abetting U.S. imperialism. Part III ends on
rather an ambiguous note, avoiding an over-optimistic impression of the ease
with which the Revolution has transformed Cuban society. Though the film concludes with a reassuring image of a young girl smiling at the sight of Tomás and
Lucía frolicking on the beach, it is important to underline that the last image we
have of the married couple is of Tomás leaning on top of Lucía, trying to impose
his will – he has not given up his *machista* beliefs – while Lucía is stubbornly
shaking her head – an epitome of female defiance. By having three historical
versions of Lucía – indicating the Cuban Revolution as emerging in stages:
failed, betrayed, successful, respectively – Solás's film offers a re-writing of
Cuban history and culture which promotes a sense of Fidel Castro's Revolution
as the culmination of a process begun by José Martí in 1895 when he attempted
unsuccessfully to rescue Cuba from imperialist domination, and half-completed

in 1932 with the overthrow of one of Cuba's most hated dictators – Machado. Barabara Weinstein has argued that, by using these three female figures in an allegorical way, Solás's films can be faulted. Solás was, she suggests, 'operating with two handicaps when viewed through contemporary eyes: the absence of sophisticated historical interpretations of women's political activity, and his conceptualization of the film around three standard "great moments" in Cuban history' (Weinstein, p. 127). As Marvin d'Lugo observes: 'For the three female protagonists in *Lucía*, transparency meant at once the social condition in which male characters did not so much see women as see *through* them' (Marvin d'Lugo, p. 280).

Imperfect Cinema

This film has been interpreted as an excellent example of the 'imperfect cinema' which was espoused by the Cuban Film School in the 1960s as a means of combatting the dominance of Hollywood. For any viewer used to the cinematic language of the Hollywood blockbuster, the camerawork will appear disjointed, jumpy, disorganised and occasionally out of focus. Imperfect cinema was espoused by a number of Latin American film directors in the 1960s as much out of necessity as for ideological reasons. The budget of a typical feature film in Latin America at that time was, obviously, minuscule compared to the enormous budgets of North-American blockbusters. This meant that film sets, lighting, multiple takes, dolleys, multiple cameras were all well beyond the budget. But, by turning necessity into a virtue, film directors such as Humberto Solás were able to use the hand-held camera, natural lighting, and the single take in such a way which was innovative and certainly began to attract the attention of a number of film directors in Europe if not in the United States. Some of the camerawork in *Lucía*, for example, uses the hand-held camera in such a way that the result achieved can be quite enthralling.

The filmic language used throughout the film is disorientating in another sense as well, since three distinct cinematic idioms are used in the three parts: symbolism, 1930s realism, and comic social realism (Martin and Paddington, p. 3). The sequence early on in Part I, for example, in which the camera whirls around La Fernandina when she begins to shout at the Spanish General provides a vivid sense of La Fernandina's unhinged mind. The battle scenes towards the end of Part I – particularly those centred on the river – provide a vibrant sense of unchannelled mayhem, and can arguably be seen as more successful than the bar brawl topos common in the Hollywood westerns of the 1960s. In these particular cases – and others could be cited, particularly those which focus on La Fernandina – the form expresses the content effectively. Indeed, one of the more intriguing parallels explored in Part I – the connection between dance, sexuality and violence – is highlighted as a result of the similar mise-en-scène employed to depict La Fernadina's rape and Lucía's seduction (La Fernandina is hunted on the battlefield in the same way that Lucía is hunted in the sugar mill), and the playful circle formed by her friends around

Lucía in the parlour party which occurs immediately before – and is therefore echoed by – the more threatening ring formed around La Fernandina by the drunk soldiers. In each case the camera weaving between the participants is an effect which could only have been produced by a hand-held camera. It also has the rather startling effect of allowing the camera – particularly during the ring of roses parlour game – to appear to turn into one of the participants playing the game. (At some points in the game of blind man's buff, for example, the POV provided by the camera can only be Lucía's, though this is 'impossible' since she is blindfolded at the time.)

Part II is less innovative than the first part and employs a more conventional filmic language to express its story. The final frame – which shows Lucía's face in frontal – echoes the final frame of Part I which is also a close-up of Lucía's face, but now it is a full frontal shot rather than a side shot of a recumbent face (as if to suggest that Lucía – and by extension Cuba – has begun to rise from its passivity in order to adopt a more reflexive stance). Similar in some ways to Part II, Part III is not as innovative as the first of *Lucía*. But it does have some extraordinarily raw scenes – such as the fist-cuff fight between Tomás and the man he 'catches' talking to Lucía. The hand-held camera approaches Lucía offering us Tomás's POV and, then, suddenly the focal point of the scene is lost as the camera loses a centre of gravity when the chaos of the fight breaks out. One particular shot is favoured in each of the three parts, and this is the close-up of Lucía's face when conflict is unleashed all around her. In Part I, for example, we focus on Lucía's anguish-ridden face during the war between the Spanish and the Cubans; in Part II we have a similar overpowering focus on Lucía's pain when she sees Aldo's dead body in the morgue; and in Part III, Lucía's breaking point is reached when Tomás and the teacher have a fight – the camera leaves the two men brawling in the background in order to home in on Lucía's tortured face and mad screams. In this way Solás is able to use Lucía as the changing but constant site of consciousness of Cuban history, thereby adding a consistency of vision and an epic depth to his film.

Works Cited

Agramonte, Arturo, *et al.*, 'Las mejores películas del cine cubano', www.iquebec. ifrance.com/particuba (consulted on 18 December 2003).

Chanan, Michael, *The Cuban Image* (London: BFI, 1985).

D'Lugo, Marvin, 'Transparent Women: Gender and Nation in Cuban Cinema', in *Mediating Two Worlds: Cinematic Encounters in the Americas*, eds John King, Ana M. Lopez and Manuel Alvarado (London: BFI, 1993), pp. 279–90.

King, John, *Magical Reels: A History of Cinema in Latin America* (London: Verso, 1990).

Martin, Michael T., and Bruce Paddington, 'Restoration or Innovation: An Interview with Humberto Solás: Post-Revolutionary Cuban Cinema', *Film Quarterly*, 54.3 (Spring 2001), 2–13.

'Moscow International Film Festival, 1969', www.miff.ru/eng/history/1969.html (consulted on 18 December 2003).

Weinstein, Barbara, *Based on a True Story: Latin American History at the Movies*, ed. Donald F. Stevens (Wilmington, Delaware: Scholarly Resources, 1997), pp. 123–42.

Xavier, Ismail, 'Historical Allegory', in *A Companion to Film Theory*, eds Toby Miller and Robert Stam (Oxford: Blackwell, 2004), pp. 333–62.

7

EL CHACAL DE NAHUELTORO (THE JACKAL OF NAHUELTORO, 1969), DIRECTED BY MIGUEL LITTÍN

Cast

El chacal, played by Nelson Villagra
Rosa, played by Shenda Román
Priest, played by Héctor Noguera

Also Featuring

Marcelo Romo
Luis Alarcón
Pedro Villagra
Luis Melo
Ruben Sotoconil
Rafael Benavente
Roberto Navarrete

Crew

Production: Luis Cornejo, Luis Alarcón
Sound: Jorge Di Lauro
Music: Sergio Ortega
Editing: Pedro Chaskei
Photography: Héctor Ríos
Scriptwriter/Director: Miguel Littín
Produced by: Cine Chileno

Awards

Awarded prize for best documentary at the Latin American Film Festival held in
Viña del Mar, Chile, in 1969

Plot

The documentary – filmed in black and white – opens with footage of the Jackal
of Nahueltoro being led away by police; the mob around are out of control,

hurling insults at him, calling him 'asesino' (murderer). We then cut to the Jackal who, in voice-over, recalls his life as a child. He drifted from various temporary jobs, and was abused by cruel employers. When he went back to his mother's house he found he had a new half-brother and half-sister. For some unspecified crime, he was jailed, and, soon after release, met up with a woman called María González. He stayed with her for a while, until he came to blows with her nephew, and was thrown out. We see him stealing some clothes in order to trade them for a drink in a bar. He arrives at a small holding where a woman, Rosa, is cutting up some wood. She offers him a drink, and tells him she has a hard life bringing up her five children; her husband, Oscar, was stabbed to death. She asks him to stay. The family is evicted because the husband is no longer working for the landowner. We cut to a new sequence in which a dead man is being carried back to the village, and Rosa being offered condolences by the priest (a recon-struction of Oscar's death and funeral). Camera cuts back to the eviction of the family, and cuts once more to the angry mobs once the Jackal is captured. Cuts back to the Jackal, now with Rosa and her family, who decide to camp in the open air. Rosa offers the Jackal some wine, which he drinks. We hear his voice-over describing his actions. Over a period of three hours while drunk, the Jackal murders Rosa and then her five children. He puts stones on their hands and chest in order to stop them moving. We cut to the Chillán prison where the Jackal is now detained. Gives up his belongings, and the 6,300 pesos he stole from Rosa after killing her. Cuts to silent sequence in which horsemen bring back the six bodies to the village; camera pans past the silent faces. News coverage; the authorities are searching for the Jackal whom they believe may be attempting to escape to Argentina. We cut to a party in a village where people are singing. The Jackal joins in, and he is challenged, and then arrested. Cuts once more to the arrival of the police van with the Jackal. A report in voice-over from the Chillán Prison which declares that the Jackal was abused as a child. A new section begins entitled 'Education and Taming'. The Jackal is taught to read, to weave, and to play football. He is given history lessons about Chile's glorious past. A prisoner's song is heard in voice-over about a man who is about to die. The Jackal is sen-tenced to death. Just before his execution he is interviewed by a reporter about his life. The film concludes with his execution.

Analytical Overview

Given that the film industry was a relatively new phenomenon in Chile in the 1960s – Chile, like many Latin American countries at the time, had been force-fed a diet of Hollywood or European cinema since the beginning of the twenti-eth century – it is not surprising that Chile's first forays into the arena of film included the documentary. The documentary, prized for its sheer recording abil-ity, has often emerged in societies eager to learn about the geography and social conditions of the world at large. And here was a story which had gripped Chilean society, an ideal subject for a documentary. José (aka as Jorge) del Carmen Valenzuela Torres, or the Jackal of Nahueltoro as he came to be known, was Chile's first ever serial killer. A drifter, he had brutally clubbed to death a defenceless mother and her five children in Chillán, in northern Chile, in what was apparently a motiveless crime. News coverage of the event and the massive police search for him traumatised Chile at the time. Miguel Littín decided to reconstruct the tragedy using the documentary genre but he introduced some innovative twists into the mix. The film was an enormous success at the Second Festival of Latin American Film held in Viña del Mar in November 1969 (Francia, pp. 162–6). By allowing Valenzuela Torres the opportunity to speak, the viewer is allowed inside the killer's mind, and we see how he is simply a product of his society. As Hennebelle and Gumucio-Dagrón point out, Littín 'affirme que le délinquent n'est qu'un produit d'une société qui a recours à l'appareil judiciare et à la peine de mort contre ceux qui osent transgresser ses lois' (Hennebelle and Gumucio-Dagrón, p. 200). As a result, Littín's gripping film is, in the words of one critic, 'one of the most significant works of the New Latin American Cinema (. . .); it was exhibited during Salvador Allende's successful election campaign by trade unions, at schools, and in open air meetings was later released to theatres in 35mm, eventually being seen by an estimated 500,000 people' (Rist, pp. 221–2).

The most striking feature of *El chacal de Nahueltoro* is the way in which it splices events from different time periods together. There are basically four self-contained time-worlds in Littín's documentary: (i) his early life as recounted in voice-over in confession mode, (ii) the reconstruction of the events leading up to the murder, along with the murder itself, (iii) his arrest, and abuse by the crowd, and (iv) his life in prison after the trial in which he is sentenced to death, culminating in his execution. But the documentary is not recounted in chronological order. Thus we begin with a sequence depicting his arrest, and then track back into the events of his early childhood – recounted in voice-over – which are reconstructed up until the point of the murder, and then the film takes up the narrative of the Jackal's life in prison during the period of rehabilitation, and concludes with his execution. During the narrative of his life, the film returns almost obsessively to the scene in which the Jackal is led away by police, signalled each time by the whine of the police siren. It is only at the end of the film when we see the Jackal being interviewed – making a final confession to a news-reporter just before his execution – that we realise that the earlier reconstruction of his childhood was elicited at this point. The documentary – rather dramatically – takes its point of departure from the Jackal's last confession, a criminal's version of the last will and testament. The narrative of the murder itself is not cleaned up in the reported version; the inconsistencies are left there. For example, at one point the Jackal says that he only used a stick on one of the daughters, but this account is contradicted by someone present who states that he is lying, and that she **was** strangled. Likewise, when describing the murder of Rosa, he again says he just used a stick, but that he was holding a knife at the time. The reporting style simply leaves these details as they are. We are not provided with a 'reassuring' analysis of what 'really' happened. The rawness of the original events is thereby retained, even while it is being reconstructed on camera. José Agustín

Mahieu has pointed out that the film does have some weaker scenes: 'El filme en sí muestra algunos desequilibrios de estructura y tratamiento entre sus partes; las vitales secuencias de la cárcel y los procedimientos curiales son a veces débiles en su *mise-en-scène*, pero la general intensidad de la interpretación (Nelson Villagra) y el rigor auténtico de los elementos (las reconstrucciones de escenas entre pobladores fueron verdaderos *revivals* de los testigos del hecho) dieron a la obra el carácter de una revelación' (Mahieu, p. 105).

As is clear from the plot summary provided above, Littín's film shuttles between various perspectives on the murder, not only in temporal terms, but also in discursive terms. Thus, we sometimes hear the voice-over of the Jackal as he recounts his life (and it is reconstructed before our eyes), and sometimes we hear the voice-over of the news reporting of the time. It is a technique which is similar to that employed by Gutiérrez Alea in *Memorias del subdesarrollo*. One of the mysteries of the murder concerns the fact – classic in this kind of sensationalist tragedy – that there was no discernible motive. He mentions that he was drunk on the wine that Rosa had given him, and that she insulted him. No more details are given. And when this scene is reconstructed, we witness Rosa shouting, but we hear nothing. The terror of the event is visibly enhanced as a result of the use of this cinematic technique. What cannot be said – the film implies – is left unsaid.

Social Commentary and Ideology

One of the important points about this documentary – one which responded to the revivified interest in the problems of contemporary social reality in Latin American cinema of the time – is the notion of blame. The narrative framework of the film echoes that of a journalistic investigation. The journalist-cum-director wants to know what the Jackal's motives were for what he did. Since the Jackal is unable to give any reason – as the voice-over puts it – it is his childhood which is, in effect, put on trial and – by implication – the society which produced an individual such as José del Carmen Valenzuela Torres. Rather like Camilo José Cela's novel, *La muerte de Pascual Duarte*, Littín's documentary concludes by placing blame for what happened at society's door. It is the lack of social care, the lack of a safety net within society that leads to the production of individuals such as the Jackal. The main idea behind *El chacal de Nahueltoro*, therefore, becomes one of pricking society's conscience, forcing the 'bien-pensant' sections of society to think again and become more active in the process of social renewal. It breaks what Hennebelle and Gumucio-Dagrón call the viewer's 'fausses conceptions humanistes' (Hennebelle and Gumucio-Dagrón, p. 200).

We should not fall into the trap of interpreting *El chacal de Nahueltoro* as the creation of a dispassionate, unpoliticised observer. Littín's left-wing credentials, indeed, were well-known. He later on became an ardent supporter of Salvador Allende, and was denounced by a neighbour soon after Pinochet's coup took place: 'ya habíamos sido denunciados por una vecina que conocía nuestra relación con el Gobierno, mi participación entusiasta en la campaña presidencial de Allende, las reuniones que se hacían en mi casa mientras el golpe militar iba haciéndose inminente' (p. 36). He was arrested at the office of Chile Films by a group of armed soldiers, and the porter tried to turn him in:

> – Ah – gritó señalándome –, ese caballero, el senor Littín, es el responsible de todo lo que ocurre aquí.
> – El sargento le dio un empujón que lo tiró por tierra.
> – Váyase a la mierda – le gritó. No sea maricón.
> – El portero se puso en cuatro patas, aterrizado, y me preguntó:
> – ¿No se toma un cafecito, señor Littín? ¿Un cafecito?
>
> (García Márquez, p. 35)

Littín was temporarily freed, but could not return home, and had to hide in a series of safe houses for a month, until he was forced into exile. He was seen as so dangerous by the military regime that he was on a list of 5,000 exiles permanently banned from Chile: 'el Gobierno chileno empezó a publicar listas de exiliados a los que se les permitía volver, y no encontré mi nombre en ninguna. Más tarde alcanzó extremos de desesperación cuando se publicó la lista de los cinco mil que no podían regresar, y yo era uno de ellos' (García Márquez, p. 12). In his essay, 'El cine latinoamericano y su público', Littín rejected the Hollywood movie industry, calling for an endogenous Latin American cinema: 'No es a través de copiar o de la imitación de los modelos ajenos como podemos encontrar nuestra verdadera identidad, es en la profundización de nuestra problemática, es en la búsqueda y encuentro de la memoria popular, en la experiencia acumulada, en la lucha por recuperar nuestro rol protagónico en la historia' (Littín, p. 42).

The Crafting of Reality

Littín saw himself above all as a documentarist and, in his memoir, he gives an insightful view of his working methodology as a documentarist: walking around the streets with a miniature recorder in his shirt pocket, relying on secret hand signals to indicate to the cameraman when to start filming, hoping to catch 'subversive' snippets of conversation, taking notes on the back of Gitane cigarette packets (García Márquez, p. 42). These cinematic techniques are very much in evidence in *El chacal de Nahueltoro* in that the reconstruction of events leading up to the murder is crafted in a vivid manner. Some details have clearly been added to increase the suspense and drama. Firstly, one should mention the way in which the narrative of past events is periodically punctured by the scene in which the Jackal is brought to justice and – more importantly – shouted at by the crowd. The film thereby focuses on the public revulsion at the events depicted, and mimics the viewer's reaction. At the same time, it moves between the past and present in a swing-saw fashion, mimicking effectively the process of memory and memorisation characteristic of the legal process. Secondly, it leaves the events as they are, and does not provide an overall frame in which they can be understood; inconsistencies are left in the narrative (see above). Thirdly, the narrative has a number of blanks – a number of points at which the Jackal says he cannot remember exactly what happened. This also adds to a sense of the rawness of the events and heightens the sense of verisimilitude. Fourthly, the camerawork during the murder scenes is extremely effective (given the time that this was filmed) in giving a sense of horror at the murder (see below, camerawork). Lastly, it should be mentioned that the narrative does not shy away from what might be called poetic details; thus, just before Rosa invites the Jackal to stay, she observes that 'the fire is going out' – on one level this is an innocent, naturalistic detail but, at a deeper symbolic level, it functions as an omen of what will befall her and her children. Their lives are about to be snuffed out. The crafting of reality we find in this film is similar in many respects to that we find in Gabriel García Márquez's *Crónica de una muerte anunciada* (1981; see Hart, *Crónica*, pp. 18–27). It is well-known that the Colombian writer is an avid fan of Littín's work and of *El chacal de Nahueltoro* in particular, so the similarities between the two should not surprise us.

Camerawork and Acting

The camerawork during the depiction of the murders is flexible and dynamic. At times the camera moves around wildly, and we lose focus, thereby echoing the wildness of the events themselves. At other times, we are invited as viewers to step into the mind of the murderer, since the murder scenes are reconstructed via the Jackal's POV. Rosa, just before she is beaten to death, looks in horror at **us**. This section of the film has the haunting obsessiveness and inescapability that we associate with films such as Robert Montgomery's *Lady in the Lake* (1946), in which the character's vision coincides relentlessly with the viewpoint of the spectator (see Aumont, p. 215). At other times, the camera looks calmly at the children before they are killed, recalling the filmic perspective of early horror films such as *Dracula* (1931) and *The Wolf Man* (1941) in which the viewer is encouraged to follow in the footsteps of the monster as he commits the terrible deed, thereby allowing the viewer into the mind of the monster (Lehman and Luhr, pp. 314–5). The important difference with Littín's *El chacal de Nahueltoro*, however, is that his documentary focuses on a real story. His monster, as it were, really existed. When the baby is killed (the last child to be murdered) we take up a different perspective; now we become the impartial observer watching the Jackal placing his foot on the baby's head. The variety of perspectives from which the murder scenes are recreated make this an extremely effective sequence, remarkable in its flexibility and visual power.

Nelson Villagra's acting performance must be credited with some of the power of these sequences. In an interview Villagra has described how he develops his characters, using a method partly inspired by Brecht and Stanislavsky. He starts off with the director's orientation, and then begins to research the socio-historical context of the character, imagining how he lived. Villagra then 'stages' a confrontation with the character, and recreates a specific scene from the script. Once he has achieved what he calls the character's 'mode', he then begins to live out the character in his daily life: 'I ride the bus in character; I speak to my wife and children in character. I become unbearable' (Villagra, p. 215). He found it a particularly sorrowful experience taking on the character of the Jackal. As he explained: 'How dismal to have to look at the world with a blunted mind, as it through a poorly focused lens, debilitated and stupefied. How else could this man walk, surrounded outside and within by underdevelopment, except so softly that he seemed to be asking permission from the very ground under his feet? I am afraid to step briskly. Perhaps the ground will rise up against me in anger, grab a stick and start to beat me, and send me away howling in pain, hopping on one foot . . .' (Villagra, pp. 216–17).

Works Cited

Aumont, Jacques, *et al.*, *Aesthetics of Film* (Austin: University of Texas Press, 1992).

Francia, Aldo, *Nuevo Cine Latinoamericano en Viña del Mar* (Santiago: CRAN, 1990).

García Márquez, Gabriel, *La aventura de Miguel Littín clandestino en Chile* (Madrid: El País, 1986).

Hart, Stephen, *Gabriel García Márquez: Crónica de una muerte anunciada* (London: Grant and Cutler, 1994).

——, 'Miguel Littín', in *An Encyclopedia of Latin American Culture*, ed. Peter Standish (Detroit: Manley Publishers, 1995–6), p. 161.

Hennebelle, Guy, and Alfonso Gumucio-Dagrón, *Les Cinémas de l'Amérique latine* (Paris: Pierre L'Herminier, 1981).

King, John, *Magical Reels: A History of Cinema in Latin America* (London: Verso, 1990).

Lehman, Peter, and William Luhr, *Thinking About Movies: Watching, Questioning, Enjoying* (Oxford: Blackwell, 2003).

Littín, Miguel, 'El cine latinoamericano y su público', in *El Nuevo Cine Latinoamericao en el mundo de hoy* (Mexico City: UNAM, 1988), pp. 41–6.

Mahieu, José Agustín, *Panorama del cine iberoamericano* (Madrid: Ediciones de Cultura Hispánica, 1990).

Rist, Peter, 'El chacal de Nahueltoro', in *South American Cinema: A Critical Filmography 1915–1994*, eds Timothy Barnard and Peter Rist (Austin: University of Texas Press, 1996), pp. 221–3.

Villagra, Nelson, 'The Actor at Home and in Exile', in *Cinema and Social Change in Latin America: Conversation with Filmmakers*, ed. Julianne Burton (Austin: University of Texas Press, 1986), pp. 211–19.

8

YAWAR MALLKU: LA SANGRE DEL CÓNDOR (THE BLOOD OF THE CONDOR, 1969), DIRECTED BY JORGE SANJINÉS

Main Cast

Ignacio Mallku (played by Marcelino Yanahuaya, communal leader of Kaata)
Paulina Yanahuaya (played by Benedicta Huanaca, a miner from Huanuni)
Sixto (played by Vicente Vernero, a miner from Huanani)

Crew

Director: Jorge Sanjinés
Scriptwriter: Oscar Soria
Cinematography: Antonio Eguino
Music: Alberto Villalpando
Producer: Ricardo Rada for Ukamau

Awards

Winner, Best Foreign Film, George Sadoul Award, Paris, 1969
Winner, Gran Premio Espiga de Oro, Valladolid, Spain, 1970
Jury Selection, San Francisco International Film Festival, 1970
Voted 59th most historically significant film by UNESCO

Plot

Ignacio and his wife, Paulina, have lost their three children and they walk to the top of a hill to bury three dolls in memory of their children. In the village they are discussing why the women appear to have become barren. Shock cut to the scene in which some villagers – Ignacio among them – are taken to the top of a hill and shot. Ignacio, who is not quite dead, is taken by Paulina to La Paz to see if Ignacio's brother, Sixto, can help them. They take him to hospital but the blood is too expensive. Sixto asks Paulina how it all happened, and – in flashback – we revisit the steps whereby Ignacio, elected head of the community, discovers that the Cuerpo del Progreso (The Progress Corps, a thinly veiled reference to the real-life Peace Corps) – under cover of providing modern medical treatment to the women in the village – has been sterilising the women in the village in their Maternity Clinic. All the while this story is being recounted we cross-cut to the desperate attempts by Sixto to get medical help for his dying brother. The community decides to attack the gringos during a party. They kill – or possibly emasculate – the gringos. Sixto returns empty-handed to the hospital and finds that his brother has already died. The film concludes with an image of rifles raised in defiance.

Analytical Overview

Yawar Mallku (The Blood of the Condor) is Jorge Sanjinés's most famous film, even if not all critics would agree it is his best. On the day of its premiere in La Paz (17 July 1969), the theatre where it was about to be shown – the 18 de Julio – was suddenly closed down as a result of the film's inflammatory subject matter; a public riot ensued and, eventually, the authorities relented and allowed the film to be screened (Hennebelle and Gumucio-Dagrón, p. 80). The film showed the trademake of Sanjinés's interest in politicised cinema. Though Sanjinés began his career with the desire to make 'film for film's sake', he gradually became more interested in creating a 'cinema for society', because art is an 'excellent instrument' with which to create a social consciousness; art plays a fundamental role in the process whereby society achieves a 'toma de conciencia' of itself (Hart, 'Interview'). During his apprenticeship as a film director in Chile Sanjinés had become interested by the methodology and techniques used by the Italian Neo-Realist school. In the post-World War II period, film directors such as Visconti were striving to give their films a more gritty realism that was currently in fashion; they wanted to show life as it really was rather than how governments wanted it to be depicted. And, as Visconti argued, if you want a realistic portrayal of a postman, why not actually use a real-life postman in the film? In Vittorio de Sica's *Umberto D.* (1952), for example, we observe 'a wealth of detail that traditional dramatic writers and directors would eliminate' (Lehman and Luhr, p. 260), and the same might be said of the drawn-out scenes in *Yawar Mallku* which portray the transportation of Ignacio by Paulina and others to La Paz.

Running very much in counter to the prevailing ideology and work practices of Hollywood which favoured the use of professional actors and indoor scenes, Sanjinés decided to base his film on a real-life event, the covert sterilisation of women in the Bolivian village of Kaata. Sanjinés went to the village with his camera crew (the Productora Cinematográfica Ukamau consisting of Sanjinés, Ricardo Rada, Oscar Soria and Antonio Eguino; Sánchez H., p. 115), but he found that it was practically impossible to persuade any of the villagers to act in his film. They were far more concerned in reaping the harvest. Finally a coca leaves ceremony was held by the local *yatiri* (soothsayer) – which had a positive result, and everything then went to schedule. The three main protagonists of the film – Ignacio, Paulina and Sixto – were not professional actors. In fact *Yawar Mallku* has Ignacio, as communal leader of Kaata, in effect (like Visconti's postman) playing himself. This was something that Sanjinés had learned from the Italian Neo-Realists. But he used this formula, and added to it one more very important ingredient, and this was the left-wing ideology of the film. The overall

1. Jorge Sanjinés on set

2. *Yawar Mallku*: The Coca Leaves' Ceremony

message of the film which emerges – and this is made breathtakingly clear by the various clips of statements by different western scientific agencies quoted at the beginning of the film, the gist of which is that genocide of inferior races is OK – is that the Peace Corps is a malevolent western influence in Latin America which is seeking to colonise the American Sub-Continent under the guise of providing medical and economic assistance. As José Sánchez-H. points out: 'As a result of the denunciation made by *Yawar Mallku*, the Peace Corps was expelled from the country by President General Juan José Torres in 1971 and did not return to Bolivia until 1990' (Sánchez-H., pp. 83–4). Given this, it is ironic that the musical score was performed by a symphony orchestra whose director, Gerald Brown, was a member of the Peace Corps at the time; Alberto Villalpando, as he has explained in an interview, enlisted the latter's help since he was a personal contact (Sánchez H., pp. 157–8). *Yawar Mallku* had far-reaching consequences in terms of the emergence of a new postcolonial consciousness among Third-World nations and, as such, the film's message resists any geographical strait-jacketing. As Gumucio-Dagrón suggests: '*Yawar mallku* is a parable of imperialism: the foreign control of fertility was a real event, but here it is taken as a starting point for a larger historical analysis. Medical mutilation is seen as a symbol of U.S. intervention in Bolivia and Latin America, and when the "Mallku" discovers this, what is really being depicted is a class awareness of this intervention. The sterilisation also serves as a powerful metaphor for the silencing of the region's culture' (Gumucio-Dagrón, p. 93).

Indeed, the events of the film are structured in such a way that it is very difficult for the viewer not to feel angry at the way in which the inhabitants of the Bolivian village have been treated; the destruction of the gringos in this sense appears to be a 'necessary murder' rather than an example of a mindless killing. The final freeze frame of the film – showing a group of the villagers holding their rifles aloft in a sign of obvious defiance – suggests that armed struggle is the only logical way forward (Mesa Gisbert, pp. 87–8). As viewers we have experienced the trauma that Sixto obviously feels as he is attempting to save his brother; we notice that at the beginning of the film he had become to an extent urbanised. He is wearing western clothes, he is seen playing football, and he rejects the notion that he is an Indian. When challenged, he says: 'no soy indio, carajo' (I'm not a bloody Indian). But in the final sequence of the film, we see Sixto who has now taken off his western clothes, he is now in traditional Indian dress, and he is walking back to his home village, quite clearly determined to carry on where his brother, Ignacio, left off. He has become, so to speak, 'decolonised'.

There is one important element of symbolism in the film and this concerns the associations connected with the condor in the film. For the Aymara indigenous populations the condor has a special role within the divine panthenon since it is associated closely with divinity. For the Incas, likewise, the condor played a crucial role; the inner sanctum of Machu Picchu, for example, is inhabited by an enormous stone sculpture of a condor. Despite the title, *The Blood of the Condor*, there are hardly any overt references to the bird itself in the film. The rare image we have of a condor occurs in the opening sequences of the film: just after the villagers are seen discussing what has happened to their women, none of whom appear able to conceive, we have a shock cut to a dead condor hanging from the community hut door. The camera does not linger on the shot, which makes it all the more resonant. As the film progresses it becomes clear that the symbolic space associated with the condor is occupied in the narrative by Ignacio who comes, thereby, to stand for the victimhood of the Amerindian peoples of Latin America. The real protagonist of the film, we might say, is the Amerindian people (Pérez Murillo and Fernández Fernández, p. 73). The time of the film is, indeed, structured around the stages whereby blood gradually seeps from his body until it reaches the climax of death. Whereas the condor on the community hut door is already dead, *Yawar Mallku* depicts the gradual death throes of its protagonist and hero. The 'blood' of the title is, therefore, clearly at once the absent blood which Sixto is attempting to find as well as Ignacio's life-force which is gradually ebbing away. It is intriguing that Sanjinés decides to avoid any overt or political reference to the Catholic rite of communion – one could imagine how a scene depicting how Sixto is turned away from the 'blood' of the Holy Communion would have immediate political ramifications – but this decision is ultimately a good one since it allows the film to focus unremittingly on the contrast between Amerindian cultural practices and gringo cultural actions.

Cultural Dilemmas

The film focuses on the cultural dilemma that Bolivia faced in the 1960s when the film first came out, and which it still does. The cultural options from which Bolivians must choose are structured around three possibilities; (i) the Quechua-speaking Aymara community focused on sharing the earth's resources between all the members of the community (as evidenced by Paulina's refusal to sell the eggs to the gringos half way through the film, since there are some people waiting for her eggs in the market square), (ii) the Spanish-speaking, white or *mestizo* people – such as the doctor in the hospital, or the Comandante who orders the execution of Ignacio after he rocks the boat, and the doctor's wife who gives Sixto a lift to the banquet – who tend to look down on the Amerindian population, and (iii) individuals from the United States – the two men and one woman who are from the Peace Corps – who are exposed as manipulative (i.e. when they try to pacify the local population by providing the children with western clothes), selfishly acquisitive (as when they attempt – in a grotesquely ironic scene – to buy all of Paulina's eggs while she is on the way to market), and ultimately destructive (since they sterilise the women of the village because they feel they are having too many children). This triadic structure is underlined by the three languages which are used in the film – Quechua, Spanish and English. Each of the three languages rub shoulders in the film, and cultural-political pointers are suggested by their respective use. It is not by chance that the Comandante should use Spanish when ordering his troops to open fire on Ignacio and his friends. It is not by chance that the doctors in the hospital in La Paz are unable to speak Quechua and therefore need a translator in order to speak to their patients. Pointing in a similar direction, it is also deeply ironic as well as highly poignant that the doctor's children – whom we see at play when Sixto is brought into the house towards the latter end of the film – are being taught English. The global societal hierarchy which would put Americans at the top and Indians at the bottom of the pile – namely, 3-2-1 – is completely reversed in Sanjinés's film, such that the third group (the Americans) has been destroyed, and the first group (epitomised by Ignacio) has now woken up to its exploitation and is now beginning to fight back. It is important to point out, though, that not all viewers are likely to be sympathetic to the political position advocated by the *Yawar Mallku*. As Bill Wadum argues: 'I must disagree (. . .) with Sanjinés's advocacy of armed revolution as the solution to the Indians' plight. I feel that an armed revolution by the Indians against the Bolivian government would facilitate the physical genocide hitherto avoided by the Indians. This contention is based on the fact that an insurrection on the part of the Indians would have international repercussions which might prompt the intervention of the United States' (Wadum, p. 107).

Filmic Devices

While the film does rely on traditional story-telling techniques – it tells the story of the tragedy experienced by a particular community via the representational narrative of one significant individual – it disrupts narratological linearity in a number of striking ways. The establishing scenes of the film proper – i.e. after the review of racist statements by various apparently *bona fide* institutions – cast us as viewers into the midst of a domestic dispute between two individuals whom we are seeing for the first time, who are quarrelling over an event that we are finding difficult to extrapolate, in a language (Quechua) that we were perhaps not expecting. The full significance of that primary scene in which, as a result of ignorance, Ignacio blames his wife for her infertility, only emerges as the plot unfolds. This fly-on-the-wall technique is successful in the sense that the film sets up a dramatic situation which the viewer is then invited to 'solve', rather like an Amerindian whodunnit (for more on this point, see Hart, 'Mama Coca', pp. 291–2). But the film also boasts one other filmic technique which is used consistently from about one-eighth into the film, and this concerns the use of flashback overlaid with cross-cutting. The flashback occurs at the precise point when Sixto asks Paulina what happened. The flashback, of course, has been a common cinematic device since the 1940s, with *Citizen Kane* (1941) being an early important example of its exploitation (Lehman and Luhr, p. 32), but *Yawar Mallku* does not use the flashback in a conventional fashion – i.e. the flashback is initiated, scrolls back to some significant moment in the past, and then gradually moves in linear fashion back up to the 'present' of the film when the flashback was initiated. Instead, it uses the flashback as in order to initiate a tightly-choreographed seesaw effect between the present (Sixto wandering around La Paz looking for blood for his dying brother) and the past (a discrete set of events during which Ignacio discovers what is happening in the Maternity Clinic). The film's cross-cuts become more intense as the plot proceeds, echoing the anxiety and suspense underlying Sixto's doomed search for blood. Because we know that Ignacio is already dying, the events as recounted already taken on a proleptic, sinister feel. This unease is enhanced by the often haunting, occasionally dissonant, external diegetic musical score which accompanies the film; as Villalpanda recalls, the music was added after Sanjinés had already produced a first-cut (Sánchez H., p. 158) and, as such, it often offers an inventive counterpoint to the story (a good example being the strident music which accompanies Paulina's POV shots of La Paz's tall buildings). Cross-cutting between the present and the past also allowed Sanjinés to build up connections between apparently unconnected events. When Sixto goes to the centre of La Paz, for example, he witnesses a military procession going past, and the camera focuses in close-up on a young girl who is also witnessing the procession; as if to underscore the sinister nature of the ceremony, we see she is crying. The camera then slips into the past time of the film, and the viewer now witnesses the Comandante who is attempting to persuade the villagers that they should accept the gringos who have just arrived in town. The gringos hand out clothes for the children to wear. This scene – which might be interpreted at face value as an example of kindness towards others – is already overlaid by the scene of the young girl crying which immediately preceded it; the gift thereby takes on sinister overtones.

It is important to point out, however, that the use of the cross-cut in the context of the flashback was not seen at the time of the film's release as an unmitigated success. Sanjinés has stated in interviews that his aim in *Yawar Mallku* was to address the Aymara population of Bolivia rather than a western audience. He discovered, soon after the film was released, however, that many Indians in the audience found the time-shifts rather confusing. Here is Sanjinés's own verdict:

> When we filmed *Blood of the Condor* with the peasants of the remote Kaata community, we certainly intended that the film should be a political contribution, denouncing the *gringos* and presenting a picture of Bolivian social reality. But our fundamental objective was to explore our own aptitudes. (. . .) the spectators (. . .) complained later when the film was shown to them.   (Sanjinés, p. 35)

Sanjinés decided, as a result of this experience, to re-formulate his cinematic vision, and thus, in later films such as *El coraje del pueblo* (The Courage of the People), he decided against using the flashback. In this later film, he argued, he was able to integrate the vision of the people into the filmic narrative rather than tying some of the community's ideas to his personal vision: 'We, the members of the crew, became instruments of the people's struggle, as they expressed themselves through us!' (Sanjinés, p. 35). There are some, though, who would argue that this was not necessarily a step forward, since few would suggest that *El coraje del pueblo* is a better film – structurally and aesthetically – than *Yawar Mallku*. It does show, however, how versatile Sanjinés was (and, indeed, still is), always seeking to change or improve his cinematic style to suit new ideological urgencies or new historical events (for more discussion of this point, see Hart, 'The Art of Invasion . . .', p. 79). It is legitimate to argue that the confusion between the two time dimensions that is inevitably created as a result of the rapid cross-cutting in *Yawar Mallku* also leads the viewer to see a great deal of similarity between Ignacio and his brother, Sixto. On a first viewing, for example, it is quite possible to mix the two brothers up. But, in the final analysis, this fusion of the two brothers is a direct outgrowth of the underlying ideological strength of the film, which seeks to combat the individualism of the West, in order to stress communal values as well as that sense in which identity is totally dependent upon – rather than separate from – the community, and indeed the family unit. The visual overlaying of Sixto onto Ignacio allows the final scenes their triumphant logic: by returning to his village to fight against the forces of imperialism, Sixto – not just metaphorically but literally – **becomes** Ignacio.

Works Cited

Gumucio-Dagrón, Alfonso, 'Yawar Mallku', in *South American Cinema: A Critical Filmography 1915–1994*, eds Timothy Barnard and Peter Rist (Austin: University of Texas Press, 1996), pp. 92–4.

Hart, Stephen, 'Interview with Jorge Sanjinés', La Paz, Bolivia, 21 July 2001.

——, 'The Art of Invasion in Jorge Sanjinés's *Para recibir el canto del pájaro*', *Journal of Hispanic Research*, 3.1 (2002), 71–81.

——, 'Mama Coca and the Revolution: Jorge Sanjinés's Double-Take', in *Contemporary Latin American Cultural Studies*, eds Stephen Hart and Richard Young (London: Arnold, 2003), pp. 290–9.

Hennebelle, Guy, and Alfonso Gumucio-Dagrón, *Les Cinémas de l'Amérique latine* (Paris: Pierre L'Herminier, 1981).

Hess, John, 'Neo-Realism, and New Latin American Cinema: *Bicycle Thieves* and *Blood of the Condor*', in *Mediating Two Worlds*, eds John King, Ana López and Manuel Alvarado (London: BFI, 1993), pp. 104–18.

King, John, *Magical Reels: A History of Cinema in Latin America* (London: Verso, 1990).

Lehman, Peter, and William Luhr, *Thinking About Movies: Watching, Questioning, Enjoying* (Oxford: Blackwell, 2003).

Mesa Gisbert, Carlos D., *La aventura del cine bolivianao 1952–1985* (La Paz: Editorial Gisbert, 1985).

Pérez Murillo, María Dolores, and David Fernández Fernández (eds), *La memoria filmada: América Latina a través de su cine* (Madrid: IELPA, 2002).

Pick, Zuzana M., *The New Latin American Cinema: A Continental Project* (Austin, TX: University of Texas Press, 1993).

Sánchez-H., José, *The Art and Politics of Bolivian Cinema* (Lanham: Scarecrow Press, 1999).

Sanjinés, Jorge, 'Problems of Form and Content in Revolutionary Cinema', in *Twenty-Five Years of the New Latin American Cinema*, ed. Michael Chanan (London: BFI, 1983), pp. 34–8.

Wadum, Bill, 'The Fictional Documentary', in *Latin American Cinema: Film and History*, ed. E. Bradford Burns (Los Angeles: UCLA Latin American Center, 1975), pp. 105–8.

9

LA BATALLA DE CHILE (THE BATTLE OF CHILE, 1975–1979), DIRECTED BY PATRICIO GUZMÁN

Crew

Assistant Producers: Patricia Boero, Alicia Crespo, Jorge Sánchez
Modernised version: Luis Matti, Sergio Pérez, Molinari S.A.
Film Teams: Pablo de la Barra. Productora América Proa
Archive: Hayowsky and Sceunmann Studios, Noticiario Chile Films; Cuban
Film Institute Archive, Pedro Chaskel, the review *Chile Hoy*, ISKRA
Editing and credits: Jorge Pucheux, Delia Quesada, Eusebio Ortiz, Alberto
Valdés, Ricardo López
Narrator: Abilo Fernández
Sound Engineer: Carlos Fernández
Filmset Managers: Ramón Torrado, José León, Juan Demosthene
Main consultants: Paloma Guzmán, Lilian Indseth, Gastón Ancelovici, Juan José
Mendi, Harald Edelstran, Roberto Matta
Script consultants: Pedro Chaskel, José Bartolomé, Julio García Espinosa,
Federico Elton, María Harnecher, Chris Marker
Executive Producer: Jorge Guzmán
Production Manager: Federico Elton
Sound recording: Bernardo Menz
Director's assistant: José Bartolomé
Montage: Pedro Chaskel
Photography and camera: Jorge Müller Silva
Screenplay and Directing: Patricio Guzmán

In Collaboration With

Chris Marker
Instituto Cubano del Arte e Industria Cinematográficas
John and Catherine T. MacArthur Foundation

Awards

Novas Teixeira Prize, French Association of Film Critics (1976, 1977)
International Film Festival, Grenoble (1975, 1976)
International Film Festival, Leipzig (1977)
International Film Festival, Brussels (1977)

International Film Festival, Benalmadena (1977)
International Film Festival, Havana (1979)

Sequencing

La batalla de Chile, one of the most famous documentaries ever to be produced in Latin America, consists of three parts, each of which has a slightly different focus on the central event of the *coup d'état* of 11 September 1973 which brought an end to democracy in Chile and ushered in Augusto Pinochet's right-wing dictatorship. Part I, *La insurrección de la burguesía* (The Insurrection of the Bourgeoisie, 96 minutes, released in 1975), opens with very dramatic footage of the bombing of the Moncada Palace, the seat of Chilean government, on the morning of 11 September. By the end of the day Salvador Allende, the first ever Marxist President to be voted into power in Latin America, would be dead. After this dramatic footage the film then tracks back to the elections of the previous year in which Patricio Guzmán and his team are seen interviewing men and women in the street asking them about who they think will win the elections, and by what percentage. The voice-over which punctuates the interviews offers comments on what is being depicted in the everyday scenes. Part I focuses on five specific events which are highlighted in subtitles: *Acaparamiento y mercado negro* (Hoarding and the Black Market), *El boicot parlamentario* (Parliamentary Boycott), *Asonada estudiantil* (Student Disturbances), *Ofensiva de los gremios patronales* (The Trade Unions Go on the Offensive), and *La huelga del cobre* (The Copper Mine Strike). It concludes with the breathtakingly stark footage of the Argentine cameraman, Leonardo Henricksen, who filmed his own death as he is shot on by soldiers who attacked the Moncada Palace in June 1973. Part II, *El Golpe de Estado* (The Coup d'Etat; 88 minutes, released in 1976), opens with the same sequence which had concluded Part I, namely the point at which Leonardo Henricksen filmed his own death, but there are a few differences (see discussion in 'Camerawork and the Documentary' below). This scene is the central one in the events of that June which last throughout the summer of 1973 and conclude with the footage once more of the bombing of the Moncada Palace. Part III, *El Poder Popular* (Power of the People; 78 minutes, released in 1979), looks at the same events but does so from the positive perspective of the way in which the people's cause will never die. This part begins with a parade of honour through the streets of Santiago in which Allende is being honoured for his achievements in the year since he came to power. The documentary subsequently follows the course of the informal debates which occur mainly within the workplace over the following two years in which the proletariat come gradually to a deeper awareness of their mission in the world. The film concludes on a message of hope for the future which repeats the words which Allende said just hours before he died.

Analytical Overview

The voice-over offers a pro-Allende version of events; this was, indeed, part of the aim of the documentary since Guzmán, in interviews, has stated that he did not intend to make a neutral documentary. The pro-Allende focus of the documentary is also engineered via the greater air time given to Allende as well as his grass roots supporters. Typically, we will see and hear the workers expressing their hopes for the future and for their children, and this will be spliced with sequences depicting the military; we do not hear their voices, we see their lips move as they talk to each other, they look distant, far removed from our world – a clever technique which invariably draws the viewer into sympathy with the workers and out of the world of the military and opposition politicians. The role of the United States – and in particular the CIA – is simply referred to in voice-over as a 'given'. In this way the objective authority of the lips-over lends further ammunition to a version of events which was – at the time – still speculative, although the publication of Kissinger's diaries since then have confirmed that the CIA were actively involved in the destabilisation of the Allende government.

Part I is arguably the most effective of the documentaries; it has been described as 'un documentaire journalistique, apologétique et spectaculaire' (Hennebelle and Gumucio-Dagrón, p. 209). Guzmán has described how the film developed: 'The "screenplay" thus took on the form of a map, that we hung on the wall. On the one side of the room, we listed the key points of the revolutionary struggle as we saw them. On the other side, we would list what we had already filmed . . . . So we had the theoretical outline on the one side and the practical outline of what we had actually filmed on the other' (quoted in King, p. 179). By emphasising five aspects of the economic life of the country (Hoarding and the Black Market, Parliamentary Boycott, Student Disturbances, The Trade Unions Go on the Offensive, The Copper Mine Strike), the documentary skilfully draws attention to the worsening relationship between the workers and their bosses, between Allende's Government and the United States, and the struggle between the office of the President Allende and the opposition-dominated Congress. The funeral of the proletarian, José Ahumada, is filmed and explored sensitively in order to promote a sense of the solidarity of the workers behind Allende. But its most effective feature is the way that it manages to suggest that a crucially important series of historical events are being caught before our very eyes; the unplanned appearance of the interviews, the rawness of the emotions expressed, the abrupt camera movements, all contribute to a sense of *cinéma-vérité* years before it had become a trend in France.

Part II arranges the material slightly differently than in Part I. Whereas the first part had used a thematic framework, Part II employs a chronological frame in order to structure its message. The struggle emerges between Allende and the people versus the Christian Democrat Party and the military. It begins with footage of the first attack on the Moncada Palace which occurred on 29 June, 1973 – the day that Henricksen died – and follows the dramatic events of the subsequent summer of discontent – each new event is punctuated by the date of its occurrence – and finally concludes with footage of the bombing of the Presidential palace on 11 September. The chronological presentation of the material contrives to give a sense of grim inevitability to the coup.

Part III has a more of a conventional documentary feel about it than the preced-
ing two parts. It has less a sense of recording reality as it is unfolding before the
camera's eyes, and more an air of a reflection with the benefit of hindsight about
the lessons learned during Salvador Allende's experiment. This reflective ambiance
is also underlined by the content matter: most of the scenes occur within the work
place, focusing on the problems involved in the inevitable difference between
workers and bosses, the problems with strikes, lock-outs, plans to create workers'
co-operatives – that is, the distribution of power within the work place understood
in concrete terms. This third part is one where the imprint of the typical Cuban documentary – as promoted by the Cuban Film Industry – is most evident.

Ideology

The interviews are said to be for Channel 13 (a ruse used by Guzmán to ensure
participation on the part of the interviewees); the Alianza Popular supporters –
Allende's party – seem quietly confident they will win, the right-wing Social
Democrat party supporters appear angry and agitated, but just as confident they
will win. For example, a woman who is clearly a right-wing sympathiser
expresses hatred for the Allende government, and her faces curls up in hate as she
expresses her disgust, calling the Marxists 'disgusting', 'corrupt' and 'dirty' ('éste
es un gobierno corrompido y degenerado, señor! . . . ¡Degenerado y corrompido!
¡Inmundo! . . . ¡Comunistas asquerosos, tienen que salir todos de Chile!'). It is
clear from the interviewing process itself that Guzmán is egging her on; Guzmán
asks her leading questions, waiting until she finally explodes on camera. In this
way a contrast is being set up between the Allende supporters who are whiter than
white and the opposition, who in effect become venomous, repulsive, scheming
Fascists. During the filming of the funeral of the high-ranking military official –
Arturo Araya – we see various members of the armed forces chatting among
themselves and, though the content of their conversation could be innocent, as
viewers we are persuaded – given the context of what is to come – that they are
conspiring the overthrowing of democracy. The fact that we cannot hear what they
are saying is used cleverly in the documentary to allow us to imagine the worst.
Given the ideology of the documentary it is not surprising that, after the coup, the
production team had to flee the country, although, as Rist points out, not all of
them made it: 'After the coup, all of the filmmakers, with the exception of Jorge
Müller, who with his companion Carmen Bueno "disappeared", were able
to leave Chile clandestinely, in prearranged order. Guzmán had been arrested
and held in the National Stadium for two weeks, while Federico Elton and
Bernardo Menz were also detained for a while, but nobody panicked and everyone was re-united in Cuba after being invited there by ICAIC' (Rist, p. 232).

Documentary and Camerawork

Guzmán has provided an excellent definition of what, for him, a documentary is:
'representa la consciencia crítica de una sociedad. Representa el análisis

histórico, geográfico, ecológico, social, científico, artístico, ensayístico, político de una sociedad. Un país que no tiene cine documental es como una familia sin memoria, sin espejo, sin álbum de fotografías' (quoted in Ruffinelli, p. 348). It comes as something of a surprise, given the grandeur of this definition, to find that Guzmán, as he has said in interviews, had no experience of how to make a documentary when he began *La batalla de Chile*, and that the only theoretical work he had read was Julio García Espinosa's 'For an Imperfect Cinema' (Ruffinelli, pp. 128–9). In the same interview Guzmán mentioned that, in effect, he and his camera team – the Equipo Tercer Año – were learning things as they went along, namely, pragmatically rather than theoretically (Ruffinelli, p. 129). 95% of the footage of *La batalla de Chile* was filmed directly by Guzmán and his camera team, Equipo Tercer Año. The external footage which was incorporated into the documentary consisted of (i) the filming of his own death by Leonardo Henricksen, (ii) the filming of the jets flying over the Presidential palace (which came from Pedro Chaskel who filmed them from his Cine Experimental offices), (iii) the bombing of La Moneda Palace, which belonged to a German film collective (Hayowsky and Sceunmann Studios), and (iv) some stills derived from Noticiarios de Chile Films (Ruffinelli, p. 134). Everything else was filmed by Guzmán himself – this is made clear in the various images when we catch the sound engineer or the interviewer Guzmán himself, on camera. These scenes lend authenticity to the documentary, providing an excellent example of the strengths of what Bill Nichols has called the interactive documentary (see Buckman, pp. 111–15). *La batalla de Chile* was re-released in 1995; the footage was left intact, but Guzmán decided to replace certain dated phrases and expressions with their modern equivalent: 'bourgeosie', 'imperialism' and 'fascism' became 'middle classes', the 'U.S. government' and the 'extreme right' (see Ruffinelli, p. 345, pp. 402–3).

The impressive feature about the live interviews is that the camera often moves from the interviewee's face to their surroundings, as if offering further commentary on what is being said. A good example of this occurs when we first see one of Allende's supporters expressing their support for Alianza Popular. The camera – which is clearly hand-held – moves from her face to the ice-cream in her hand, providing a sense of unplanned spontaneity – and by implication truth – about the filming. We should not be fooled, however, into thinking that this film is like an eye simply recording what comes in its way (the best example of which is, perhaps, Michael Snow's *La Région centrale* (1970) in which the camera, from a fixed position, simply sweeps about for three hours in front of a Canadian landscape; see Aumont, p. 215). In *La batalla de Chile* the camera becomes the mobile, roving eye which keenly observes what is before it. At a meeting of Allende sympathisers the camera flits from face to hand effortlessly, creating a fluid, dynamic sense of reality being created before our eyes. On another occasion we are led into the home of a Christian Democrat sympathiser; we see her coyly not wishing to answer all the interviewer's questions, and yet her coyness is belied by the wealth which surrounds her, the accoutrements of a culture which is undeniably bourgeois. As a result of the camera panning around the room it seems almost redundant to ask her why she is in favour of the opposition. Objects speak louder than words. The first 30 minutes of Part I – though they have that unforced spontaneity we associate with *cinéma-vérité* – are examples of sophisticated camerawork, allowing a message to emerge *malgré soi*.

One of the filmed incidents for which the documentary is justifiably famous is the 30-second or so sequence – already mentioned – in which the Argentine film director films his own death. There are two versions of this same event. The one which occurs at the conclusion of Part I shows the camera focusing on a soldier in a truck who notices the camera and then begins firing, until one of the bullets hits its target, and the camera falls to the ground and blurs over. The second version, which occurs at the beginning of Part II, shows the same soldier firing from the truck at the camera, but it appears that the fatal bullet is fired not by the soldier but by his military superior. In an interview Guzmán explained why he decided to use both versions. The first, he says, is the unedited version, and is the footage which was recovered – after the event – in Henricksen's camera. The second was footage which had been edited and was subsequently broadcast on national TV and on the international media, and Guzmán suggested that, though it appears to have been edited, he decided to retain it because it showed that the real guilty party was not the soldier but his superior who had ordered the soldier to open fire (Ruffinelli, pp. 146–7). The first version, we might say, has a 'raw' truth, the second a 'poetic' truth.

Works Cited

Aumont, Jacques, *et al.*, *Aesthetics of Film* (Austin: University of Texas Press, 1992).
Buckland, Warren, *Film Studies* (London: Hodder and Stoughton, 1998).
Hart, Stephen, 'La batalla de Chile', in *An Encyclopedia of Latin American Culture*, ed. Peter Standish (Detroit: Manley Publishers, 1995–6), p. 30.
Hennebelle, Guy, and Alfonso Gumucio-Dagrón, *Les Cinémas de l'Amérique latine* (Paris: Pierre L'Herminier, 1981).
King, John, *Magical Reels: A History of Cinema in Latin America* (London: Verso, 1990).
Rist, Peter, 'La batalla de Chile', in *South American Cinema: A Critical Filmography 1915–1994*, eds Timothy Barnard and Peter Rist (Austin: University of Texas Press, 1996), pp. 229–32.
Ruffinelli, Jorge, *Patricio Guzmán* (Madrid: Cátedra, 2001).

10

LA ÚLTIMA CENA (THE LAST SUPPER, 1977), DIRECTED BY TOMÁS GUTIÉRREZ ALEA

Cast

The Count, played by Nelson Villagra

Also Featuring

Silvano Rey, Luis Alberto García, José A. Rodríguez, Samuel Claxton, Mario Balsameda, Idelfonso Tamayo, Julio Hernández, Tito Junco, Andrés Cortina, Manuel Puig, Francisco Borroto, Alfredo O'Farril, Mario Acea, Peki Pérez, Mirta Ibarra, José Díaz, Elio Mesa, Luis Salvador Romero, Leandro M. Espinosa

Crew

Director: Tomás Gutiérrez Alea
Director's assistants: Constante Diego, Zita Morrina, and Roberto Viña
Script: Tomás Gutiérrez Alea
Screenplay: Tomás González and Tomás Gutiérrez Alea, with collaboration from María Eugenia Haya and Constante Diego
Director of Photography: Mario García Joya
Camera operators: Mario García Joya, Julio Valdés
Music: Leo Brouwer
Sound: Germinal Hernánez
Editing: Nelson Rodríguez
Scenography: Carlos Arditti
Wardrobe Design: Jesús Ruiz, Lidia Lavallet
Make-up: Magdalena Alvarez and Marta Rosa Vinent
Head of production: Santiago Llapur, Camilo Vives
Produced by: Cuban Cinema Institute

Awards

Golden Columbus Jury's Prize, III Week of Latin American Cinema, Huelva, Spain, 1976
First Golden Hugo Prize, XIII International Film Festival, Chicago, USA, 1977
Notable Film of the Year, London Film Festival, UK, 1977

Best Foreign Film exhibited in Venezuela, Venezuelan Film Critics, Caracas, 1978
Grand Prize, VII International Film Cinema, Figueira da Foz, Portugal, 1978
First Prize, Iberian and Latin American Film Festival, Biarritz, France, 1978

Plot

The film is set just after the Haitian revolution of 1795 on a sugar plantation in Cuba, taking place over Holy Week. **Wednesday in Holy Week**. The Count of Casa Bayona arrives at the plantation and hears from his overseer (mayoral) that a slave has escaped. Tour of the sugar refinery in which the Count is introduced to the educated French sugarmaster, Don Gaspar. Cut to a scene in which Manuel drags the runaway slave (Sebastián) back to the plantation, and cuts his ear off, throwing it to the dogs to eat it. The Count – taken aback by this barbarity – decides to make amends by treating his slaves better, and in particular by re-enacting the Last Supper. In the chapel the Count washes the slaves' feet, echoing the Last Supper. Manuel leaves the chapel in disgust. **Maundy Thursday**. The Count wines and dines his twelve 'disciples' in a re-enactment of the Last Supper. The Count has Sebastián seated on his right hand side, but Sebastián spits in his face. The Count petulantly compares Sebastián to Judas, and tries to lecture the slaves on the virtues of putting up with one's lot in life. He says that everyone will have the day off the following day. Drunk, he finally retires to bed. **Good Friday**. The Count leaves and Manuel, despite the Count's promise, forces everyone to go to work. The slaves rebel, and put Manuel in the stocks. The priest rushes to catch up with the Count, asking him to authorise the holiday he promised to the slaves, which he refuses to do. Two slaves tie up the woman at the 'trapiche' and she is killed when the rope around her neck is tightened. Back at the plantation, Sebastián kills Manuel. The Count and his soldiers arrive, see Manuel with his outstretched arms and compare his death to that of Christ. The Count orders all of the twelve disciples to be hunted down one by one. The Count is laying the foundation for a church in Manuel's honour; the foundation is surrounded by twelve pikes on which the disciples' heads are affixed. Cut to Sebastián who is seen running through the jungle.

Analytical Overview

In what could almost be seen as a politicised reading of *Babette's Feast*, *La última cena* was Alea's first venture into the world of colour, and it was the culmination of a long line of distinguished Cuban films which re-visioned Cuba's history and attempted to give a new meaning and relevance to the events which had eventually led to the Cuban Revolution (an excellent example was *El Otro Francisco* (1975) by Sergio Giral). Following in the vein of the 'testimonio' genre about the life of the slave which grew in popularity in the 1960s and 1970s as a result of Miguel Barnet's classic biography of a runaway slave, *Cimarrón* (1966), *La última cena* is based on a short reference that Alea came across in a historical work by one of Cuba's most eminent historians, Manuel Moreno Fraginals, and which reads in English translation as follows:

> His Excellency the Count de Casa Bayona decided in an act of deep Christian fervour to humble himself before the slaves. One Holy Thursday he washed twelve Negroes's feet, sat them at his table, and served them food in imitation of Christ. But their theology was somewhat shallow and, instead of behaving like the Apostles, they took advantage of the prestige they thus acquired in their fellow-slaves' eyes to organise a mutiny and burn down the mill. The Christian performance ended with rancheadores (hunters of escaped slaves) hunting down the fugitives and sticking on twelve pikes the heads of the slaves before whom His Excellency had prostrated himself.   (quoted in John Mraz, pp. 112–13)

This in itself was not enough to provide the material for the film, so Alea enlisted the help of some researchers to help him fill out the historical backdrop. His description of this process is worth quoting in full:

> The storyline was constructed beginning with a very simple paragraph that appears in *The Sugarmill* by Moreno Fraginals. Fortunately, the book offered a suggestive vision, rich in data, and superbly elaborated in relation to the moment which the anecdote recounts. We then had to engage in a more detailed investigation of the epoch, that is, provide ourselves with sufficient details and documentary information in order to arrive at a more concrete image of the reality we wished to depict. In this aspect we counted on the help of María Eugenia Haya, who also collaborated on the script. She efficiently researched documents and organised a file which was most useful not only in constructing the script, but in the later phases of production too (wardrobe, machinery and work tools, scenery, characters, working with the actors, etc.).
> (quoted in Mraz, p. 114)

The aim of the film, according to Alea, was to question the conventional way in which the slave had been portrayed: 'Se trata de custionar la imagen tergiversada y prejuiciada que del esclavo construyó la cultura del opresor, y también de revelar en toda su complejidad los disímiles y contradictorios aspectos de su personalidad, provocados por su situación de sojuzgamiento social: su espíritu supersticioso y al mismo tiempo realista, su mezcla de desconfianza y credulidad' (Évora, p. 40). Given that this film is set in a specific time period, the 1790s, it refers to a specific historical event (a slave rebellion), and follows a linear format, we would expect it to be reasonably straightforward. But there are a number of features of this film which render its meaning ambivalent if not contradictory. This is demonstrated above all by the figure of the Count. There does seem to be a contradiction between a person who would prostrate himself before some slaves and yet, later on, would order their violent execution? How do we explain this?

The film enacts a gradual process of demystification in a way which is similar to *Memorias del subdesarrollo* (see discussion in chapter 5). Whereas the establishing scenes of *La última cena* allow the viewer to take up a sympathetic view of the Count (as opposed to the barbaric slaves, and the brutal foreman), we gradually realise that his life is based on a façade. Yet it is not simply that his humility is a show, and that later on he shows his merciless side. It is true that there are hints in the Last Supper scene that he is not as Christian as he says. He mocks Pascual cruelly when the old man says he has nowhere to go, and therefore his freedom is meaningless. When carried off to bed at the scene by Edmundo, the Count looks at the slaves and says: 'Que no se despierten nunca' (May they never wake up!), which is hardly a Christian sentiment. But there is quite a step from his peevishness and irritability to the man whose cruel vindictiveness means that he wants every single one of his 'disciples' shot, and their heads put on pikes to commemorate the foundation of a new Church. The change in his character – though presented by gradual accretion – is, nevertheless, a shocking one. It is very removed from the Hollywood film which lulls the viewer into a cocoon of security; it does precisely the opposite, in effect, throwing the reader back onto an analysis of his/her unquestioned assumptions.

In his elegant essay, *Dialéctica del espectador* (Dialectic of the Spectator), Gutiérrez Alea sets out the case for the filmic strategies he uses in his films. As one might expect from a communist, Alea rejects Hollywood cinema (he believed that the intended audience of a Hollywood classic has the age of 12!), arguing that Hollywood is a mass art based on a contemplative and passive spectator. While it is designed for the masses, it is not 'popular' in the true sense of the word; truly 'popular' is Soviet film, which is: 'destinado a las masas – y por ende, popular – porque expresaba los intereses, las aspiraciones y los valores de los grandes sectores del pueblo que en ese momento hacían avanzar la historia' (p. 13). Alea goes on to discuss the two main inspirations for his work, to which he devotes a chapter each, Bertolt Brecht, and Sergei Eisenstein. From Brecht he takes the idea of 'distancing-effect', which is used in order to produce a distance between the audience and the actors on the stage in order to allow them to think critically about what they are witnessing rather than being immersed in it. Rather than Aristotelian theatre, Brecht favoured what he called an epic theatre, and Alea certainly took this idea on board; he wanted his audience to reflect on history rather than consume it. From Eisenstein he took the idea of montage as conflict, and what might be called the dialectic underlying the spectator's reaction to the images on the screen before him.

We can see a number of these techniques in operation in *La última cena*. Alea, for example, uses Eisenstein's dialectical approach to film form by forcing the viewer to reflect upon the contradiction at the centre of the Count's existence. There are two good instances in the film. The first occurs in the long drawn-out scene in which petals are spread on the floor, accompanied by loud rousing music, which is just before the scene in which the Count washes the slaves' feet, echoing the Last Supper. The audience is drawn into the Count's mind; we see his highly emotional caressing of the flowers; the music drives up to a crescendo; we capture his sense of pain and delight as he contemplates the statue of Christ. We are brought down to earth with a bump, however, because the scene is followed by a long silence, which is then abruptly punctured by the sound of laughter of the slave as his feet are being bathed, and tickled in the process. Another similarly bathetic scene occurs when, during the Thursday evening meal, the Count tells the story of St Francis, which justifies suffering as the only true religion. Again his account is accompanied by grand, melodramatic music. Since we do not see anyone's face but the Count's, we assume that the slaves share his expression of love for others. Yet the music is followed by an ominous silence. And then the slaves simply burst out laughing, because they have been told to 'enjoy' their beatings. This is a very Sartrean moment in the film, echoing the French philosopher's unpacking of the insidious links between colonialism and Christianity (Sartre, p. xxxviii). Another good example of ironic contrast occurs when the Count's story of the Last Supper is spliced with references to the Carabalí tribe who practise cannibalism. Contrasts between sequences of this kind are good examples of what Eisenstein meant by conflict within the work of art. They force the reader to reassess his or her views about religion, mysticism, and suffering. The viewer is forced to perceive directly the conflict between the two worlds, holding both in dialectical tension, and he is unable to give precedence to either. We therefore experience the work of art dialectically.

Alea rams his de-mythifying ethos home by consistently using the handheld camera, and thereby subverting the device of continuity editing we associate with classic Hollywood cinema. But what Alea lost in cinematic continuity he gained in fluidity, a characteristic of his films he owed, in his opinion, to the skills of his main cameraman, Mayito (Mario García Joya):

> His camera is very steady. In addition, Mayito uses some devices that he has invented. For instance, he or an assistant places a rod underneath the camera when it must be stationary, and that rod is removed when the camera must begin to move and follow a character. His inventions work marvelously. You see a tremendous fluidity in these different mises-en-scène. I would go so far as to say that the fluidity is even more perfect than if he had used a Steadicam, because when a Steadicam is used the camera floats a bit.   (West, p. 18)

At times it must be said that the camerawork is a little too 'imperfect' for the modern viewer. For example, the scene in which the female hostage dies instantly when the rope around her neck is tugged backwards by the mutineers is not very verisimilous, and is one of those rare occasions when some special effects would not have gone amiss.

Caliban, the Subaltern and Political Symbolism

The film is skilful at presenting the different versions of the subaltern. It is not only a case of master versus slave, since there are a number of gradations in between. The social scale presented in *La última cena* is a complex one. At the pinnacle of the social pyramid is the Count, closely followed by his cruel foreman, Manuel. The priest and the sugarmaster act as intermediaries with the subaltern classes; the priest, for example, pleads with the Count to keep to his word about letting the slaves have the day off, but to no avail. Don Gaspar offers a more complex picture. He is, we remember, the educated French sugarmaster with a scientific mind. He mocks the priest's statement to the effect that the slaves have witchcraft while the Church has truth, saying both systems deal in magic. He compares what he is doing (by changing sugar beet into white refined sugar) to the Christian theory of redemption of souls (purged by suffering in the fires of hell). He also seems to be mocking, perhaps, the racist basis of the Church's and society's views; i.e. by drawing attention that he is producing white out of black. He tells the priest that the real secret to the refining process is in the little bag which contains 'caca de poule' (humour at the priest's expense). Don Gaspar is a Voltaire-like figure, well aware of the excesses of colonial administration. He warns about what happened on Haiti. And, most importantly of all, he is seen to be hiding Sebastián during the uprising. To some degree he is 'in league' with the subaltern slaves.

It is clear that Alea has refused to content himself with a stark 'us against them' version of social conflict in *La última cena*. The subaltern takes many forms in the film, ranging from the old man, Pascual, who is powerless and could not accept freedom even if it were given to him; the deferential subaltern, Edmundo, who works as the Count's personal servant, and refers to the other slaves as 'negros'; Antonio, who is desperate to exchange his labours in the sugar cane fields for the easy life in the Big House as a domestic servant; the proud subaltern, Bangoché, from the Congo, a man who is now a slave but was once a king, and therefore has innate dignity; and the dancer who – as his story about the son who sells his father rather than being sold himself aptly illustrates – is the witty rather than rebellious subaltern, namely the slave who works the system rather than challenging its raison d'être.

Sebastián is the true figure of the subaltern in the film. Like Shakespeare's Caliban, Sebastián with his severed ear, is 'a thing most brutish' (Prospero), and very ugly: 'a villain, sir, / I do not love to look on' (Miranda) (Shakespeare, p. 7). Relating him specifically to the Cuban context, it is legitimate to see Sebastián as the personification of the Caliban described in Roberto Fernández Retamar's influential 1971 essay *Calibán*; he is an apt symbol 'for the people of Latin American since they were enslaved and taught a foreign language by their conquerors' (Hart, p. 143). Intriguingly he is the slave who was definitely Alea's addition to the historical account which only mentioned twelve slaves. The Count asks Manuel to choose twelve slaves, which he does, and then includes Sebastián. Sebastián is at once magical and rebellious. His association with magic is confirmed when he takes out a pouch containing powder which, he suggests, will ensure that he will not be caught, and blows it over the Count as if asserting his power over him. His rebelliousness is epitomised when – after being asked by the Count '¿quién soy, Sebastián?' (who am I Sebastian?) – there follows a pregnant seventeen-second pause before Sebastián spits in the Count's face. The Count accuses him of being a Judas figure, and this is in a sense confirmed when he murders Manuel during the uprising (i.e. this scene recreates the 'murder' of 'Christ'). But Sebastián is more complex than this; he epitomises something of the enimga we associate with the subaltern. Gayatri Spivak has argued that the 'subaltern cannot speak' (Spivak, p. 27), by which she meant that his voice, if expressed, would not be understood by the society in which he lives, and therefore he is disqualified from having a voice. It is surely not coincidental that the only time we really hear Sebastián speak is precisely when the Count is asleep. A true subaltern, his speech is grammatically incorrect, mixing genders and endings ('lo hizo completa', '**lo** cosa fea', '**lo** cosa buena'). As Alea has pointed out: 'Sebastián, el negro que se ha rebelado, se apropia del lenguaje del conde para dirigirse también a los otros: el mito del cuerpo de la Verdad con la cabeza de la Mentira es la respuesta que hará tambalearse los valores y los razon-amientos que el conde presenta como inconmovibles' (Évora, p. 42). The African parable he tells his audience, which is about the struggle between 'Verdad' and 'Mentira', is a postcolonial version of the struggle between colonised and colonising peoples which acts as a counter-response to the Count's parable of human suffering: 'When Olofi made the world he made it complete with day and night, good and bad. Truth and Lie. Olofi was sorry for Lie, who was ugly, and gave him a machete to defend himself. One day Truth and Lie met and had a fight. Lie cut off Truth's head. Headless, Truth took Lie's head. Now Truth goes around with the body of Truth and the head of Lie.' In order to demonstrate this idea, Sebastián picks up the pig's head and places it in front of his own – the clear message is that the Christian West has been passing off lies as truth in order to guarantee its ideological superiority over the rest of the world. Sebastián fur-thermore tells the group of slaves that he has magical powers which allow him to change into an animal or a tree – an idea reinforced by the final, uplifting sequence of the film. In that concluding scene we see Sebastián running free through the jungle, and this sequence is spliced with lush, flowing images of the jungle (a flying bird, a running river, running horses), and accompanied by stir-ring, triumphalist music. We do not know Sebastián's fate, but these final images and sounds of the film suggest freedom and a return to the laws of nature. He has finally escaped his political oppressors.

It is clear that the film bears the imprint of political symbolism. One way in which this film can be related to the experience of Cuba in the 1970s is to see it as what Jerome Branche calls 'a metaphor for Cuba's present struggle against contemporary Yankee imperialism' (Branche, p. 3). Throughout the 1960s – par-ticularly as a result of the Tricontinental Conference of Solidarity of the Peoples of Africa, Asia and Latin America held in Havana in January 1966 – and during the 1970s, Cuba became a crucial player within the growth of anti-colonialist sen-timent around the world (Young, p. 213). *La última cena* could be seen, thus, as an allegory of the political status inflicted on Cuba during the 1970s as the sub-altern of the United States. Gutiérrez Alea's film, given its upbeat ending, can thus be seen as an elegiac response to what Fidel Castro memorably called 'toiling humanity, inhumanely exploited (. . .), controlled by the whip and the overseer' which, at long last via the Revolution, was beginning to have its say: 'But now (. . .) this anonymous mass, this America of colour, sombre, taciturn America, which all over the continent sings with the same sadness and disillusionment, now this mass is beginning to enter conclusively into its own history, is beginning to write it with its own blood' (Castro, pp. 165–6). The promotion of an Afro-Hispanic legacy in *La última cena*, thus, contains a covert political layer, providing the film with a concrete and contemporary relevance.

Works Cited

Branche, Jerome, 'Barbarism and Civilisation: Taking on History *in The Last Supper*', *The Afro-Latino Forum*, 1.1 (1997), 9 pp. Occasional Papers published by the African American Studies and Research Program and the Latin American Studies and Research Program, University of Kentucky, College of Arts and Sciences.

Castro, Fidel, *Fidel Castro Speaks*, ed. M. Kenner and J. Petras (Harmondsworth: Penguin, 1972).

Évora, José Antonio, *Tomás Gutiérrez Alea* (Madrid: Cátedra, 1996).

Fernández Retamar, Roberto, *Caliban and Other Essays*, trans. Edward Baker (Minneapolis: Minnesota University Press, 1989).

Gutiérrez Alea, Tomás, *Dialéctica del espectador* (Havana: Unión de Escritores y Artistas de Cuba, 1982).

Hart, Stephen, *A Companion to Spanish-American Literature* (London: Tamesis, 1999).

Mraz, John, 'Recasting Cuban Slavery: *The Other Francisco* and *The Last Supper*', in *Based on a True Story: Latin American History at the Movies*, ed. Donald F. Stevens (Wilmington, Delaware: SR Books, 1997), pp. 103–22.

Sartre, Jean-Paul, 'Orphée Noir', in *Anthologie de la nouvelle poésie nègre et malgache de langue française*, ed. Léopold Sédar Senghor (Paris: Presses Universitaires de France, 1969), pp. ix–xliv.

Shakespeare, William, *The Tempest*, in *The Works of William Shakespeare* (London: The Queensway Press, n.d.), pp. 2–23.

Spivak, Gayatri, 'Can the Subaltern Speak?', in *The Post-Colonial Studies Reader*, eds Bill Ashcroft, Gareth Griffiths and Helen Tiffin (London: Routledge, 1997), pp. 24–8.

West, Dennis, 'Strawberry and Chocolate, Ice Cream and Tolerance: Interviews with Tomás Gutiérrez Alea and Juan Carlos Tabío', *Cineaste*, 21.1–2 (1995), 16–20.

Young, Robert J.C., *Postcolonialism: An Historical Introduction* (Oxford: Blackwell, 2003).

11

PIXOTE: A LEI DO MAIS FRACO (PIXOTE: THE LAW OF THE WEAKEST, 1980), DIRECTED BY HÉCTOR BABENCO

Cast

Pixote, played by Fernando Ramos da Silva
Sapato, played by Jordel Filho
Dito, played by Gilberto Moura
Chico, played by Edilson Lino
Garatão, played by Claudio Bernardo
Lilica, played by Jorge Juliano
Fumaça, played by Zenildo Oliveira
Deborah, played by Elke Maravilha
Sueli, played by Marília Pêra
Almir (the Policeman), played by João José Pompeo
Judge, played by Rubens de Faldo
Psychologist, played by Isadora de Farias

Crew

Screenplay: Héctor Babenco and Jorge Durán, based on novel *Infância dos mortos* by José Louzeiro
Photography: Rodolfo Sancho
Producer: Luiz Elias
Music: John Neschling
Executive Producer: Silvia Naves
Associate Producers: Paolo Francini, José Pinto, Embrafilme
Director: Héctor Babenco

Awards

Winner, Best Foreign Film, New York Film Critics and Los Angeles Film Critics, 1981
Nominee, Golden Globe, Best Foreign Film, 1981
Winner, Silver Leopard, Locarno, 1981
Winner, Critics' Prize, San Sebastian Film Festival, 1981
Winner, Best Film, Sydney Film Festival, 1982
Winner, Best Actress (Marília Pêra), National Society of Film Critics, USA, 1981

Plot

Film opens with a scene in which some young men are watching a violent scene from a film on TV, which they subsequently imitate. We are in a police station, where we see a woman report her son who has been missing for a month. A group of children are brought in by the police, their names checked, and then they are driven to the reformatory, which is called Pavilhão Euclides da Cunha. The Chief Superintendent, Sapato, explains the rules to them. That night we see a young boy being raped by some of the older boys; Pixote watches, but refuses to reveal the identity of the culprit (it was Garatão), when questioned by the Prison Warden. Pixote's new friend, Fumaça (who loves marihuana, hence his name which literally means 'smoke') introduces Pixote to drugs. That night the two boys see a police officer attempting to find out from the prison inmates who killed the judge the previous week and robbed him of his wallet. They refuse to tell; the transvestite, Lilica, is picked on, but he also refuses to spill the beans. Lilica's lover, Garatão, forces Pixote to eat the food he has spat on at breakfast. Garatão's sadistic nature is further illustrated when he tortures Fumaça by sticking a needle into his arm, forcing him to tell all he knows about what happened to the judge; because of the pain Fumaça has no choice but to 'squeal'. Dito's mother comes to see Dito and he, at first, refuses to see her; then, when she kisses the Chief Superintendent, we realise she is probably having an affair with him. Roberto sings a song for everyone, and despite his terrible voice everyone enjoys it. Pixote is visited by his grandfather; Pixote asks him to get him some marijuana but the latter refuses. Then a group of the boys are taken off by the police officer for identification. Despite pressuring them, the police officer is unable to persuade the family that the blond-haired boy – Fumaça – is the one they are after. Fumaça's mother comes to look for her son, but he is nowhere to be found. We hear a radio report saying that two boys have been found. Journalists come to the hospital and want to know what happened to Fumaça. They imply that the police killed him, but the Boss and the Chief Superintendent deny this, and emphasise what a good job they are doing. While Pixote is cleaning the toilets he is given some glue to sniff. He does so, becomes ill, is sent to the medical unit, and while there he sees Fumaça who is on the point of death. He hears the authorities arguing about what has happened; why, the Boss asks, did they accept Fumaça in this state? Fumaça's body is found on a rubbish tip. The boys subsequently see a news report in which the Boss states that Fumaça was killed by Garatão. The boys are all shocked; Garatão freaks out and demands to see Sapato. Sapato says everything will be OK; that night, though, Garatão is murdered. There is a riot as a result, and the reformatory is nearly burnt down. A judge arrives attempting to find out what is going on; he interviews Lilica but the latter refuses to say anything. Out of despair at what has happened to his lover, Garatão, Lilica slashes his wrists. The boys break out from the reformatory, all except Roberto who decides to stay behind. At this point Part II of the movie begins. We see Dito and Pixote stealing on the streets of São Paolo. Dito and Lilica fall in love, and make love. Lilica meets up with an old friend, Cristal, a drug peddler and pimp. He gives them a lead to a prostitute called Deborah. They meet her, but she takes their drugs, promising to pay them later though she clearly has no intention of doing so. The boys go swimming on the beach of Rio de Janeiro, and everything seems idyllic. But they realise that they have been double-crossed. They go to see Raimundinho in his dance club; Chico and Pixote take the drugs in, and Raimundinho takes it off them. The deal is interrupted, though, by Deborah. They follow her out of the office, demand their money. She refuses and, in the ensuing struggle, Pixote stabs Deborah in the stomach, and then robs her. Chico is also killed in the struggle. They now become the pimps of a prostitute called Sueli. She is in the toilet, having just had an abortion, and she shows Pixote the dead child's body. Dito, Lilica and Pixote begin mugging Sueli's customers at gun-point. Sueli falls for Dito and takes him away from Lilica, who becomes jealous, and eventually leaves. Finally Pixote kills a North-American customer, killing Dito as well during the struggle. The film concludes with Pixote suckling at Sueli's breast, in a scene which verges on the sexual. She throws him out on the streets and the film ends with an image of Pixote walking along the railway tracks back into the city.

Analytical Overview

Susan Ryan explains the background to the film: Babenco's first concept for Pixote was to make a documentary about a reform school, but the authorities denied him access to the school. Still intrigued by the idea of a film about children living on the margins of society, Babenco turned to José Louzeiro's documentary novel, *Infância dos Mortos* (1977), as the basis for a fictional film about street children (Ryan, p. 195). Louzeiro's novel – strictly speaking it was a work of documentary fiction, the 'romance-reportagem' – was, as Randal Johnson has pointed out, 'motivated by what is known as the Camanducaia incident, in which dozens of imprisoned minors were taken from Rio de Janeiro jails and literally dumped over a cliff near a town called Camanducaia in the state of Minas Gerais. It is a denunciation of a violent, hierarchical and closed society that forces many homeless or less fortunate children into a life of crime' (Johnson, p. 38). The end result was stark; *Pixote* can almost be described as the Brazilian version of Buñuel's *Los olvidados*, since it offers a dispiriting vision of the lives of a number of young men who are the outcast of a large Latin American city (this time it is Rio de Janeiro), and whose lives soon lead to crime. The film opens by evoking the language of the documentary. As Marc Lauria points out:

> The film begins [in the version released in the U.S.] as a documentary. Babenco addresses the camera, and states that 50 percent of the population in Brazil is under 21, and this includes three million homeless children. Brazilian law prevents anyone under the age of 18 to be prosecuted for criminal offences; older criminals prey on these youths. Babenco, standing in front of a slum area, then introduces Fernando Ramos da Silva, who lives there as 'Pixote' in the film proper. ('Pixote')

What follows is 'one of the most haunting portrays of childhood ever filmed' ('Rotten Tomatoes Review'). *Pixote* traces the troubled childhood of a young boy in a reformatory in a way which is redolent of Truffaut's New Wave masterpiece, *Les Quatre cent coups* (1959) (Armes, pp. 177–8). Christopher Null has argued that *Pixote* is unsuccessful as a film because Babenco 'muddles the story with no sympathetic character at all' such that 'we've judged Pixote as just another gutterpunk, not a victim' ('Review'), but surely this is just the point that Babenco is attempting to make: we can't gloss over the reality being depicted. It **is** horrible.

Babenco and Jorge Durán used Louzeiro's *Infância dos Mortos* in order to create a screenplay which differed in some key respects from the original documentary novel. As Johnson points out, 'Pixote ("Pichote" in Louzeiro) is a minor character in Louzeiro's book who dies in the first chapter, gunned down as he and other marginalised children run through a cemetery to avoid being abused by pimps and drug pushers' (Johnson, p. 43). A number of the film's episodes, though, such as the prostitution/hold-up racket, are taken straight from the novel, though it is character called Dito who is the protagonist. The theme of the corruption of the authorities likewise originated in the book; this, indeed, is a common motif of Brazilian literature and film (see the discussion of *City of God*, chapter 25). Sapato is a prime example of this. While he pretends to be on the boys' side, he is always planning ways in which he can use his position to good account. He does not attempt to punish the perpetrator of the rape in the rooms during the night – he simply shouts at the boys, deliberately covering up any wrong-doing. Thus, when he picks up the young, naked boy who had been kept in the cell with the others, he puts him quickly into bed before anyone discovers what has happened. In order to stop the reporters asking any awkward questions, Sapato says the boy has a contagious disease. And it is clear – though not stated – that he is behind the dumping of Fumaça's dead body on the rubbish tip in the suburbs. His name is well chosen; as the 'sapato' (shoe) of the authorities, he is their lackey, but also the one who implements their repressive policies, keeping the boys under lock and key. Because he is so duplicitous Sapato can be seen as the villain of the piece. His villainy fully emerges in his treatment of Garatão, who is sacrificed for the 'greater good'. The children are 'disappeared' as soon as there is a problem; they become pawns in a larger social power game. When, for example, Sapato says to Garatão that he will soon be eighteen, and that he 'doesn't exist', his words may be taken on a number of levels. First of all they are meant to stand for encouragement in that Garatão's record will be wiped clean. But they also mean that – in society's eyes – the delinquents really do not exist. On a third level, they are a chilling omen of what will happen to him that night. He will be murdered; Sapato knows that this is going to happen, and he is a willing accomplice in that murder.

The film is split into two quite separate halves. In the first part, we witness Pixote's life in the reformatory. As Marc Lauria points out: 'As in the Hollywood prison genre (except in this case, the protagonists are children), the point of view is exclusively of the inmates, and emphasis is placed on power structures operating within personal relationships' ('Pixote'). The second part of the film shows the gang now on the outside, and much of what was being worked out in the first part of the film (social culpability, police corruption, etc.) is left unresolved. The culpability of the authorities – though underlined – never re-enters the frame, thereby subverting the Hollywood formula in which evil is punished with retribution. As in a picaresque novel where the energy is in the episodic, ever-moving nature of the narrative, Pixote simply moves on to pastures new. It is interesting that Roberto, the singer, should stay behind. He does so for empirical reasons in that he has a broken leg. But his refusal to leave can be interpreted on a symbolic level as well. For him, the world of the imagination – the world of the asylum and the institution palliated by unrealistic dreams – is better than the real world.

The film repeatedly re-enacts the drama of the dysfunctional family, focusing in particular on the absence of any positive female figures. The 'femme', indeed, in *Pixote* is always 'fatale'. Sexuality is never presented within a normative, heterosexual context. It appears either in the guise of prostitution – there are two prostitutes in the film, Deborah and Sueli, and both offer sordid views of sexuality – or male rape (as when Garatão rapes the young boy in the reformatory), or male-male sex (when Dito and Lila have sex soon after their arrival in São Paolo). Mothers are either absent (as in Pixote's case, since he does not know where his mother is, as his grandfather comments to him during the prison visit), or they are two-timers (as Dito's mother shows herself to be, when she begins kissing the Chief Superintendent), or they are heartless prostitutes (as Sueli reveals herself to be, when she kills her child with a knitting needle).

As the above suggests – in its creation of gritty reality – *Pixote* clearly evokes the rhetoric of the 'romance-reportagem'. Yet it should be stressed that Babenco's film also employs those techniques we associate more readily with feature films, such as foreshadowing. Thus while Pixote is cleaning the toilets we get a close-up of his foot squashing a cock-roach, which is an omen of what will happen to Fumaça. In a clever pun, he will be squashed under Sapato's shoe.

Criminality, Voyeurism, Symbolism

It is clear right from the beginning of the film that the film is enacted along a scopophilic axis, with the criminal being put forward as the epitome of the voyeur. The film opens with the young criminals in the reformatory watching a violent scene from an action film on TV. Pixote watches when the young black boy is raped by Garatão in the reformatory. His expressionless face – in that it does not express horror – suggests that he is beginning to derive a scopophilic pleasure from watching the 'private' – we might call them virtual nowadays – lives of others. He watches the pornographic film with the other boys in Cristal's apartment – and, like them, begins to masturbate. He also watches when Sueli and Dito make love, and – the first time that his evident pleasure is shown by the camera eye – he licks his lips. He watches through the curtains when Sueli is with her Brazilian client, and the POV shots are his, when they are not focused on his own face watching what is going on very intently. The final voyeuristic scene occurs when he is sitting watching some dancers on TV. In a deliberately contrived two-shot he is shown watching the TV while Sueli – depressed now that Dito is dead – is captured sitting behind him, watching him watching. A gesture echoed on a number of occasions in the film, Pixote turns from the TV programme and settles his eyes on Sueli. This transference from the TV to the nearest individual in the room is a rhetorical move which occurs again and again throughout the film. It suggests that the boys have an unmediated vision of the filmic image. Thus, if they see pornographic images they immediately masturbate, if they see violence they react violently. They are unable to cut themselves off from the media. They are its victims, and its playthings.

In the 'climax' of the film, Pixote turns from watching some beautiful women on the TV, and feels desire for Sueli. In a scene that 'meshes sexuality and maternal desire in a highly confusing and destabilising way' (Kantaris, p. 181), Sueli attempts to mother Pixote, and he takes advantage of this fact in order to suck her nipple sexually. When Sueli realises Pixote is not acting as her 'baby', she screams at him to stop, and orders him to leave. Her final words to him – 'I'm not your mother!' – sum up the underlying rhetorical move of the film. The protagonists – and Pixote foremost among them – search for their mother in different people, but all they find are 'false' mothers. Lilica attempts to 'mother' Garatão and then Dito. Deborah attempts to mother Pixote (she asks him if he wants to come round and play with her son, thereby in effect mothering a motherless boy), and Sueli does the same. But this gesture always leads to failure or death. The relationship between Sueli and Pixote is the most poignant since there are a number of pointers that suggest that the mother-son relationship is being worked at in the film's symbolics. In a visually unpleasant scene – the abortion scene in the toilet – Sueli says that the aborted child looks a bit like him (see discussion in Kantaris, p. 180), and this scene is especially important since – as the concluding scene of the film makes clear – she pointedly refuses to be his mother. She sends him out into the world; he is, in a sense, not only a dead man walking (we are reminded of the pertinence of the title of the documentary novel on which the film is based – *Infância dos mortos*), but, as it were, an abortion walking. Sueli has, in fact, expelled Pixote from her home, her womb, and has condemned him to an early death.

As one might expect in such a gritty film, it is the grim harvester which provides the symbolic resonance behind the different scenes. There is, for example, a deliberate parallelism between the needle which Garatão uses to torture Fumaça early on in the film and the needle which Sueli uses to kill her unborn child. The torture of Fumaça thereby becomes, in retrospect, a grim omen of what is to follow. Just like the aborted child, he will end up dead. This parallelism has a number of implications for how we interpret the film. Given that Garatão is a rapist, and given the phallic resonance of the needle, it is clear that a web of association is being built up in the film which aligns male sexuality with torture, rape and death. This pessimistic assessment of human sexuality is balanced by the repetition of the moif of the absent mother (see above).

Acting

The children in the film were non-actors, and were given crash courses in acting before and during the shoot: 'Babenco trained each child from scratch, thereby avoiding the stereotypical mannerisms that likely would have come from using professional child actors' (Levine, p. 203). The actors were allowed to extemporise and change the script; as Babenco said: 'They gave me the right words, the right sentences' (quoted in Shaw, p. 147). Sometimes their input even changed the perspective on a given episode; as a result of Fernando's input, Pixote was drafted in as a witness to the sex scene between Chico and Sueli; in the original script he had been in another room (Shaw, p. 147). As Marc Lauria puts it, 'incidents in Pixote don't seem to be set up for the cameras; the film seems to follow the characters no matter what they do or say' ('Pixote'). Unlike the children, though, some of the adult performances are a little exaggerated. One reviewer, for example, speaks of the acting being a little 'over-done', and this would seem to be the case with Sapato, whose performance is theatrical rather than filmically seamless. The detective is also presented in rather Gothic, overdone tones. But there are some fine haunting performances by Lilica. Sueli's is a rough, believable performance, and Pixote's, though not spellbinding, is understated enough to allow the terrible nature of his psyche to shine through.

The terror of this film is not what we have seen but what will happen next when Pixote goes to Rio. The final image of the film is extraordinarily haunting; Pixote walking along a railway track with a gun in his belt, back to Rio de Janeiro. Having murdered three people already, though only a minor he is already a 'hardened' criminal, experienced in violence, extortion, the use of firearms, and with a worryingly precocious interest in sex. The fate of the main character in the film after its release in 1980 is a testimony to its verisimilitude. After the film was released Fernando Ramos da Silva, who played Pixote, was persistently harassed by the police, arrested on two occasions, tortured and – on 25 August 1987 – he was gunned down by police (Levine, pp. 208–11). A film, *Quem matou Pixote?* (Who Killed Pixote?, 1996), directed by José Joffily, has been made about the life of the actor who was gunned down (Carboni), revealing this as a story that runs and runs. There is, indeed, no greater testimony to the true-to-life grittiness of Babenco's film.

Works Cited

Armes, Roy, *French Cinema*, 3rd ed. (London: Secker and Warburg, 1985).

Carboni, Ciça, 'Quem matou Pixote?' www.cinemando.com.br/arquivo/filmes/quemmatoupixote.htm.

Johnson, Randal, 'The *Romance-Reportagem* and the Cinema: Babenco's *Lúcio Flávio* and *Pixote*', *Luso-Brazilian Review*, 24.2 (1987), 35–48.

Kantaris, Geoffrey, 'The Young and the Damned', in *Contemporary Latin American Cultural Studies*, eds Stephen Hart and Richard Young (London: Arnold, 2003), 177–89.

King, John, *Magical Reels: A History of Cinema in Latin America* (London: Verso, 1990).

Lauria, Marc, 'Pixote', www.senseofcinema.com/contents/03/25/cteq/pixote.html (consulted on 23 December 2003).

Levine, Robert M., 'Fiction and Reality in Brazilian Life', in *Based on a True Story: Latin American History at the Movies*, ed. Donald F. Stevens (Wilmington, Delaware: Scholarly Resources, 1997), pp. 201–14.

Null, Christopher, 'Review: Pixote', www.filmcritic.com/misc/emporium.nsf/0/373d26efcbf353e488256c9f0017247c?OpenDocument (consulted on 23 December 2003).

Rotten Tomatoes Review, 'Pixote', www.rottentomatoes.com.m/Pixote-1016381/about.php (consulted on 23 December 2003).

Ryan, Susan, 'Pixote, a Lei do Mais Fraco', in *South American Cinema: A Critical Filmography 1915–1994*, eds Timothy Barnard and Peter Rist (Austin: University of Texas Press, 1996), pp. 195–7.

Shaw, Deborah, *Contemporary Cinema of Latin America: 10 Key Films* (London: Continuum, 2003), pp. 144–58.

12

EL NORTE (THE NORTH, 1983), DIRECTED BY GREGORY NAVA

Cast

Rosa, played by Zaide Silvia Gutiérrez
Enrique, played by David Villapando
Arturo Xuncax (Rosa's father), played by Ernesto Gómez Cruz
Lupe Xuncax (Rosa's mother), played by Alicia del Lago
Nacha, played by Lupe Ontiveros
Pedro, played by Eradio Zepeda
Josefita, played by Stella Quan
Monty, played by Trinidad Silva
Raimundo, played by Abel Franco
Jaime, played by Mike Gomez
Ed, played by John Martin
Joel, played by Ronald Jospeh
Bruce, played by Larry Cedar
Karen, played by Sheryl Bernstein
Len, played by Gregory Enton
Carlos, played by Tony Plana
Jorge, played by Enrique Castillo

Crew

Screenplay: Gregory Nava and Anna Thomas
Director: Gregory Nava
Producer: Anna Thomas
Sound Producer: Robert Yerinton
Cinematography: James Glennon
Film Editor: Betsy Blankett
Set direction: David Wasco
Editing: Betsy Blanket
Music Composers: Gustav Mahler, Guiseppe Verdi, Samuel Barber, The Folkloristas, Melecio Martinez, Emil Richards, Linda O'Brien

Awards

Winner, Best original screenplay, Academy of Motion Picture Arts and Sciences, Hollywood, 1983
Winner, First Prize, Montreal Film Festival, 1983
Best original screenplay, Writers' Guild of America, 1983
Official Selection, Cannes Film Festival, 1983

Plot

The film is split into three parts, the first set in Guatemala, the second in Mexico and the third in the United States, mainly in Los Angeles. The film opens with breathtaking shots of rural Guatemala. Arturo Xuncax works at a coffee plantation and he is involved in the workers' resistance movement; the Army arrives during one of their meetings and kills everyone. Because Arturo Xuncax killed one of the soldiers, el Puma, they decapitate him and hang his head from a nearby tree. The mother, Lupe, is subsequently taken away by the army, and Enrique and Rosa, their children, decide to make their way to the United States. They get money to finance the trip from Rosa's godmother. In Part II Rosa and Enrique travel by bus through Mexico until they get to the border town, Tijuana. They are befriended by a man called Jaime from Zacatecas who offers to take them across the border. However, he attacks them in the forest. They meet up with Raimundo Gutiérrez who agrees to takes them across; he advises them to go through the sewers. While crawling through, they get bitten by rats. In Part III, Raimundo takes them to Lazy Acres Motel where they are provided with a room. Raimundo starts working in a restaurant, and Rosa in a sweat factory where she is befriended by Nacha. The sweat factory is raided and Nacha and Rosa start cleaning a rich lady's house. Enrique is promoted and, to get even, the Chicano working there informs the Immigration Unit. Enrique and his friend, Jorge, have to escape. Rosa falls ill and is taken to hospital by Nacha. She is diagnosed with typhus. Enrique is offered a job in Chicago but he comes back to be with Rosa in hospital, where she dies. The next day Enrique is back in the queue waiting for work; he starts working on a building site.

Analytical Overview

El Norte won a number of prizes on its release in 1983 – it took first prize at the Montreal Film Festival and scooped an Oscar for best original screenplay in Hollywood – which immediately alerts us to the fact that it needs to be taken seriously in its own right. But Nava's movie is also significant as a cross-over film, not only in thematic terms (it focuses on a journey across the border between Mexico and the United States), but also in terms of the interplay between U.S. and Latin American film. On a more obvious level it reverses the trend – evident in Hollywood from the early 1920s – of presenting Mexicans as 'greasers' (Monsiváis) and 'bandidos' (King, p. 17), as criminals from 'down there' who threaten the stability of the 'American dream' (for further discussion see Noriega). It builds on the evolution of a national identity created by New Latin American Cinema in the 1960s (Pick, pp. 38–65; and Chanan, passim). Most importantly, *El Norte* offers a sneak preview of the more dynamic and creative interaction between Latin American filmmakers and Hollywood which has emerged in the twenty-first century (in the work of film directors such as Alejandro González Iñárritu; see Smith), since *El Norte* came from within the U.S. movie industry.

The above should not be interpreted, though, to suggest that *El Norte* offers a rosy view of the relationship between the United States and Latin America. Quite the opposite is the case. With hindsight it seems difficult to square the rather glamorous view of Gregory Nava presented by his Fans' Web Site ('Nava Web Page') nowadays with the rather sniffy reviews that *El Norte* elicited soon after its release in 1983. Christine Ricci called the film 'uneven', 'overdone' and 'overwhelmingly sentimental' ('Review: El Norte'), while Dave Kehr criticised it for downplaying realism in favour of producing a tear-jerker: 'Nava is clearly less interested in exploring the tragic reality of the situation than in wringing a few tears from Anglo audiences. Though his subject is a serious one and has intentions that are apparently noble, Nava has made a film that is essentially indistinguishable from *Love Story*' ('Review: El Norte'). The allusion to *Love Story* in *El Norte* occurs, of course, in the hospital scene where Rosa says farewell to her brother – and here comment should be made of Zaide Silvia Gutiérrez's strong acting performance; she went on to star in a number of other movies (see 'Filmography') – but the adverb within the expression 'apparently noble' says it all. It is clear – though not explicitly stated – that it is the mixture of love and politics and, more importantly, the anti-American-dream ethos of the film that Kehr has baulked at. Even if a hostile stance is taken to the film, it is surely **not** the case that the film does not explore 'the tragic reality of the situation'. Even Fredric and Mary Ann Brussat's positive review of *El Norte* effectively damns by faint praise: 'Nava's attention to details, particularly the authentic and religious beauty of Indian culture, and his sympathy for the protagonists' inner lives lift this story above its melodramatic moments and make this tale a memorable one' ('Review: El Norte'). The implication is that *El Norte* needed a lift from its melodrama. It was essentially the mixture between melodrama and politics – itself a hallmark of Latin American cinema (see López) – that the U.S. critics found uncomfortable. Michael O'Brien, for example, argued that 'there's no propaganda in the movie, just visual poetry, suspense and emotional force' ('Review: El Norte') – a view which I will be contesting below – while Janet Maslin was rather bemused that 'this is one movie in which the white, English-speaking characters are strictly walk-ons' ('Review: El Norte'). For his part, Michael Canby hit the nail on the head when he referred to the film's 'arbitrarily tragic ending' ('Review: El Norte'). This is, indeed, the real problem with the film. While it evokes the rhetoric of the American dream with its paraphernalia of an upbeat story of rags to riches (Hayward, pp. 45–9), it dashes completely that dream in the closing sequence of the film: Enrique is right back where he started. Rather than upward social mobility and success as per the American dream, *El Norte* expresses downward mobility and failure.

As we can see, *El Norte* certainly offers a new perspective on the American dream, one which might be characterised as the Mexican version of that dream. From the beginning 'El Norte' functions as an image of an earthly paradise, more concretely, as a haven of escape from the harrowing politicised environment of Guatemala. Given that both of their parents have been killed (we know that Arturo has been murdered, and although we cannot know for sure, our assumption as viewers is that Rosa's mother is also taken away to be murdered) Enrique and Rosa have to flee, and cannot return to Guatemala. Their imagination about the North is fired by the various back numbers of *Buen hogar* that Rosa's godmother keeps in her back room. She captivates the villagers with her stories of the interior design of houses in the United States, focusing in particular on their flush toilets and electric lights. In some respects *El Norte* follows the Hollywood formula in the sense that it describes two individuals who overcome adverse circumstances in order to achieve their dreams. Thus Rosa and Enrique overcome the death of their parents, the trauma of travelling through Guatemala until they get to Tijuana, they elude murder at the hands of Jaime the trickster, they overcome the trauma of making their way through the sewage tunnels (even being bitten by rats in the process), and – despite their illegal status – they finally get jobs (Enrique as a waiter and Rosa as a cleaner). The scene where Enrique proudly tells Rosa that he has been promoted is the point at which they are the nearest to the American dream. As we soon discover, however, this is the apex of their good fortune for, almost immediately afterwards, their lives change dramatically for the worst. Enrique is turned in by the Chicano waiter at the restaurant they both work in because of jealousy and Rosa suddenly falls ill. Though different phenomena – one is the result of human action, the other the result of disease – they are twinned in the film because of their simultaneity. The suggestion is that, whatever they do, Latin American refugees will find it almost impossible to create a new life in the United States; the inevitability of Rosa's illness (it was only a matter of time before the typhus finished her off) is thus grafted metaphorically onto Enrique's predicament – it was only a matter of time before he was going to be shopped. It is from this point onwards that their fate seems sealed. Rosa dies in hospital and her death-bed speech refers to how there is 'no room' for either of them ('no hay lugar aquí para nosotros') and, when we see Enrique reduced to going back to queue outside the Lazy Acres Motel, we know that it is just a matter of time before he succumbs as well to adverse circumstances. It is in this sense that we can describe *El Norte* as a film which conjures up the American dream, only finally to tear it to tatters. The conclusion the viewer draws about the film is, thus, a profoundly ironic one about the accessibility of the American dream for 'wetbacks'.

Symbolism

El Norte is almost a classic example of continuity editing; it tells a story from beginning to end and does so chronologically. There are no flashbacks and it even keeps internal monologue/dream sequences to a bare minimum. But there are junctures in the film in which various events are tied together and shown to have a more symbolic connection. The most obvious example of this is the scene which concludes the film in which Enrique shouts out to the building site foreman that he has 'fuertes brazos' (strong arms) to work with, since this alludes – ironically – to the conversation Enrique had with his father just before the latter was murdered, in which he says that he is fighting against the ideology of the rich for whom the peasants are 'puros brazos para trabajar' (simply arms for labouring). Other allusions are more subtle. Much is made throughout the film about the gringos' ability to flush their excrement away; as Rosa's godmother suggests, 'se puede mear como una reina' (you can piss like a queen). And the first thing that Rosa and Enrique do when they go to the North is flush the toilet. This mechanisation, however, has its more negative side since it is part and parcel of a mind-set which sends in trucks and arms soldiers with guns to destroy 'civil unrest', destroying families in the process; it is for this reason that when Lupe is taken away in a truck that we hear the following words pronounced by a soldier: 'arranca toda esa mierda' (take all that shit away). Rosa's mother is being 'flushed' away as if she were no more than excreta. In this context, we may surmise, it is not by chance that Rosa and Enrique have to get to the United States via the sewage system.

There are a number of scenes in the film which allude subtly to the discourse of magical realism and it is worthwhile examining them in greater detail. The epitome of magical realism is that fusion of the magical and the real that we would find in the visible image of a ghost (Hart), and this classical sense of the magical real finds its way into the filmic repertoire of *El Norte*. Magic appears in the film often in the context of death and crisis; logically this is the time when the other side 'comes over'. The first indication of the crisis which has blighted the family occurs when Rosa returns to the house and finds it filled with butterflies; she follows their trail and discovers they are emerging from her mother's silver necklace which is among the lit candles on the family altar. In symbolic terms this scene functions as an omen of her mother's soul emerging, like a butterfly, from her body. Then Rosa hears the dreadful news from a neighbour – her mother has been abducted by the Army. Soon afterwards we see her sitting peacefully in a clearing near a forest; atmospheric music is used, and suddenly a deer appears, followed by Rosa catching sight of a group of white cut flowers nearby, and finally we see – almost as if he were an apparition – Enrique. In an interview Gregory Nava has mentioned that he is fond of using pre-Columbian motifs in his film since they are intrinsic to the culture from which he comes. He has suggested that *Mi Familia, my Family* (1995) 'has a strong pre-Columbian mythic structure' expressed particularly via a 'tremendously, strong and deep pre-Columbian spirituality' (West, p. 28). We find a similar mythic structure in *El Norte*. For the Quiché-Maya who inhabit Guatemala the deer is a sacred animal and also associated with an individual's 'nagual' or animal-soul; flowers are associated in the Aztec and Mayan cosmology with the souls of the departed. This scene therefore suggests that – in a mysterious way – Rosa is communing with her parents.

Enrique's appearance simultaneously confirms and re-structures this moment of 'inscape' (to use Gerard Manley Hopkins's term) since Rosa believed that he too had been killed. Soon after this scene – when she has decided that she will take her chances and go to the United States with Enrique – she goes to light some candles for her parents in the local church, and, as she is coming back, she is suddenly confronted by the two old women sitting outside their house who ask her in Quiché where she is going; the door subsequently bangs shut, and they are revealed to be no more than a magical-realist vision – their appearance combines the supernatural (ghosts appearing during the night) with the quotidian (old women sitting on their chairs outside their house).

Other symbolic uses of mise-en-scène deserve mention. There are various junctures in the film when the director has chosen to depict Enrique as – metaphorically speaking – behind bars. This entrapment occurs literally when he, and Rosa, have to crawl their way to San Diego along the tunnel, but it also occurs when Enrique looks at the villagers' legs going past the barred window in Tijuana, when the shadow of bars are reflected on his face when he pleads with the owner of Lazy Acres Motel to give him another chance at the Chicago job, and, finally, when he is shown – right at the end of the film – in a rear-view crane shot in a line of workers shovelling out a trench – we see him through wooden rafters which act metaphorically as bars confining him, and indicating that Enrique is as imprisoned by his circumstances at the end of the film as he was at the beginning. The strongest symbol used in the film, however, is that of the cyclical nature of life, a notion deeply seated in the Amerindian world-view and one which does not mesh well with the linear conception of time and history favoured by the West. Nava has referred to how, in *Mi familia, my Family*, the corn field 'is regeneration (sic) and cyclical' (West, p. 28), and a similar motif appears in *El Norte* and here it is expressed visually by means of various images of cyclical phenomena. The first image of the cyclical occurs in the water wheel on which the camera focuses almost obsessively when Enrique is receiving much-needed advice from Ramón about the tricks to watch out for when going North. The image recurs in the film's concluding sequence when the camera obsessively dallies on the concrete mixer. The message here – it appears – is, to use a Beckettian metaphor, 'plus ça change, plus c'est la même chose'.

The image which is put to the most varied use is that of light, either natural or mechanical. Like the sewerage system, electric lights are selected as a synecdoche of urban modernity; Rosa and Enrique are amazed by the electric lights they encounter in their room in Lazy Acres Motel. And, like the sewerage system, they have a negative symbolic side. In a very deliberately choreographed sequence the lights of the Immigration Unit's helicopter hovering overhead are grafted onto the light of Enrique's torch as they are being 'tortured' to death by the rampant hordes of rats climbing over them and biting them as they go. Soon after they emerge from the tunnel, Enrique and Rosa marvel at the lights of downtown San Diego at night. The notion of social control associated with lights even appears in the seemingly anodyne details – when Enrique is picked up for his first job in a restaurant, we get a close-up of the front light of the Mercedes.

Before moments of danger, the moon is often shown in an establishing shot, often half-covered, and acting as an omen. The light of the moon thereby functions as a natural corollary – with deep associations in Amerindian cosmology with death, since the Moon 'lives' during the night – of the threatening lights of modern civilisation epitomised by the urban life in the United States. Details such as these – while they might be unimportant when taken separately – prove to be important symbolic structuring devices when understood contextually.

Cultural Conflict and Humour

In a film such as *El Norte*, it is clear that cultural conflict is a central theme. Yet this conflict is not voiced as an 'Us-versus-Them' contest, of Guatemalans pitted against the United States. *El Norte* cleverly avoids the stereotyping about 'latinos' which had characterised Hollywood cinema for decades before this film came out; it was a filmic set-up which relied for jokes as much as for the excitement of the forbidden on the image of the Mexican, for example, as an oversexed, dangerous 'bandido' living in a lawless region 'somewhere down South' (see above). Since we follow the protagonists' journey through the length of Mexico, we are also introduced to some of the views that Guatemalans have about Mexicans (they swear a lot, saying 'chingar' every other word, and are often crooks – as indeed turns out to be the case, as Jaime the Trickster's actions prove), the ideas that Mexicans have about Guatemalans (they are all dumb Indians from a tiny village), as well as the views that Mexicans have about Chicanos (watch your back, because they'll turn you in at the drop of a hat, as indeed happens in the film). We also find out what Chicanos think about Mexicans (they are needed to provide cheap labour to keep the U.S. economy going, but they have to be put in their place if they get ideas above their station), what Chicanos think about gringos (they are all mad and you will never understand them), as well as what the U.S. population think about foreigners (they are exploitable, a bit backward, and they swear a lot, etc.). This variety of views is introduced very skilfully, thereby making it in effect impossible for the viewer to adopt a stereotypical view of what latinos are like.

Language plays an important role in this cultural conflict. The Xuncax family – along with the villagers – speak Quiché to each other; the use of the indigenous language is reserved pointedly for moments of tenderness between family members, the best example being when Rosa persuades Enrique to take her with him to the North. Part of the persuasiveness of her rhetoric – the scene makes clear – is rooted in the fact that she uses Quiché rather than Spanish. Often intra-cultural as well as extra-cultural conflicts are expressed in terms of humour. The scene when Ramón teaches Enrique to swear in Mexican is a delightfully humorous one; when Rosa and Enrique meet their first Mexican – the truck driver – he produces a string of swear words on cue. Likewise some of the jokes that the Mexicans in Tijuana use to poke fun at Enrique and Rosa just after they have got off the bus in Tijuana ('they don't know their arses from a hole in the ground', etc. etc.), though cruel, are amusing. Other examples of cultural conflict – such as when the Immigration

Officer tries to establish whether Enrique is Mexican, or when Mrs Rogers is explaining how the washing machine works to Rosa and Nacha, or when Jorge and Enrique laugh at the Mocho because he can't understand Spanish – are innately comic. Gregory Nava, as we can see, is quite prepared to use humour as a means of making serious points about the ways that cultures collide with each other; *El Norte*, after all, is also a story about people missing the point.

Works Cited

Brussat, Fredric and Mary Ann, 'Review: El Norte', www.rottentomatoes.com/ click/movie_1015251/reviews.php (consulted on 8 January 2004).

Canby, Michael, 'Review: El Norte', www.galegroup.com/free_resources/chh/ bio/nava_g.htm (consulted on 8 January 2004).

Chanan, Michael (ed.), *Twenty-Five Years of the New Latin American Cinema* (London: BFI, 1983).

'Filmography',   www.movies.go.com/filmography/Filmography?person_id= 268328 (consulted on 8 January 2004).

Hart, Stephen, *Reading Magic Realism from Latin America* (London: Bloomsbury, 2001). ISBN: 0747556202. Internet book.

Hayward, Susan, *Key Concepts in Cinema Studies* (London: Routledge, 1999).

Kehr, Dave, 'Review: El Norte', www.rottentomatoes.com/click/movie_1015251/ reviews.php (consulted on 8 January 2004).

King, John, *Magical Reels: A History of Cinema in Latin America* (London: Verso, 1990).

López, A.M., 'Tears and Desire: Women and Melodrama in the "old" Mexican Cinema', in E.A. Kaplan (ed.), *Feminism and Film* (Oxford: Oxford University Press), pp. 505–20.

Maslin, Janet, 'Review: El Norte', www.galegroup.com/free_resources/chh/bio/ nava_g.htm (consulted on 8 January 2004).

Monsiváis, Carlos, 'Mythologies', in *Mexican Cinema*, ed. Paulo Paranaguá (London: BFI, 1995), pp. 117–27.

Noriega, Chon A. (ed.), *Visible Nations: Latin American Cinema and Video* (Minneapolis: University of Minnesota Press, 2000).

'Nava Web Page', www.angelfire.com/celeb2/gnava (consulted on 8 January 2004).

O'Brien, Michael, 'Review: El Norte', www.galegroup.com/free_resources/chh/ bio/nava_g.htm (consulted on 8 January 2004).

Pick, Zuzana, *The New Latin American Cinema: A Continental Project* (Austin: University of Texas Press, 1993).

Ricci, Christina, 'Review: El Norte', www.rottentomatoes.com/click/movie_ 1015251/reviews.php (consulted on 8 January 2004).

Smith, Paul Julian, *Amores perros* (London: British Film Institute, 2002).

West, Dennis, 'Filming the Chicano Family Saga: Interview with Director Gregory Nava', *Cineaste*, 21.4 (1995), 26–9.

13

CAMILA (1984), DIRECTED BY MARÍA LUISA BEMBERG

Cast

Camila, played by Susú Pecoraro
Ladislao, played by Imanol Arias, and dubbed by Lellio Incrocci
La Perichona (Camila's grandmother), played by Mona Maris
Adolfo (Camila's father), played by Héctor Alterio

Also Starring

Elena Tasisto, Carlos Muñoz, Héctor Pellegrini, Juan Leyrado, Cecilio Madanés, Claudio Gallardou, Boris Rubaja

With

Alberto Busaid, Lidia Catalano, Zelmar Gueñol, Jorge Hacker, Carlos Marchi, Roxana Berco, Alejandra Colunga, Alejandro Marcial, Oscar Núñez, Jorge Ochoa, Fernando Iglesias (Tacholas)

Crew

Director: María Luisa Bemberg
Screenplay: María Luisa Bemberg, Beda Docampo Feijoo, and Juan Bautista Stagnaro
Cinematography: Fernando Arribas
Editing: Luis César D'Angiolillo
Art Directors: Miguel Rodríguez and Esmeralda Almonacid
Assistant Director: Alberto Lecchi
Camera: Daniel Karp
Production Delegate: Paco Molero
Wardrobe: Graciela Galán
Make-up: Oscar Malet
Hairdresser: Rodolfo Spinetta
Production Managers: Martha Parga, Clara Zappettini
Sound: Jorge Stavropulos
Music: Luis María Serra
Producer: Lita Santic for Gea Producciones (Argentina) and Impala (Spain)

Awards

Nominee, Best Foreign Film, Academy of Motion Picture Arts and Sciences, Hollywood
Winner, Best Actress (Susú Pecoraro), Karlovy Vary, 1984
Winner, Best Actress (Pecoraro, shared), Havana, 1984

Plot

Film opens with establishing shot of the pampas; panning shots of the O'Gorman estate. Camila's grandmother, La Perichona, alights from her horse-drawn carriage; is greeted by her son Adolfo, who wishes her well during her house arrest in the tower. Domestic scenes around the estate. In church Camila is seen confessing the contents of a sexual dream; Camila sees the new priest and asks who he is. Camila buys a prohibited book in Mariano's bookshop. During a party at the O'Gorman household Camila falls in love with the new priest, Ladislao. Mariano is murdered, and Ladislao uses his sermon to criticise the perpetrators. Camila praises his action at dinner, and is asked to leave the table by her father. Camila gives some clothes to the Church. In a highly charged confession she confesses her love to Ladislao. Ladislao and Camila have a secret rendez-vous in the belfry and snatch their first kiss. They elope and settle in Goya City, miles from Buenos Aires, and set up a school. Some strains appear in their relationship. Ladislao is discovered by Padre Gannon in a tavern. They are offered horses to flee, but they remain and the Comandante arrives and arrests them. They are both imprisoned, and sentenced to death because of their sacrilegious actions. Despite the possibility of a reprieve for Camila because she is pregnant, they are both shot by firing squad on Rosas's explicit orders. The two bodies are put in the same coffin. Voice-over suggests that they are joined in death.

Historical basis

Intriguingly enough, the actual events which led to the discovery of Camila's and Uladislao's hideaway in the summer of 1848 were even more melodramatic in real life than they were in the film version. (I use Ladislao to refer to the film character and Uladislao Gutiérrez to refer to the historical individual who eloped with Camila O'Gorman in December 1847, since that is how the earliest historical documents spell his name.) Camila O'Gorman, a 20-year-old woman from a wealthy, respected Irish-Argentine family, and Uladislao Gutiérrez, a 23-year-old priest and nephew of the Governor of Tucumán, eloped from Buenos Aires on the night of 11/12 December 1847, and by March of the following year they were teaching at a school they had founded in Goya, in northern Argentina, under the assumed names of Máximo Brandier and Valentina Sanz. The Justice of the Peace in Goya happened to be Esteban Perichón, the brother of Ana María Perichón de Vandeuil (O'Gorman), that is,

Camila's grandmother, La Perichona, who had created a scandal in Buenos Aires over her affair with the Viceroy Santiago Liniers, for which she had been ostracised from Buenos Aires high society. Esteban Perichón had seen Camila only as a baby and the two lovers therefore thought they were safe. But their identities were discovered during a party held at the house of Esteban Perichón to honour Camila's pregnancy, at which, as bad luck would have it, Father Gannon was in attendance. Bemberg chose to drop some of these details no doubt in order to simplify the plot but she thereby passed up the rather intriguing possibility of having the Justice of the Peace discover that he had invited to his house not only an outlaw on the run, but a woman who had run off with a priest, but, to top it all, his grandniece. In its irony this is almost like the reversal-scene of a Greek tragedy; the fall from grace could not have been any more striking. Life sometimes is stranger than art (for more on the historical basis see Ruffinelli, pp. 11–14).

Analytical Overview

The story of the love-affair between Camila and Uladislao was a contentious one which reflected badly on an important figure of Argentina's republican history (Rosas) as well as the Church, and, for reason, although a short film had been made in 1912, 'every director since then had been forbidden to tell their story' (Stevens, p. 87). It was a result of Bemberg's extraordinary determination to tell Camila and Uladislao's story that the film finally came about. Intriguingly, *Camila* cost a mere $370,000 to make (Bach, p. 23), which, by Hollywood standards (Simens), is a minuscule budget. And yet it became one of the best box-office hits of all time in Argentina; its sales in Argentina even surpassed those of *E.T.*, released in the same year (1983). Why was this so? It is important to bear in mind that – on one level – the film definitely panders to the popular taste – it has a good mixture of love, suspense, drama, death. Bemberg decided to emphasise the melodramatic elements of the original events of 1847–1848 in her film version. Her aim in filming *Camila*, as she pointed out in an interview, was as follows: 'I want a melodrama. I don't think it's a bad word' (Bach, p. 23). For that reason, as she went on to say, *Camila* 'was shot in a highly romantic style because I felt that in that way I could really hit the audience, in the heart and in the pit of their stomach. Melodrama is a very tricky genre, because at any minute it can turn into something sentimental, which I detest. So it had all those little tricks, such as the handkerchief, the gold coin, the priest who's sick with love, and the thunder when God gets angry. They're all like winks at the audience' (Whitaker, p. 293). It is easy to point to a number of stock melodramatic elements in the film, ranging from those mentioned by the director herself to the 'coup de foudre' when Camila takes off her blindfold and sees Ladislao's face, the dramatic discovery of Ladislao by Father Gannon in a 'pulpería' in Goya, the suspense when Camila is 'saved' when it is discovered she is pregnant, the suspense during the execution, and, most extreme of all, the voice-over when Ladislao's voice speaks to Camila from

3. *Camila*: Camila's Scream

beyond the grave ('a tu lado, Camila'; 'I'm beside you, Camila'). *Camila*, indeed, has all the hallmarks of what Warren Buckland has identified as the 'fallen woman melodrama', namely the melodramatic film which focuses on a woman who commits a sexual transgression, is expelled from the domestic space, and is eventually punished with death (Buckland, pp. 82–6). True to type in other ways as well, *Camila* is also, like many melodramas, based on an 'omniscient form of narration' (Buckland, p. 81). In his 1981 article, 'The "Force-Field" of Melodrama', Stuart Cunningham has argued that melodrama is best seen as a reponse to modernity and its shift from 'the traditional Sacred and its representative institutions (Church and Monarch)' to a new democratic society that is obliged to 'propagate the new "sacred" in purely ethical and personal terms' (Cunningham, p. 348). This is essentially the struggle which occurs in the film between Ladislao's more traditional notion of the Sacred (evident when he turns back to God) and Camila's own more subversive view of the Sacred which, for her, is tied to the personal, the erotic – love. As Ruby Rich has suggested, Bemberg used 'seamless art cinema (lush, transparent, and perfect periodicity) in the service of a new idea' (Rich, p. 286). *Camila*, indeed, offers a vivid contrast to Carlos Carrera's recent re-vamping of Eça de Queiroz's nineteenth-century story about a wayward priest in *El crimen del Padre Amaro* (2002); whereas Carrera's film offers a secularised, de-sensationalised version of a priest's peccadillo, Bemberg pulls out all the stops to underline the melodramatic, 'sacrilegious' nature of the lovers' crime.

The Two Levels

Camila works on a number of levels. On its most obvious level – which coincides with its level as entertainment – the film is a tragic love story set in mid-nineteenth century Argentina. For the more perspicacious viewer, however, there are enough hints – and winks as Bemberg calls them – for the audience to realise that *Camila* also allegorises a particularly unpleasant slice of recent Argentine history, the Dirty War of the mid-1970s to the early 1980s, in which thousands of political subversives were captured by the authorities and 'disappeared'. Bemberg has pointed to the dual level of the film in interviews: 'It's a very Romantic story in which fear and menaces are also present, something which we've very much lived with in Argentina and it's there, just beneath the surface' (Torres, p. 78; my translation). It is in this sense that we can say that the politics of the Dirty War is encrypted within the narrative of love story set in nineteenth-century Argentina. Camila, as Ruffinelli has pointed out, is as much a modern woman as a nineteenth-century historical figure (Ruffinelli, p. 22). For contemporary audiences, indeed, the association between the two historical events was made crystal clear by the posters advertising the film which carried the caption 'Nunca más' (Never Again), the words used as the title of the official Truth Commission report on the atrocities of the Guerra Sucia (King, 'María Luisa Bemberg and Argentine Culture', pp. 23–4). The film was therefore clearly using the distant past in order to shape a vision of the recent past. As King suggests: '*Camila* and *The Official Version* also allowed the Argentine audience a form of collective catharsis, enabling them to experience, in public, emotions that had remained private during the years of the dictatorship. Over two million people wept at the story of Camila O'Gorman, which was their story' (King, *Magical Reels*, p. 96).

Bemberg chose certain details from the nineteenth century story and highlighted them since they worked well for her allegorising intention. Bemberg wished to present Rosas as a distant, unreachable figure; thus he is present in *Camila* via the letters he sends and, above all, in the portraits which adorn the Church and the Prison of Santos Lugares. It is significant that Rosas never appears in the film; he is all-perceiving eye, present in the portrait which 'watches' Camila when she confesses her sexual emotions in the confessional (she thinks it is Father Félix, but it is not), which 'watches' Ladislao when he gives his sermon, which 'watches' the jailer when he receives the letter which condemns Camila to death, despite her pregnancy.

Rosas is present also in Bemberg's shrewd portrayal of him in the 'divisas' (large ribbons) which the population are obliged to wear (Father Gannon obligingly places a ribbon on Ladislao's chest when it is discovered he is not wearing one), and, tellingly, in the emblems of Rosas worn on the chest by a number of the characters, notably the religious. Despite this overwhelming visual iconic presence, Rosas never once makes an appearance – not even off-stage – in the film. Bemberg chose this device in order to remind her audience of the sinister techniques of the Asociación Anticomunista Argentina which, unseen by its victims or their next-of-kin, 'disappeared' 30,000 people from 1976 until 1983.

In this way the melodramatic features of *Camila* have been modernised, and, in the process, given a harder political edge.

Feminism

Bemberg once declared that she became a film director because she wanted to give women the chance to speak rather than be spoken for: 'My films are an attempt to make women recognise themselves and learn more about themselves through the protagonists' predicament. This is my ethical commitment, helping them to be free' (Graham-Yooll). This is very important because, in Bemberg's view, Argentina is 'one of the most *machista* countries in the world' (Bach, p. 27). 'Since childhood', she has suggested, 'I had felt a sense of frustration, a double standards between my brothers and I.' Her entry into the film world was 'a rebellion I had had since being a girl, and it manifested itself especially after reading Simone de Beauvoir's *Second Sex*' (Bach, p. 22). So the film is itself a blueprint for Bemberg's own rebellion against her family, her society, and sexual oppression. *Camila*, indeed, like Douglas Sirk's early melodrama *All that Heaven Allows* (1953) develops a social critique of woman's place in society (Lehman and Luhr, p. 107), though it does so specifically by presenting a more positive view of womanhood than it does of manhood. It is true that Ladislao openly criticises the Rosas regime when Mariano, the bookseller, is murdered in his Church sermon, and he subverts the social order as much as she does when he runs off with Camila. Yet the film is very careful to point out that, of the two, Camila is the strongest. In her films, Bemberg had said that she wanted to 'propose images of women that are vertical, autonomous, independent, thoughtful, courageous, spunky', and this is certainly the case with Camila (Bach, p. 22). After all, it is she who is portrayed as initiating the love-affair in the film. Traditional versions of the story had an innocent woman seduced by a lecherous priest. 'I think it was a good idea to have the priest seduced by the woman', recalled Bemberg wryly. 'It helped me with the Church' (anonymous review in the *Daily Telegraph* [9 June 1995]).

Quite consistently throughout the film, Camila takes centre stage and thereby marginalises Ladislao (the acting performance by Susú Pecoraro, as Douglas suggests, is 'exemplary'; Douglas, p. 62). Bemberg's revision of the traditional melodramatic formula centres on the fact that Camila breaks the rules: 'Camila was a transgressor, she broke the received pattern of Argentina, not to mention feminine decorum. Not only does she enjoy a love-affair with her priest, but her action fought against the paternalistic order of family, church and state' (Bemberg interview; see Caleb Bach, p. 23). Camila is more independent-minded and rebellious. When push comes to shove, Ladislao turns to God. Camila, however, has nowhere to turn. When she discovers from the doctor that she is pregnant, we cut to a shot in which Camila is screaming through her prison bars to Ladislao that they have a child. The camera cuts to Ladislao's cell; we see him in long shot; he is hunched over, clearly oblivious to her words. Our sympathy is engineered for Camila during the prison sequences in that the microphone has been placed close to her mouth; we hear her nervous breathing, we hear the water going down her throat – in cinematic terms we hear her body from the inside.

Camila's love is far stronger than Ladislao's because it is uninhibited by the confines of religion. Ladislao's love comes with strings attached, and there are indications of this early on in the love-affair. When the Easter procession goes past the lovers' house, Ladislao is visibly disturbed, yet he drowns his remorse in the passionate seduction of Camila on the kitchen table. This is, indeed, the most erotic love scene in the film (the earlier love scene which occurs in the carriage is delicate in its Flaubertian resonances). Ladislao's sexual love reveals itself to be a **substitute** for divine love. His Catholicism is always hovering in the background. As if to underscore this point, Ladislao becomes very lifeless at the end of the film, being almost reduced to a set of monosyllables (see Torres, p. 78). Camila, however, desperately wants to live, rejects the intercession of the Church, wants her baby to live, and yet, even so, she is executed. For this reason she becomes the tragic heroine of the film. Ladislao's is the necessary murder; Camila's the tragedy (Hart, p. 81).

Camila can be read – as we have seen – on the one hand, as a love story and, on the other, as a tale about nation-building in nineteenth-century Argentina (see Sommer for the use of this motif in the nineteenth-century novel), the clear implication being that the unborn child that Camila is carrying when she is executed allegorises the fledgling nation of the 'unitarios' mercilessly crushed by Rosas's iron fist. Superficially, the execution of the lovers would tend to suggest that the film is a maudlin lament on behalf of a lost political opportunity but it can be argued that the very presence of the voice-over ('A tu lado Camila'), which, as suggested above, is an overt allusion to a Romantic notion of post-corporeal love, itself suggests a transcendence of those powers which have crushed Camila's and Ladislao's vulnerable bodies. The film, therefore, has a positive political message. The way in which the film actually came into being points to not only its political resonance but also the sense in which its gestation period accompanied the birth of a new political era. As Lila Stantic recalls:

> It's 2.30 in the morning and I'm with María Luisa (. . .) Marta goes off and comes back a few minutes later with the papers under her arm. In banner headlines all the papers proclaim: 'Argentina has invaded the Malvinas'. (. . .) We did not know that at this precise moment the right conditions were being created for María Luisa's third film, *Camila*. This is because almost all the critics agreed that in María Luisa's films to date (*Momentos* and *Señora de nadie*), there was no belief in the possibility of love. This *machista* interpretation of María Luisa's female characters led me, a few days later, to throw down the big challenge: 'now you have to do a love story. You have to do a love story. You have to tell the story of Camila O'Gorman.' (Stantic, p. 33)

The filming of Camila began – significantly enough – on 11 December 1983, that is the day after Alfonsín became the first civil president in almost a decade in Argentina (Ruffinelli, p. 11). Put in another way, it was the day on which Argentina emerged from the nightmares of the Guerra Sucia. This day also happened by pure coincidence to be the anniversary of the day when Camila and Uladislao eloped (it was on the night of 11/12 December 1847). These omens were not fortuitous.

In this way, it is possible to argue that the film presents a positive ideological statement given the structural significance of its ending. The transcendence of death by virtue of love suggested by the voice-over must logically be seen as an allegory of the transcendence of the dirt of war through the hope inspired by the new democracy ushered in by the demise of the Guerra Sucia. Camila's child – the body of Argentina – dies in her womb but the voice-over of love ('a tu lado Camila') suggests hope for the future, 'another rhythm of breathing and loving' (Bemberg, p. 222).

Works Cited

Anonymous, 'María Luisa Bemberg', *Daily Telegraph* (9 June 1995), p. 27.

Bach, Caleb, 'María Luisa Bemberg tells the untold', *Américas*, 45.2 (March/April 1994), 21–7.

Bemberg, María Luisa, 'Being an Artist in Latin America', in *An Argentine Passion: María Luisa Bemberg and her Films*, edited by John King, Sheila Whitaker and Rosa Bosch (London: Verso, 2000), pp. 216–23.

Buckland, Warren, *Film Studies* (London: Hodder and Stoughton, 1998).

Cunningham, Stuart, 'The "Force-Field" of Melodrama', *Quarterly Review of Film Studies*, 6.4 (1981), 347–64.

Douglas, David, 'Camila', in *South American Cinema: A Critical Filmography 1915–1994*, eds Timothy Barnard and Peter Rist (Austin: University of Texas Press, 1996), pp. 61–3.

Foster, David William, *Contemporary Argentine Cinema* (Columbia: University of Missouri Press, 1992).

Graham-Yooll, Andrew, 'María Luisa Bemburg', *The Independent* (24 May 1995), p. 16.

Hart, Stephen, 'Bemberg's Winks and Camila's Sighs: Melodramatic Encryption in *Camila*', *Revista Canadiense de Estudios Hispánicos*, XXVII.1 (2002), 75–85.

King, John, *Magical Reels: A History of Cinema in Latin America* (London: Verso, 1990).

——, 'María Luisa Bemberg and Argentine Culture', in *An Argentine Passion: María Luisa Bemberg and her Films*, edited by John King, Sheila Whitaker and Rosa Bosch (London: Verso, 2000), pp. 1–32.

Lehman, Peter, and William Luhr, *Thinking About Movies: Watching, Questioning, Enjoying* (Oxford: Blackwell, 2003).

Rich, Ruby, 'An/Other View of New Latin American Cinema', in *New Latin American Cinema: Volume One: Theory, Practices and Transcontinental Articulations*, ed. Michael T. Martin (Detroit: Wayne State University, 1997), pp. 273–97.

Ruffinelli, Jorge, 'De una *Camila* a otra: historia, literatura y cine', in *Estudios Iberoamérica y el cine*, ed. Francisco Lasarte & Guido Podestá (Amsterdam: Rodopi, 1996), pp. 11–25.

Simens, Dov S-S, 'Two-Day FilmSchool', Raindance, London, 29–30 November 2003.

Sommer, Doris, *Foundational Fictions: The National Romances of Latin America* (Berkeley: University of California Press, 1991).

Stantic, Lita, 'Working with María Luisa Bemberg', in *An Argentine Passion: María Luisa Bemberg and her Films*, edited by John King, Sheila Whitaker and Rosa Bosch (London: Verso, 2000), pp. 33–40.

Stevens, Donald F., 'Passion and Patriarchy in Nineteenth-Century Argentina: María Luisa Bemberg's *Camila*', in *Based on a True Story: Latin American History at the Movies*, ed. Donald F. Stevens (Wilmington, Delaware: Scholarly Resources, 1997), pp. 85–102.

Torres, Miguel, 'Camila', *Cine Cubano*, 113 (1985), 77–9.

Whitaker, Sheila, 'Pride and Prejudice: María Luisa Bemberg', *Monthly Film Bulletin* (October 1987), pp. 292–4.

14

LA HISTORIA OFICIAL (THE OFFICIAL VERSION, 1984), DIRECTED BY LUIS PUENZO

Cast

Alicia, played by Norma Aleandro
Gaby, played by Analfa Castro
Roberto, played by Héctor Alterio
Benítez, played by Patricio Contreras
Ana, played by Chunchuna Villafane
Macchi, played by Jorge Petraglia
Father Ismael, played by Leal Rey
Enrique, played by Hugo Arana
Sara, played by Chela Ruiz

Crew

Director: Luis Puenzo
Screenplay: Aída Bortnik, Luis Puenzo
Administration: Carlos Fernández
Technical Supervisor: Orlando Rodríguez
Production Chief: Carlos Latreyte
Assistant Director: Raúl Outeda
Scenography: Abel Facello
Wardrobe: Ticky García Estevez
Make-up: Blanca Olavego
Camera: Héctor Morini
Sound: Abelardo Kuschuir
Mixing: Juan Carlos Macías
Photography: Félix Monti
Production Manager: Marcelo Piñeyro
Associate Producer: Progress Communications
Music: Atilio Stampone
Song: 'En el país de Nomeacuerdo' by María Elena Walsh

Awards

Oscar for Best Foreign Language Film, Academy of Motion Picture Arts and Sciences, Hollywood, 1985

Best Film, Best Supporting Actress (Chunchuna Villafane), Chicago, 1985
Second Prize, Best Screenplay, Havana, 1985
Best Film, Quito, 1985
Best Actress (Norma Aleandro), Best Film, Cannes, 1985
Best Actress (Norma Aleandro), Special Mention, Cartagena, Colombia, 1985

Plot

The film opens with a school assembly in which teachers and pupils are singing the national anthem, followed by a history lesson given by Alicia. Cuts to Alicia's home; her daughter, Gaby, is in the bath. Her husband, Roberto, comes home with a present for Gaby, a big doll. Roberto and Alicia go out to dinner with some business associates, during which we hear that Alicia is sterile. Classroom scene of English lesson by Benítez. Alicia's friend, Ana, explains to Alicia that she left Argentina because she had been tortured; Alicia is shocked. In the history lesson, Alicia's students are beginning to rebel, questioning her version of history. Benítez invites Alicia for coffee and presents her with a file on the 'desaparecidos'. Alicia goes to see Roberto at work; he is leaving on a business trip; tension is mounting. Alicia looks at Gaby's clothes. She begins her search for Gaby's true identity, visiting hospitals as well as the local priest, but without much luck. In a scene at Roberto's father's house, Roberto's father accuses his son of being corrupt. Roberto has started drinking heavily, while Alicia is more responsive to her students' questions about real history. Alicia meets Sara and finds out that Gaby is Sara's granddaughter. Alicia takes Sara to confront Roberto but he throws her out angrily. When he discovers that Gaby is not in the apartment, he loses his temper, bangs Alicia's head against the wall, and breaks her hand in the door hinge. Roberto receives a phone call from Gaby, while Alicia is soothing her hand under the cold tap. Alicia hugs Roberto, and then leaves.

Analytical Overview

In 1985 *La historia oficial* won an Oscar for the Best Foreign film at the Hollywood Awards Ceremony ('Awards Database'), and as such became the first Latin American film to do so (Barnard, p. 65); as a result the Argentine film industry grew famous overnight. As John King points out, the film 'deals with a society's guilt at its complicity with the military's "dirty war" against "subversion", which led to so many deaths and disappearances' (King, p. 1). *La historia oficial* specifically portrays and analyses the social conflict which produced the Guerra Sucia in Argentina from 1975 until 1982; it was a dirty war in which as many as 30,000 people were kidnapped and subsequently disappeared (the so-called 'desaparecidos') by the military leaders. As such the film 'is a wrenching and painful drama that crystallizes the horror and the obscenity of political activities that annihilate family solidarity in the name of ideology' (Frederic and Mary Ann Brussat). It was a crime punishable by 10 years in prison openly to criticise the military regime; as many as 100 journalists 'disappeared' during this period.

One of the events which this film picks on – rather than say, the fight against terrorism, the portrayal of torture and how it destroys the mind, in the manner of a Hollywood thriller – which characterised the war, and was particularly painful for Argentines during the period of consolidation which occurred once democracy had been re-established after the Falklands War, was the abduction of the children of subversives, and the providing of these children for adoption often by high-ranking militaries who were unable to father children. Once the child was taken, the parents were often murdered in their prison cells. So the film takes as its theme one particularly unsavoury event of what was going on clandestinely during the Dirty War. And it also makes the choice of focusing on the drama of one particular child, Gaby, as a symbol of what was happening at the time. As Ismail Xavier points out, *La historia oficial* 'adopts a melodramatic tone in its discussion of the kidnapping of children born inside the dictatorship's camps of torture and execution. The female protagonist condenses, in her own experience and in her "will to know" the truth, the experience of Argentine society after the 1983 redemocratization occurred. The film places family affairs at the center of a humanist approach to the political tradition of melodramas that work out social questions, taking a nuclear family as the exemplary microcosm that condenses the entire nation' (Xavier, p. 357). It is the 'clarity of vision of an exiled friend [Ana] that helps the protagonist become aware of the true nature of recent Argentine history' (King, p. 22). Its allegorical treatment has led some critics, such as Vicente Zito Lema and Raúl Filipelli, to see it as only 'brushing over' the political dimension of the 'guerra sucia', rather than dealing with it in a profound way (Manrupe and Portela, p. 280). Other critics, however, such as José Augustín Mahieu have referred to the film's 'eficacia narrativa y excelente interpretación' (Mahieu, p. 48).

Suspense and the Official Story

The action of the film centres on the gradual discovery by Alicia, a history teacher in a secondary school, that the child that her husband, Roberto, a high-ranking businessman with links to counter-espionage, the USA, and the military, gave to her, some four or five years before the film narrative proper begins, is in fact a child abducted from her parents, two subversives killed while emprisoned by the military regime, soon after the child is born. This knowledge is produced as a result of Alicia's research, and, especially, by her fortuitous meeting with Sara, who is the child's grandmother. The historical backdrop to the film is provided by the gradual demise of the business community, whose corruption Roberto symbolises and epitomises. From a successful businessman at the beginning, we see him sink progressively lower and lower as the truth gradually comes out, until he is forced to flee his offices taking files with him (as in the scene when he meets Alicia's friend, Ana, in the car basement). The basic plot of the film is (i) the gradual discovery of Gaby's true identity, i.e. growth of truth, and (ii) Roberto's gradual demise, i.e. diminution of his power. By the end he is revealed to be one of the key men in the corrupt military regime. As Mark Szuchman suggests,

'Much in the same way as the lead actress's hair unravels over the course of the film (in contrast to the tightly controlled bun she wears at the start), the official history of events in the Argentina of military governments unravels at the end, loosened from the weight of fear and political naïveté' (Szuchman, p. 191).

The film opens with a portrayal of Alicia as a naïve, middle-aged, bourgeois woman who believes everything she is told. Thus she says to her friend, Ana, when told about the latter's torture ordeal: 'why didn't you report it to the relevant authorities?' As the scene makes clear, Alicia is the history teacher with a stiff, upper lip who accepts, disseminates and expects others to accept the 'official story' about what is happening in Argentina. But her conversation with Ana is the first moment of what David William Foster calls her 'moral anagnorisis' (Foster, p. 38). In another scene of exceptional naïveté Alicia advises her school colleague, Benítez, to report what he has found out to the authorities. But Benítez gets annoyed with her. 'What do you really care about the truth?' he shouts at her as he goes off to join the Mothers of the Disappeared who congregate in the Plaza de Mayo on Thursdays to protest about the unknown fate of their children. It is no coincidence that Benítez is the literature teacher, since literature, unlike history, is portrayed as the true version; history, as one of the students points out, was 'written by assassins', and therefore is a glorified lie. The contrast between the two teachers is presented in the memorable shot in which Benítez is lying on the table – in a scene redolent of Peter Weir's *Dead Poets' Society* (1989) – having just read from the conclusion of *Juan Moreira* (1879), a novel about a Gaucho with a good heart who was killed by the police (Hart, pp. 680–6), and thus highly relevant to the circumstances of the 'guerra sucia'. Gradually, however, Alicia comes to adopt Benítez's critical stance, and she begins her own investigation of what really happened and, in particular, where Gaby came from. A strong acting performance by Norma Aleandro engineers the audience's sympathy and, in the process, leads, as Timothy Barnard has pointed out, to a loss of identification with the real victims of the piece (Gaby's parents): 'the film manages to convince us, through its melodramatic treatment of Aleandro's dilemma and our identification with her, that her plight is more traumatic than those of the characters who have a marginal existence in the film, like her daughter's natural grandmother. In this way the film accomplishes the bizarre feat of shifting the burden of suffering under the dictatorship from those who lost family members through torture and execution to those who adopted their children' (Barnard, p. 64).

Roberto, of course, is the villain of the piece, though an important feature of the film centres on the fact that we do not really know what he does for a living. The first real clue that his job is not completely above-board occurs during the lunch at his father's house when his father – a Spanish expatriate who fought on the losing side during the Spanish Civil War – accuses him of being obsessed with money. How is it, his father asks, that, while everyone else is going under, only the 'hijos de puta' and his son, are doing well for themselves? – at which point Roberto lets rip about his family being a bunch of losers. But the scene when the veil finally drops off is when Alicia decides to give him a bit of his own medicine by hiding Gaby from him, and he loses his temper completely: he grabs

4. *La historia oficial*: Roberto the Torturer

her, hits her, bashes her head against the door, and then breaks her fingers in the door. Peter Lehman and William Luhr have pointed out that 'many films have vivid scenes that, once seen, the viewer finds difficult to forget: viewers of *Titanic* might be fuzzy in their remembrance of the various character interactions but are unlikely to forget the spectacular overhead shot in which the stern of the ship rises almost vertically out of the water, with people and objects suddenly plummeting down as if falling from a tall building' (Lehman and Luhr, p. 53). And this scene in which – against all expectations – Roberto rams his wife's fingers into the doorframe and breaks her hand, is just one of those memorable scenes in Latin American film. At this point, we realise that Roberto has been involved not only in dodgy business deals, and with the military, but also is very likely to be a torturer. His earlier comment, '¿Soy yo su torturador?', in reference to what happened to the parents of Gaby, is revealed to have been a crucial slip of the tongue. There are enough clues to suggest he may be not only a crook and an informer, but even a torturer as well. But, in the final analysis, Roberto's true identity is not made entirely explicit – we can guess but we'll never know – and this is one of the strengths of *La historia oficial*.

Blocking, the Long Shot, and Montage-in-Depth

There is no doubt that *La historia oficial* is in many respects a conventional film. Its traditional format has led Manrupe and Portela, for example, to see it as 'más valiso por su contenido histórico que por lo cinematográfico' (Manrupe and Portela, p. 280), and Dennis West has suggested that the film does not really depart from the viewer expectations of a commercial film (Manrupe and Portela, p. 280). As Tim Barnard suggests: '*La historia oficial* spearheaded, by virtue of its bland international style and thematic attention to the Argentine middle class, the Argentine film industry's reorientation towards the national middle class and the European and the U.S. market. (It is interesting to note that Puenzo came to film from a background in publicity, common enough in Argentine cinema but evident nonetheless in the film's style.)' (Barnard, p. 61). But there are three cinematic devices used in *La historia oficial* which, though not innovative in a *cinéaste* sense, enhance the film's intended meaning. Blocking, the long short, and montage-in-depth acquire a specific atmospheric resonance in Puenzo's film.

The establishing shot of the film, for example, gives a hint of what is to come. We witness the playing of the national anthem in the school playground at which Alicia and Benítez teach but for those viewers who expect a Hollywood-style master shot the results are rather surprising. The film begins with the title ('La historia oficial') being ripped up, at which point the camera focuses on the loudspeaker, and then – in an obsessively deliberate way – on the individuals in the school playground, but our view is consistently blocked by the concrete structure of the roof behind which the camera is placed. This blocking shot, i.e. there is something interrupting the vision of the spectator from the main action, is an early indication that we will be seeing a behind-the-scenes version of Argentine reality. This establishing shot, indeed, draws attention to one of the key techniques used in the film, namely, snares which offer a tantalising view of an event but without telling us the whole truth (for more on snares used in films, see Lehman and Luhr, pp. 37–8). The feeling of unease the viewer experiences is compounded by the sound of the aeroplane going overhead and the train passing by in the distance as well as by the bum notes played by the orchestra as it massacres the national anthem. It soon becomes clear that blocking is used quite deliberately to support the basic message of the film: the State obstructs the public from seeing its actions.

It is not coincidental, indeed, that the first time we see Roberto (soon after the establishing scene described above) he is not viewed openly in the centre of the camera space; rather he is glimpsed obliquely. Our view of him is blocked by the wall behind which he scurries after entering the house. Of course, in pragmatic terms, his actions are quite understandable since he is attempting to hide the present he has bought for Gaby – it's a doll – so it can be a surprise, but, as the film progresses, the prevalence of blocking takes on a more sinister resonance. He is the character, after all, whom we know the least about. As we realise at the conclusion of the film when – quite out of the blue – he attacks his wife, his past may have been very murky indeed. That Puenzo has deliberately chosen to block the viewer's perception at certain crucial junctures is suggested by what might at first seem innocuous decisions about mise-en-scène. Thus, when we see Roberto and Alicia leave the restaurant and walk along the pavement to their car (we hear their conversation, and can see that Alicia is visibly agitated about being insulted as a result of her infertility), it is striking that the camera tracks them as they walk along the pavement from behind a hedge on the other side of the road; the long shot combined with the fact that we can hear their voices perfectly – as if they were close by – inevitably evokes the atmosphere of secrecy and covert spying, techniques which were part and parcel of the culture animating the 'guerra sucia'.

Pointing in a similar direction to the use of blocking and the long shot is the use of the device of montage-in-depth in *La historia oficial*. The technique of montage-in-depth, though a standard cinematic device within the film director's repertoire since Orson Welles's *Citizen Kane* (1941), is used in Puenzo's film to underline the theme of the mystery of the State's machinations. The best example occurs when Alicia turns up unexpectedly at Roberto's office and witnesses a showdown between her husband and a business associate called Macchi. Macchi loses his temper and shouts at Roberto that he is not prepared to take the blame for the latter's misdemeanours. Roberto tries unsuccessfully to placate him, and then we see Macchi being bundled into a nearby office. The following sequence of shots are seen via Alicia's POV; the door is opened and then closed, and a final glimpse of what is going on in the room terminates when the lift door closes. One of the men seems to have his hand around Macci's neck: is he loosening his collar or strangling him? Surely the latter, we say to ourselves, cannot be happening? Because the scene in the office is portrayed as occurring in the most distant segment of cinematic space from the camera eye – namely further than the lift door, than the intervening space in the office, and than the office door – it is difficult to pick out what precisely is happening. The machinations of Roberto's business company are blocked from our sight. Montage-in-depth has in this scene effectively produced a sense of greater depth of the cinematic space we perceive as viewers, yet it has done so in order to underline the motif of clandestinity. We find a similar exploration of cinematic space in the scene towards the end of the film set in Roberto's home when he is entertaining his American guests and Argentine business associates. The older American is complimenting Gaby; the younger American is using the phone trying to locate his wife who seems to have disappeared; Roberto is boasting about his prowess; and his two associates are playing pool. This sequence is characterised by deep focus cinematography in which 'a great deal of space is not only visible within a shot but also clearly in focus' (Lehman and Luhr, pp. 65–6); in particular three cinematic spaces are combined – foreground, middleground and background – in such a way that the viewer used to the Hollywood formula of explicit foregrounding may be confused. Should we be listening to the Argentine men arguing about their pool game or listening to the younger American who is becoming increasingly agitated as his attempts to locate his wife prove unsuccessful? Where is Alicia? To further compound the viewer's disorientation, at one point in the sequence the 180-degree rule is broken, and we see the American behind rather than in front of Roberto (for more on the code of the 180-degree rule, see Lehman and Luhr, pp. 59–60). Though not as dramatic as the scene is which Macchi is bundled into a nearby office, this sequence demonstrates that Puenzo deliberately used montage-in-depth in order to underline the theme of the deliberate blocking of the truth. Like the next-of-kin of the 'desaparecidos' we don't know what to look for or where to look.

Symbolism

On two separate occasions, the spilling of liquids is used as a symbolic indication of the destruction of the world that Alicia has carefully constructed for Gaby. The best example occurs when Gaby startles Alicia while she is looking through some files (obviously to do with Gaby), and the orange juice is spilled, and it goes on some photographs. The shot is like a photographical still showing – in visual terms – the destruction of Gaby's world, and by extension the political space of Argentinean identity; the melodrama of the moment is complemented by the drawn-out rendition of Stravinsky.

One of the best examples of symbolism occurs during the birthday party held for Gaby. When the children, and particularly, Gaby, becomes distraught at the idea of the rabbit having the pin stuck in it (like the balloon), this is a displaced image of the torture of her parents, which exists, as it were, in her subconscious; this idea is reinforced when the boys break into her bedroom, playing war games. Again this is a pointer to the ways in which the world of the children is a displaced version in symbolic form of the world of adults in which war and torture are part of everyday life. The film works, it might be added, in terms of a cumulative use of symbols; thus it is not fortuitous that the background music which occurs when Sara tells Alicia who Gaby really is, is that of machine gun fire. In this way, Puenzo is able to make us feel the physical effects of war, in displaced form, in terms of the use of noise and games. This, indeed, is more effective than the actual depiction of the armed struggle during the Dirty War. In this way, the Dirty War is ever present, even though it is not directly presented. It is there by allusion, by suggestion rather than by direct representation.

Perhaps the best example of symbolism in the film is the doll. Gaby is often associated with the doll which she is given as a present by her father in the establishing scene of the film. Although the doll is a 'free' rather than a 'bound' motif (Gaby the child is a bound motif, since without her the film would lack an important plot element; see Lehman and Luhr, pp. 33–4), its inclusion in the story is a master touch. Gaby is – symbolically speaking – the dead doll of her disappeared parents, and when Roberto brings a doll home, he is, in effect, repeating the event of Gaby's inclusion into the family home a few years before. Even in the touching scenes in which Gaby is pictured cuddling her doll (and remember the last scene in which she sings her song about the song of 'En el país de Nomeacuerdo'), there is a sinister undertone, since this is a repetition of what Alicia is doing, since she is – in a real sense – cuddling a doll, someone else's baby.

Works Cited

'Awards Database [Academy of Motion Picture Arts and Sciences, Hollywood]', www.awardsdatabase.oscars.org (consulted on 18 December 2003).

Barnard, Timothy, 'La historia oficial', in *South American Cinema: A Critical Filmography 1915–1994*, eds Timothy Barnard and Peter Rist (Austin: University of Texas Press, 1996), pp. 63–5.

——, 'Popular Cinema and Populist Politics', in *Argentine Cinema*, ed. Timothy Barnard, pp. 5–63.

Brussat, Frederic and Mary Ann, 'Movie Review: The Official Story' www.rottentomatoes.com/m/TheOfficialStory-1015424/reviews.php.

Foster, David William, *Contemporary Argentine Cinema* (Columbus: University of Missouri Press, 1982).

Hart, Stephen, 'Public Execution and the Body Politic in the Work of the Argentine *Folletinista* Eduardo Gutiérrez', *Bulletin of Hispanic Studies*, LXXXVI (1999), 673–90.

King, John, *Argentine Cinema* (Plymouth: Plymouth Arts Centre, 1986).

Lehman, Peter, and William Luhr, *Thinking About Movies: Watching, Questioning, Enjoying* (Oxford: Blackwell, 2003).

Mahieu, José Agustín, *Panorama del cine iberoamericano* (Madrid: Ediciones de Cultura Hispánica, 1990).

Manrupe, Raúl, and María Alejandra Portela's *Un diccionario de films argentinos (1930–1995)* (Buenos Aires: Corregidor, 2001).

Szuchman, Mark D., 'Depicting the Past in Argentine Films: Family Drama and Historical debate in *Miss Mary* and *The Official Story*', in *Based on a True Story: Latin American History at the Movies*, ed. Donald F. Stevens (Wilmington, Delaware: Scholarly Resources, 1997), pp. 173–200.

Xavier, Ismail, 'Historical Allegory', in *A Companion to Film Theory*, eds Toby Miller and Robert Stam (Oxford: Blackwell, 2004), pp. 333–62.

15

CARTAS DEL PARQUE (LETTERS IN THE PARK, 1989), CO-DIRECTED BY TOMÁS GUTIÉRREZ ALEA AND GABRIEL GARCÍA MÁRQUEZ

Cast

Pedro, played by Víctor Laplace
María, played by Ivonne López
Juan, played by Miguel Paneque
Prostitute, played by Mirta Ibarra
René Simon, played by Adolfo Llaurado

With

Elio Mesa, Paula Alí, Amelia Pita, Dagobero Gainza, José Pelayo, Raúl Eguren, Jorge Alí, Daniel Jordan, Justo Fonseca, Pedro Fernández, Peggy Gómez, Miriam Dávila, Ileana Leyva, Elvira Valdés, José Hernández, Esteban Saldiguera

Crew

Director: Tomás Gutiérrez Alea
Director's assistant: Ana Rodríguez
Plot: Gabriel García Márquez
Screenplay: Eliseo Alberto, Tomás Gutiérrez Alea and Gabriel García Márquez
Additional texts: Eliseo Diego
Photography: Mario García Joya
Camera: Mario García Joya
Music: Gonzalo Rubalcaba
Sound: Germinal Hernández
Editing: Miriam Talavera
Scenography: Fernando Pérez O'Reilly
Wardrobe: Miriam Dueñas
Make-up: Graciela Crossas, Lisette Davila and Aymara Cisneros
Producer: Santiago Llapur
Executive Producer: Max Marambio
Produced by: Televisión Española, along with the New Latin-American Film Foundation

Plot

Cartas del parque is set in Matanzas, a provincial town in Cuba, in 1913. The film is split into four sections, each based on the name of a season. The film opens with a scene in which René Simon is preparing to take off in his hot-air balloon. Juan, an apothecary's assistant, is a member of the crowd; he is making eyes at a pretty young girl called María. Juan hitches a ride by clinging onto the rope hanging down from the hot-air balloon. Juan decides to woo María in earnest, but since he is not very eloquent he enlists the services of a local poet, Pedro, to write love letters for him. In a curious twist of fate, María also decides to hire Pedro's services in order to respond to the same letters. As a result of the growth of their mutual love, Juan invites María to accompany him on a romantic boat-ride around a nearby lake. We find out more about Pedro the poet's amorous activities with a ravishing prostitute in the local brothel; this earthy love contrasts with the love he describes in his letters which is ethereal and Platonic. María's mother, meanwhile, is not impressed by her daughter's interest in Juan, and tries to persuade her to take an interest in a young career-minded man called Marcelo. María and Juan go to the cinema, and Juan seems more interested in the documentary about flying than in María. María's mother intercepts one of Juan's letters, reads it out loud, and then ceremoniously tears it to bits in front of her daughter. Juan is refused entrance to María's house, and decides to go to Havana to study with René Simon. He leaves his farewell note with Pedro. Pedro, though, has fallen in love with María, and he carries on writing to her using Juan's name, sending her postcards from various exotic locations around the world. He is rumbled, however, when the local newspaper carries a story of Juan flying over Matanzas. Pedro confesses his deception in a letter to María. María, however, discovers that he is in fact in love with Pedro, and goes to see him. The film concludes just before they take their first kiss.

From Life to Novel to Film

In his memoirs, *Vivir para contarla* (2002) García Márquez provides an account of his parents' courtship. His mother, Luisa Santiaga, was a young woman living in Barrancas when a young, handsome man, Gabriel Eligio, arrived from Cartagena de las Indias. They first met at a funeral wake for a child, and Gabriel began to woo her from that point onwards. He gave her a rose with the words ('Le entrego mi vida en esta rosa'; *Vivir*, p. 60), wrote her a letter confessing his love for her, and he invited her to dance at a party, saying: 'Ya no tiene que decirme que sí, porque su corazón me lo está diciendo' (*Vivir*, p. 63). Because Gabriel Eligio was a member of the Conservative Party, and given his lowly social position – he was a telegraph operator – he was rejected by Luisa's parents, and – to make their point – they took Luisa away on a long journey over the Andes. Despite the distance and the length of time (Gabriel and Luisa were apart for a year), they kept in contact, and their love stayed alive. The lovers communicated via cards left in presents, via telegraph messages in code, and even by sign language (an idea that finds its way into the film version, see below). Finally Luisa's parents relented and gave their consent to the wedding, though they did not attend the ceremony (*Vivir*, p. 75). García Márquez has admitted that, after hearing the story so many times from his parents, he began to forget where 'life' left off and where 'poetry' began (*Vivir*, p. 59). Though his father was at one time considering using the love-affair as a basis for a novel, it was García Márquez who eventually used the drama for his fifth novel, *El amor en los tiempos del cólera* (1985).

A number of things are striking about how García Márquez transposed his parents' experience within the novel. Whereas some scenes were lifted straight from life to novel (compare *Vivir*, p. 69, and *El amor*, p. 99), crucial elements were transformed (see Simons). Firstly, he moved the action from the more provincial setting of Aracataca and Barrancas to the rather more grand backdrop of Cartagena, although the city is never specifically named in the novel (Hart). Secondly – and much more importantly – the separation period between the lovers has been extended by fifty years. *El amor en los tiempos del cólera* describes the love-affair between a dreamy poet and professional love letter writer, Florentino Ariza (based on Gabriel Eligio), and a beautiful young lady of the upper classes, Fermina Daza (based on Luisa Santiaga). Their love-affair blossoms during their adolescent years, fades during the fifty or so years when Fermina Daza is married to Juvenal Urbino, a well-connected local doctor, and then resumes after the latter's tragicomic death (he dies falling off a ladder when trying to retrieve an escaped parrot; see Bell). The novel is not narrated chronologically; instead the episodes are contained within the two defining moments in Florentino's existence: when he is rejected by the love of his life, Fermina, and the day, fifty-three years, seven months, and eleven days and nights later, when they sail off into the sunset together (*El amor*, p. 493). In the meantime the reader is regaled with tales of Florentino's plentiful sexual adventures while waiting for this true love to happen. It is important to note that the novel introduces two male lovers rather than one – Juvenal Urbino, the safe bet, and Florentino Ariza, the visionary romantic; this duality would find its way into the film version, as we shall see.

The film, *Cartas del parque*, as one might expect, changes the focus of the original love-affair once more. The film reduces the picaresque complexity of the original plot, editing out most of the characters. As such *Cartas del parque* deserves to be seen in its own terms as a new cinematic creation. This is – despite the quibbles of fidelity criticism – a positive idea since, as the experienced Bolivian *cinéaste*, Jorge Sanjinés, has pointed out, transferring a novel to the big screen often does not work:

> Literature has its own universe and film another. Perhaps the mistake of the films that have been made from his [i.e. García Márquez's] work is that they have been an attempt to transcribe his novels to a cinematographic level and this hasn't worked well. Film has its own universe that should generate its own stories, its own plots. García Márquez is also a screenwriter, he has written

> scripts for films from his novels. I think the best that has been made in film
> from his work has been exactly those films that are based on his screenplays.
>
> (Sánchez H., pp. 106–7)

This is precisely what happened in the case of *Cartas del parque*. Gutiérrez Alea
and García Márquez worked together – with some help from Eliseo Alberto – to
produce a new script, one which has a distinctly Cuban flavour. Certain motifs
are downplayed (the theme of cholera is reduced to a mere gesture in the film;
Juan is an apothecary's assistant), while others are highlighted (Florentino's role
as a 'professional' love letter writer becomes the central motif of the film). Some
scenes are added (part of the plot is enacted in the brothel, which functions as
shorthand for physical love), while certain motifs are addressed in a different
way; thus travel introduces the same basic idea in both novel and film (love feeds
on imagination, fantasy and escapism), but the film focuses on this idea mainly
via the motif of the hot-air balloon. The duality of love expressed in the novel
via the contrast between bourgeois respectability (Juvenal Urbino) and bohemian
romanticism (Florentino Ariza) is reconfigured in the film as a dialectic between
youthful but unreflective passion (Juan) and a mature and deeply 'literary' love.
The message of both *El amor en los tiempos del cólera* and *Cartas del parque*,
though, is that true love can stand the test of time; both works conclude with a
scene of reunion produced by true love.

Love, Travel and Escapism

The most important theme explored in *Cartas del parque* is, of course, love. As
Alea himself pointed out: 'tengo el tiempo vivido, lo cual quizás nos ayuda a dis-
frutar plenamente y a comprender mejor, desde una prudente distancia, ese universo de flores, postales iluminadas, corazones bordados y ángeles caprichosos
que no siempre aciertan cuando disparan sus flechas; un universo fascinante en el
que la poesía se muestra como común denominador entre las maravillosas inven-
ciones que le han ido dando su fisonomía al siglo y el gran descubrimiento de
todos los tiempos: el amor' (Évora, pp. 50–1). A related motif is that of escapism;
thus the film explores the different ways in which we seek refuge from the
mundaneness of everyday life by recourse to travel (boat-ride, train journeys, and,
most importantly, the hot-air balloon which Juan is obsessed with), literature
(which transports us into another world), and love (which transports us into an
ideal world). During scenes in which the lovers are talking about love we often
hear the sound of a train whistle or a boat's fog horn, as if underline the connection between travel and love. The danger implicit in the connection between travel
and literature is epitomised by Pedro's description of himself as Icarus ('Ícaro
soy . . .'), the well-known figure from Greek mythology who, through pride and
arrogance, flew too near the sun and crashed to the earth. The film, though,
subverts the notion of tragedy portended by the reference to the Icarus myth. For
while Juan becomes a literal Icarus – in that he goes to Havana and learns to fly
as René Simon's apprentice, Pedro is the metaphorical Icarus in that he has flown

too close to the fire of love, and – to pursue the metaphor – has got his fingers burnt in the process. He has ignored his own advice – which he shares with his prostitute-lover – of not falling in love with one's clients. Though we, at first, will interpret his commissioned love letters as essentially fraudulent, we soon realise that they are a truthful depiction of his emotions. Thus when Juan – just before he is about to leave for Havana – accuses Pedro of writing letters which are full of lies, Pedro angrily retorts that not one word he has written is untrue.

This fact explains why Pedro takes the foolhardy decision of adopting Juan's persona, continuing to write María postcards from all over the world. This leads to some deliciously comic-ironic scenes in which we see María ecstatically discussing letters apparently from Juan with Pedro. (Humour of this kind is quite common in the film; in, for example, a witty reference to one of García Márquez's earlier works, *El coronel no tiene quien le escriba*, Pedro says that the role of a writer is that of sending messages to others, but without ever getting a reply, because 'no tengo quien me escriba'.) The conclusion of the film, despite its rather burlesque treatment of love, makes a serious point, namely, that María has fallen in love with the author of the love letters, rather than Juan, and she therefore accepts Pedro's offer of love. Redolent in some crucial ways of Benjamin Constant's classic novel, *Adolphe* – which wittily demonstrates how human beings fall in love with the idea of being in love; Ellénore forbids Adolphe from even mentioning the word love because she fears the inevitable consequences (*Adolphe*, p. 79) – *Cartas del parque* shows how words sometimes create rather than simply describe love.

The Visual Language of Film

There are also some more subtle differences between the novel and the film. Unlike Carlos Arau's film version of *Como agua para chocolate* (see chapter 21) which sticks very closely to the original, *Cartas del parque* makes a significant departure from the original novel. Seymour Chatman, in his essay, 'What Novels Can Do that Films Can't (and Vice-versa)', makes some points about the translation of novel to film, which are worth mentioning here. He argues, for example, that there are always two temporal dimensions in any narrative:

> A salient property of narrative is double time structuring. That is, all narratives, in whatever medium, combine the time sequence of plot events, the time of the histoire ('story-time') with the time of the presentation of these events in the text, which we call 'discourse-time'. What is fundamental to narrative, regardless of medium, is that these two time orders are independent. In realistic narratives, the time of the story is fixed, following the ordinary course of a life; a person is born, grows from childhood to maturity and old age, and then dies. But the discourse-time order may be completely different: it may start with the person's deathbed, then 'flashback' to childhood; or it may start with childhood, 'flashforward' to childhood, then end with adult life. This independence of discourse-time is precisely and only possible because of the subsumed story-time. (Chatman, pp. 435–6)

Thus the time of the story in *El amor en los tiempos del cólera* begins with Florentino's early life, his love-affair with Fermina, her travels, and subsequent rejection of Florentino, her marriage to Juvenal Urbino, the latter's affair with Barbara Lynch, and then Jeremiah de Saint-Amour's death, followed by Urbino's own death while chasing the parrot, Florentino's subsequent wooing of Fermina, and finally their journey on the boat, Nueva Fidelidad. But the discourse-time has a different order, beginning with Jeremiah de Saint-Amour's death, Juvenal Urbino's death, followed by Florentino's decision to woo Fermina after fifty years of unrequited love, a depiction of his earlier love-affair with Fermina, Fermina's travels, and her spurning of Florentino's love, her subsequent marriage to Urbino, the latter's affair with Barbara Lynch, his death, and concluding with Florentino's re-appearance on the scene, and Fermina's and Florentino's honeymoon on the Nueva Fidelidad. García Márquez's novel has, in effect, two times – the story-time and the discourse-time – which do not coincide. The use of the flashback opens up the novel to the play on different levels of time, and also to the motif of reincorporation of the earlier love-affair within the frame of the second love-affair, as a result of the proximity caused by the narrative (rather than the 'real-time') order. An interlocking time sequence of comparable complexity would be almost unthinkable in a film, and we can therefore understand why the scriptwriters decided to adopt a simpler temporal sequencing. *Cartas del parque* instead cross-cuts between the two 'love-affairs', namely between Juan and María on the other hand, and Pedro and the prostitute on the other (with Pedro acting as a pivot between the two plots).

What it loses in terms of layered temporality, though, the film gains in visual suggestiveness. As Seymour Chatman explains: 'Film narrative possesses a plenitude of visual details, an excessive particularity compared to the verbal version, a plenitude aptly called by certain aestheticians visual "over-specification", a property that it shares, of course, with the other visual arts' (pp. 438–9). *Cartas del parque* introduces a layeredness into its visual dimension. Films, after all, use a visual medium which depicts rather than asserts a reality. As Chatman puts it:

> When I say, 'The cart was tiny; it came onto the bridge', I am asserting that certain property of the cart as being small in size and that certain relation of arriving at the bridge. However, when I say 'The green cart came over onto the bridge', I am asserting nothing more that its arrival at the bridge; the greenness of the cart is not asserted but slipped in without syntactic fuss. It is only named. Textually, it emerges by the way. Now, most film narratives seem to be of the latter textual order; it requires special effort for films to assert a property or relation. The dominant mode is presentational, not assertive. A film doesn't say, 'This is the state of affairs', it merely shows you that state of affairs. (. . .) So in its essential visual mode, film does not describe at all, but merely presents; or better it depicts, in the original etymological sense of that word: renders in pictorial form.   (pp. 439–40)

If we focus on the establishing scene of the film we can see how the film 'presents' rather than 'describes' its message about love. We see René Simon about to take off in his hot-air balloon, we experience the crowd's noisy expectation, and these background scenes are cross-cut with the depiction of the growth of Juan's love: we see him falling in love with the sight of her, rather like Frédéric in Flaubert's *L'Éducation sentimentale* who falls in love with Madame Arnoux and feels as if he has seen an 'apparition' (Flaubert, p. 40). What the novel takes pages to describe is something that happens in Frédéric's mind in one mind-shattering instant. The film focuses obsessively on María's appearance; dressed elegantly in white, with her white hat that she pulls coyly over her eyes, María looks like a luscious female from an Impressionist painting. It is important to emphasise here that Juan has not been smitten by her words, but by her appearance. Indeed, it is when the lovers are forced to talk to each other that the elusive grandeur of love seems to slip through their fingers. This recognition-scene is repeated a few scenes later when Pedro first glimpses María emerging from beneath the arcades of the main square. Like Juan his breath is taken away by the image of European fin-de-siècle femininity that she encapsulates. The choice of cultural code for her dress in the film is quite deliberate; it offers a fierce contrast with the vibrant, defiantly Cuban dress of the prostitute with whom Pedro is – in his own way – in love.

That the love which María incites in her male admirers is based on her visual reality – rather than by what she says, for example – is demonstrated in the delicate scene in which the two young lovers go on a boat-ride around the lake. During that scene both of the lovers show themselves to be totally denuded of any ability to express their love. They simply look at each other, in a rather daunting sequence of low-angle, close-up shot-reverse shots, and have nothing to say. María simply laughs out loud rather inanely, while Juan – unable to work out why she is laughing – commits some buffoonery when he loses the paddle. The voice-over declaims Poem LII of Gustavo Adolfo Bécquer's *Rimas*, each stanza of which concludes with the rousing line, addressed to the waves and the wind: '¡llevadme con vosotras!' (Carry me off with you!; Bécquer, p. 77). Bécquer's poetry is the linguistic frame which Pedro has used to guide the growth of the lovers' relationship up until this point – he at one point thought of using Quevedo's poetry, but then decided against it – and this scene expertly demonstrates that the two lovers are sending each other sublime messages whose import they do not really understand. Juan and María function, as this scene makes clear, rather like telegraph operators sending messages but without understanding what they are sending. The event has been organised by Pedro, as is made clear after the photo session when the camera zooms in on Pedro in the background. Pedro is the puppeteer – as the film suggests in its gently mocking allusion to the plot prompts characteristic of the silent movies of the 1920s – who is bringing the two 'puppets' together. Pedro also uses other types of sign language to express love; he tells Juan about the language of flowers, and María about the language of fans and handkerchiefs.

The intriguing part about this film is how it shows the puppeteer being caught within his own 'play', since this love-affair is a drama which he has created. Pedro is, as it were, framed by his own words. Pedro begins the film as a puppeteer, gradually becomes a voyeur (as is made clear by the concluding shot of the lake episode), and finally is converted into the lover. Each of the three phases of 'love' is characterised by absence which, indeed, is not presented as an obstacle to love but as its very life-blood. I have already noted that there are important junctures of the film when the physical beauty of María is highlighted, and this *topos* reaches its visual climax when we notice her figure, again in long-shot, again in white, when she goes to Pedro's apartment, and waits for him. It becomes clear that the camera eye is being used to make a profound and interesting point about love, which includes Platonic tenderness and erotic urgency: namely, distance is the fuel on which love feeds itself. Precisely that distance is conveyed in cinematic terms by the adroit use of the long shot. The language of film is, therefore, able to do something the novel cannot, and this is to focus visually on that absence that underpins love. It is within the space between word and object, between the written word and the spoken word, between the love letter and speech, that the whole dynamics of love is able to operate, and finally, generate itself. The psychological subtlety of what is going through the characters' minds as they are falling in love, may have been lost in the transfer from novel to celluloid, but what *Cartas del parque* is able to express is the manner in which true love – of the Romantic, namely, unrequited and desperate type – is predicated on the unattainability of the beloved.

Works Cited

Bécquer, Gustavo Adolfo, *Rimas*, ed. José Luis Cano (Madrid: Cátedra, 1976).

Bell, Michael, 'Not Flaubert's Parrot: Love in the Time of Cholera', in *Gabriel García Márquez* (London: Longman, 1995), pp. 106–26.

Chatman, Seymour, 'What Novels Can Do that Films Can't (and Vice-versa)', in Leo Braudy and Marshall Cohen, *Film Theory and Criticism: Introductory Readings* (Oxford: OUP, 1999), pp. 435–51.

Constant, Benjamin, *Adolphe* (Paris: Flammarion, 1965).

Évora, José Antonio, *Tomás Gutiérrez Alea* (Madrid: Cátedra, 1996).

Flaubert, Gustave, *L'Éducation sentimentale* (Paris: Garnier-Flammarion, 1969).

García Márquez, Gabriel, *El amor en los tiempos del cólera* (Barcelona: Plaza y Janes, 1998).

García Márquez, Gabriel, *Vivir para contarla* (Barcelona: Mondadori, 2002).

Hart, Stephen, 'Love in the Time of Cholera', in *Cyclopedia of Literary Places*, ed. R. Baird Shuman (Englewood Cliffs, NJ: Salem Press, 2003), vol. II, pp. 668–9.

Sánchez-H., José, *The Art and Politics of Bolivian Cinema* (Lanham: Scarecrow Press, 1999).

Simons, Marlise, 'The Best Years of His Life: An Interview with Gabriel García Márquez', *New York Times Book Review* (10 April 1988), 47–9.

16

LA TAREA (HOMEWORK, 1989), DIRECTED BY
JAIME HUMBERTO HERMOSILLO

Main cast

Virginia, played by María Rojo
Marcelo, played by José Alonso

Crew

Director: Jaime Humberto Hermosillo
Produced by: Clasa Films Mundiales, S.A.
Executive Producer: Lourdes Rivera
Producers: Pablo and Francisco Barbachano
Cinematography: Tony Kuhn
Sound: Nerio Barberis
Art Director: Laura Santa Cruz
Songs: 'Bonita' and 'Superstición' by Luis Arcaraz; 'Momento' by Los Hermanos Martínez Gil

Plot

Set in a middle-class apartment in Mexico. We see a woman dressed in black tights and a red skirt concealing a camera under a table in the front room. A man arrives. From their conversation it transpires that she is a woman living on her own, he is divorced and the father of a six-year-old son, and they had a sexual relationship four years ago. She says she has called him because seeing a film had sparked her memory of how they had made love on the floor, and she had had a wet dream. She tries to persuade him to make love in the same place but he wants to go into the bedroom. He puts his jacket on the chair in front of the camera and blocks out the viewer, but – once she realises it – she removes it. He phones up his son who is at home alone, and reassures him that he will be home soon. They have a drink, dance, then start making love. But he says that he feels as if they are being watched. Then he sees the red light of the video camera. He asks why she has been filming him in secret and she says that it is for a home-work assignment. He reacts angrily, knocks the camera, and then storms out in a huff. She then sits in front of the camera talking about her sexual hang-ups. He returns because he has forgotten his briefcase, and then is flattered to hear from her how good he is in bed. He says that he has got nothing against pornography, and then agrees to take part in her homework assignment. They strip and then make love in the hammock. Afterwards he gets up to leave, saying he has to go home to see his son. She sits in front of the camera, crying. He bursts back into the room, with two children. We discover that they are husband and wife, that they have two children, and that they have been trying to make a movie. She criticises him for being over-dramatic, and he criticises her for some of the ideas in the film. They then decide that, to help their family finances, they should turn try their hand at producing pornographic movies.

Analytical Overview

Before it was filmed professionally, *La tarea* was a home-made video. As Hermosillo points out: 'The idea for the film originally came from a super-eight video, which I made in 1989 by myself and two actors. (. . .) Economically speaking, it was a miracle costing only the price of a video cassette. There was no sound person, no light person, no cameraman, just a fixed camera, two actors, myself and an art director. We rehearsed in the evenings for a month in our free time' ('Interview', Tartan Video Sleeve). Amazingly, given its slender budget, it was a success; as Hermosillo suggests, 'the video ended up winning first place in a national competition and was considered by film critics to be among the best exhibited that year' ('Interview'). In order to turn the home-video into a professional movie, however, some changes were inevitable: 'The movie was shot in four days with a one-week rehearsal period. It is more complicated technically and we had to construct an elevated set so the camera would appear at floor level. Every ten minutes we had to change rolls, so we used moments when the actors were absent from the set' ('Interview').

Like the majority of Hermosillo's films, *La tarea* focuses overwhelmingly on sex (Hart). Unlike some of his other films, though, which home in on the ways in which sex and violence overlap, *La tarea* analyses sexuality in a humorous context. This includes slapstick comedy, as when the two lovers fall out of the hammock when trying to make love, and bathetic humour (as when the two lovers make lots of grunting noises when making love – in direct contrast to the conventional, U.S. version of pornography with its repertoire of staged screams of excited pleasure). The script in fact recognises this when we hear the words 'el erotismo y el buen gusto no se llevan' (eroticism and good taste do not mix), which are repeated. This is why Virginia is horrified when she sees herself for the first time on camera with no clothes on; she runs into the bedroom in disgust. The film panders to this notion since – just before Virginia and Marcelo make love in the hammock – a veil is draped over the camera eye. Hermosillo is pointedly drawing attention to the idea that unveiled sexuality is ugly, and that only veiled sexuality is acceptable – either in the form of the veil on the character, or in the form of Virginia's 'hang-ups' which she tells the camera about, or in the form of the fig-leaf which covers Adam and Eve's pudenda (and which is referred to in the scene directly before Marcelo and Virginia have sex). It is important to underline that Hermosillo is pointing to the ways in which sexuality is structured in bourgeois society; the middle-class veil of respectability – in its myriad forms – becomes the butt of his satire.

The Soap Opera

The film is very keen to point to the ways in which middle-class Mexicans escape from the drudgery of everyday life by creating fantasy worlds which are, themselves, heavily dependent on the world of the mass media. Virginia says that she first thought of the idea of inviting Marcelo round because of a film she saw starring Marcelo Mastroianni. The clear implication is that love affairs in films inspire love-affairs in real life. The film actor, after all, has the same first name as Virginia's ex-lover. Virginia – as we later discover – is a film student who is attempting to pull a fast one on an ex-lover and, thereby, create a 'racy' homework assignment. In a deeper sense, though, Virginia is also attempting to re-enact a film-inspired fantasy in her front living room. This is also indicated by the two film posters which are placed on the wall at different times. Virginia asks Marcelo if he remembers an actress with red hair called Deborah Kerr. All of these pointers suggest that Virginia is re-enacting the seduction techniques glorified in movie culture. This is, indeed, where Hermosillo's critique lies. He is making fun of the middle classes in Mexico who model their life styles on the glamour of films. *La tarea* in effect debunks the myth of film.

Voyeurism and Pornography

La tarea focuses on two inter-related themes: voyeurism and pornography. By keeping the camera steadily in one place – such that, after the first few establishing shots, we never see any camera shots which are not via the film under the table – Hermosillo is drawing attention to the ways in which films – because they offer access to peoples' lives in a way that would not be possible in real life – offer a thrill to the viewer which is rooted in the voyeuristic. *La tarea* also delves into the overlap between the film and pornography, deliberately introducing themes which are no-go areas in the seamless world of pornography – the need for condoms, and the discussion of the dangers of illicit sexual activity and AIDS. The theme of AIDS was in fact added when the film was filmed professionally. As Hermosillo pointed out: 'I proposed doing a film version to producers Francisco and Pablo Barbachano and, although the video only lasts an hour, I felt I could enrich situations on film. But I had to be careful not to lose the rhythm. Because of the deplorable presence of AIDS today, I found it necessary to heighten awareness by insisting that condoms be used' (Hermosillo, 'Interview').

In this way *La tarea* will catch the unsuspecting viewer off his or her guard, upsetting expectations. The first expectation revolves around gender: the audience's expectation will no doubt be that the man will be the instigator of the voyeuristic trap. In the original, home-made movie version of the film, it was the man who initiated the voyeurism rather than the woman. As Hermosillo suggests: 'the biggest change was switching roles as to which person in making the videotape. The change was inspired by Howard Hawks in *His Girl Friday*. As a filmmaker, I did not want to repeat what I had done earlier and thought it would be more interesting to have the woman making a porno film with the male used as a sex object' ('Interview').

Hermosillo's film also deconstructs the viewer's expectation by playing on the difference between the real and the illusory, everyday reality and filmed reality. *La tarea* does this by setting up a dramatic scene – a woman traps an ex-lover in a game of voyeuristic exploitation – which is then deconstructed to produce another – the man agrees to go ahead with the illusion of the film – which is, itself, deconstructed since the two previous scenes are, themselves, being acted out. As David William Foster points out, *La tarea* is 'very much of an exercise in metafilmmaking while at the same time continuing the general interest of Hermosillo's films in questions of contemporary urban sexuality in Mexico' (Foster, p. 123). On each occasion, the film suggests, we 'drop down' a level, coming one step closer to the truth. By creating scenes which – in a game of Chinese boxes – are shown to be fictitious, Hermosillo is drawing attention to the illusionism of film. And he directs his satiric gaze at two genres which require absolutely that the viewer should not suspend the illusion – the soap opera and pornography. There is, after all, nothing more ridiculous than a behind-the-scenes view of a melodramatic scene from a telenovela or a scene from a pornographic film. Both genres are highly sensationalist and any break in the game of illusionism creates highly comic situations. It is precisely the point at which illusionism breaks down and humour protrudes that Hermosillo homes in on in *La tarea*.

Social Commentary and the Camera Eye

La tarea is a light-hearted attack on the Mexican middle classes, on their addiction for mass-media produced illusions of happiness, and the ways in which these obsessions are encased within respectability. He therefore uses the critique of the illusionism of film in order to draw attention to the blindness underlying the laws of social decorum. It is ironic, of course, that – as a result of their failed experience in filmmaking – Virginia and Marcelo decide to make a go at producing pornographic films for the local market. The new title to the film – which is added in the final clip (*La tarea o de cómo la pornografía salvó del tedio y mejoró la economía de la familia Partida*) – finally exposes the hollowness of the value systems of the Mexican middle classes.

The fact that the camera stays in one spot throughout the whole film is its main cinematic innovation. The action is viewed monotonously from one camera which is placed at floor level. This device is in some ways reminiscent of Yasujiro Ozu's films in which the camera is placed at about three feet off the floor at about the eye level of someone sitting on the floor, thereby giving a realistic POV of a person in a Japanese house sitting on a mat. But whereas Ozu's aesthetic derives from Zen Buddhism, Hermosillo's guiding preoccupation is much more earthy; as mentioned above, *La tarea* focuses on sexuality and exhibitionism.

Perhaps even more intriguing is the way that this film opens up the mystique of filmmaking. As Dov Simens has pointed out, the best way for a budding film director to put together his/her first film is to create a living room drama (as occurs here) which takes place over a limited period of time (as occurs here) with a limited set of actors (again, as occurs here) (Simens). From a production point of view *La tarea* de-mystifies the creation of a film by producing a minimalist version which unveils the nuts and bolts of how it is put together. But whereas the Dov Simens formula encourages drama which occurs within one room as a means of re-enacting a drama which occurred, as it were, off-stage (as the court-room drama typically does), Hermosillo twists the focus by allowing the drama to occur before our very eyes – that drama which revolves around deception, voyeurism and sexuality. The almost unbearable nature of the unflinching camera eye which records the action as it unfolds in the cinematic space, in effect, hollows out from within the need for 'cat-in-the-window' shots which are used to cover up the imperfections inherent in filming. As well as offering an intriguing insight into the machinations of sexual deception, *La tarea* is also a clever deconstruction of the myth of filmmaking which simultaneously offers a bottom-of-the-basement snapshot of human psychology.

Works Cited

Foster, David William, *Mexico City in Contemporary Mexican Cinema* (Austin: University of Texas Press, 2002).

Hart, Stephen, 'Cinema in Mexico', in *Dictionary of Twentieth Century Culture: Hispanic Culture of Mexico, Central America, and the Caribbean*, ed. Peter Standish (Detroit: Manley Publishers, 1996), pp. 78–81.

Hermosillo, Jaime Humberto, 'Interview', Tartan Sleeve Jacket, *La tarea.*

King, John, *Magical Reels: A History of Cinema in Latin America* (London: Verso, 1990).

Simens, Dov S-S, 'Two-Day FilmSchool', Raindance, London, 29–30 November 2003.

17

YO, LA PEOR DE TODAS (I, THE WORST OF ALL, 1990), DIRECTED BY MARÍA LUISA BEMBERG

Cast

Sor Juana, played by Assumpta Serna; voice dubbed by Cecilia Roth
The Vicereine, played by Dominique Sanda
The Viceroy, played by Héctor Alterio
Archbishop, played by Lauturo Murúa
Sor Úrsula, elected abbess, played by Graciela Araujo
Bishop Santa Cruz, played by Alberto Segado
Miranda, sor Juana's confessor, played by Franklin Caicedo

Crew

Screenplay: María Luisa Bemberg, Antonio Larreta
Director's assistant: Marcello Rembado
Production Managers: Marta Paga, Miriam Bendjuia
Camera: Jorge Guillerno Behnisch
Setting: Esmeralda Almonacid
Wardrobe: Graciela Galán
Sound: Jorge Stavropulos
Music: Luis María Serra
Editing: Juan Carlos Macías
Design: Voytek
Photography Director: Félix Monti
Executive Producer: Gilbert Marouani
Producer: Lita Stantic
Director: María Luisa Bemberg

Plot

The film opens with a conversation between the Viceroy and the Archbishop of Mexico in which the rivalry between them is obvious. Cuts to convent in which the nuns are standing in the courtyard and then to sor Juana's cell in which she is busy writing. News arrives that the Viceroy will be visiting the convent and wishes to meet sor Juana. The Viceroy and his wife come to the convent, see sor Juana's latest play and decide to 'adopt' her. The Archbishop meets sor Úrsula and arranges for her to be the new abbess, encouraging her to crack down on discipline. The Vicereine comes to meet sor Juana and says they are more similar than is first apparent; the beginning of a deep friendship. During a conversation between sor Juana and Sigüenza about literary matters, the Vicereine brings sor Juana a beautiful Quetazalcoatl feather. The Vicereine protects sor Juana from Úrsula's influence, and the Viceroy reverses the Archbishop's order to have sor Juana banned from her library because of the licentious nature of her verse. The Vicereine asks sor Juana to take off her unveil and she kisses her. The Viceroys are recalled to Madrid, and Bishop Santa Cruz encourages sor Juana to write against the Archbishop's favourite theologian, the Portuguese Jesuit, Antônio Vieyra. He promises not to publish it, but when she leaves, he goes back on his word, publishing the essay, the *Carta atenagórica*, and including in the edition a preface rebuking sor Juana for her interest in mundane matters under the pseudonym, sor Filotea de la Cruz. The Archbishop is furious at sor Juana's rebuttal of Jesuit theology, and demands an explanation. Sor Juana decides to try to defend herself by writing her *Respuesta de la poetisa a la muy ilustre Sor Filotea de la Cruz*. She insults the Archbishop by forcing him to smell her hand. Miranda rejects sor Juana and says she must find another confessor. Graphic scenes of the plague in Mexico City. Sigüenza brings sor Juana the edition of her poetry, *Inundación castálida*, which had been published in Madrid. Miranda sees sor Juana scrubbing the floor, and agrees to be her confessor once more. He persuades her to sell all her belongings including her library. Final scene in which – in a room surrounded by the nuns and her confessor – she makes a final confession, beginning with the words, 'Yo, la peor de todas . . .', which she writes in her own blood. Cuts to empty library, and view of sor Juana in an empty room. Film concludes and a message appears on the screen informing the viewers that sor Juana died shortly afterwards by contracting an illness from the plague.

Analytical Overview

The important point about the film is that it offers a modern, twentieth-century reading of the life of a seventeenth-century Mexican nun. There was initially some resistance to the film in that it is totally set in Argentina. Though Bemberg was offered the possibility of filming the story in Mexico she got cold feet, feeling that she would lose control over the script. For this reason it is possible to read *Yo, la peor de todas* on two different though complementary levels. On the first more obvious level it is a reconstruction of an historical reality: the life of a nun in seventeenth-century Mexico; on a second level – one which is enhanced by the geographical setting in which it is filmed – the film functions as the exploration of the pressures and restrictions operating in the life of a young woman in Argentina. This is a way of saying that the film is about sor Juana but also a biographical exploration – Bemberg, therefore, is using sor Juana in order to talk about her own life. This is suggested by the elements of sor Juana's life which are foregrounded at the expense of others. There is nothing, for example, about sor Juana's spirituality – which, we speculate, would have been part of her life. We see little of the tasks which were part of the everyday life of a nun in the seventeenth century. Rather, the sor Juana we see is a rebellious soul whose aims are secular, and who is cruelly mistreated by her male superiors simply, it would appear, for the fun of humiliating her. Even if these points concern emphasis rather than departure from established historical truth, there is one area in which Bemberg departed from the historical account in order to pursue a different agenda. In a number of scenes the suggestion is raised that sor Juana was – emotionally if not actively – a lesbian, and that her closeness to the Vicereine had a sexual latency to it. This is suggested in two scenes in particular. The first concerns the scene in which the Vicereine – her eyes dripping with lust – asks sor Juana to remove her veil. She does so, and this scene can be interpreted as the unveiling of not only the Vicereine's but also sor Juana's lust. The second occurs when the Vicereine asks sor Juana to release her girdle. Though this could be interpreted as one woman helping another there is a tenseness about the request which suggests sexual latency. But it does not go further than this. Some have criticised the film for introducing this non-historical element into the plot; however, it is clear that the strand works well in the film as a whole and is furthermore delicately done. There have been other criticisms of the film. One, the most common, has concerned the tempo. As Andrew Graham-Yooll suggests: 'Her life of Sister Juana Ines de la Cruz, *I, The Worst of All* (1990) was not a success. Longwinded, slow it was, but it was also a magnificent historical recreation of colonial Mexico in the 17th century, and of the repression suffered by a woman who is now celebrated as one of the founding poets and writers of Latin America' (Graham-Yooll). This is perhaps a little harsh since it underestimates the iconic fascination that sor Juana exercises on Latin American women in the modern era, similar in some ways to the fascination that Shakespeare exerts on Englishmen. From the outside it seems a little quaint. Graham-Yooll has, though, pointed to something distinctive about this film and that is the way that it seems to slow its tempo to a degree which many will find uncomfortable. By slowing down the pace of the narrative Bemberg was emphasising the atmosphere of the time, but – as the stage sets suggest – she was doing so not in order to attempt to recreate the splendours and miseries of colonial New Spain but rather to provide a minimalist setting against which the existential, feminist anguish of the woman of the modern world is silhouetted in graphic, contrasting tones.

Feminism

It is clear that Bemberg picked on the story of sor Juana in order to pursue a point about the dilemma faced by women in patriarchal society. In a lecture she gave in 1992 at the University of Warwick, Bemberg made the following telling comment: 'To be a woman in a patriarchal society is still to be considered inferior. In England you may not perhaps realise how extreme such conditioning can be in a land of fearless gauchos and *compadritos*, where brute strength is encouraged. These lands gave us a particular kind of man, a sad archetype called *machismo*, which is an attitude that blends boasting, indifference, misogyny and stupidity. It is true that the century old mirror of oppression in which we were reflected has now broken. Yet, despite this fracturing, we still have not reconstructed an image of freedom from the bits that would be valid for all of us' ('Being an Artist in Latin America'). In *Yo, la peor de todas* Bemberg is attempting to bring about just this type of 'reconstruction' of an 'image of freedom' via her portrayal of sor Juana. The film is certainly not lacking what Bemberg calls that 'sad archetype called *machismo*'; the Archbishop is the epitome, indeed, of 'boasting, indifference, misogyny and stupidity'. Some of his statements are almost case-book examples of women-hatred: 'la mujer es más amarga que la muerte' (women are more bitter than death). His woman-hatred is graphically suggested in the scene in which, after the secret discussion with sor Úrsula, incense is released into the air to destroy the smell of the women.

Bemberg's sense of the feminist ideal involved creating a culture which rebelled against patriarchal culture. In her 1992 lecture, Bemberg referred to the social conditioning which often holds women back: 'We are limited by psychological conditionings that conspire against women: an absence of inner confidence and the authority to restrict cultural models; an absence of the motivation needed to create art, like a competitive spirit, the urge to differentiate yourself through what you do, and a liking for complex issues. On top of this man has cannibalized womanhood and tries to speak for both' ('Being an Artist in Latin America'). What Bemberg wanted to do was to wrest culture back from its patriarchal mould, and to do so she sought strong images of women: 'However, some women have managed to get round these obstacles like the following writers from the southern tip of my continent: Alfonsina Storni and Juana de Ibarbourou from the River Plate and Gabriela Mistral from Chile. These women, like many others from all five continents, have achieved their goal of creating a well-finished art, even if at times you can glimpse their Chesire cat's smile of apology for having dared to be daring' ('Being an Artist in Latin America'). Bemberg mentions the three most important female poets of the turn of the nineteenth and early twentieth centuries – Storni, Ibarbourou, and Mistral – and her film *Yo, la peor de todas* indicates that the Mexican nun has pride of place in this canon of women who 'dared to be daring'. In the film there are a number of points which indicate sor Juana's daring. The first – which we only see in flashback from the side of her dying mother's bed – occurred when she dressed in boy's clothes in order to try to go to university, and for which she earned her mother's anger. Others concern her direct rebellion against the Archbishop. When her library is closed, for example, she tells Úrsula to pass on the following message: 'Dígale al Arzobispo que estudiaré en el cielo, en la hierba, en la cocina' (Tell the Archbishop I will study in the sky, in the grass, in the kitchen), a telling allusion to sor Juana's comment in *Respuesta de la poetisa a la muy ilustre Sor Filotea de la Cruz* that Aristotle would have understood more about the natural world had he taken up cooking (Hart, p. 52). In her last lesson to the nuns she advises them to reject anyone who says that intelligence is the preserve of men: 'la inteligencia no tiene sexo' (intelligence has no gender). But her most transgressive act occurs near the end of the film when she is sitting behind bars, judged by the unholy trinity of Archbishop, Confessor and Bishop, all of whom have mercilessly betrayed her. She reaches through the cell bars and grabs hold of the Archbishop, forcing him to smell her hand, in a melodramatic scene towards the end of the film, thereby reversing the logic which had used incense to cover up the smell of women. It is not by coincidence that all hell is let loose from that point onwards; the melodrama is rolled out, as so often occurs in the *desenlace* of Bemberg's films, and the thunder, lightning and torrential rain lash down on Mexico City, producing the plague which seems to be a direct manifestation of God's ire.

This means that, in *Yo, la peor de todas*, Bemberg is – as suggested above – talking about the plight of women in modern-day Argentina as well as the past in Mexico. This was always a central theme of work as *The Daily Telegraph* obituary suggested, since her films were often 'poignant studies of the isolation of women which were also satires on the *machismo* of Latin American society' (Anonymous). One of the aims of her films, as she stated in an interview, was to bring greater awareness of women's plight: 'My films are an attempt to make women recognise themselves and learn more about themselves through the protagonists' predicament. This is my ethical commitment, helping them to be free' (quoted in Andrew Graham-Yooll). One area in which Bemberg took her lead from Paz but extended it in an innovatory way concerned the ways in which the relationship between sor Juana and the Vicereine blossomed. It is important to recall, first of all, that there is no historical evidence of an affair developing between the two individuals, although there is enough quantifiable evidence of their deep friendship (the evidence are the poems sor Juana wrote to the Vicereine; see Shaw, p. 128). Bemberg takes the evidence a step further and fashions Paz's masculinocentric reading into a lesbian re-vision. As Emilie Bergmann suggests: 'Although Paz insists she could not possibly have had homoerotic desires, her lesbianism is taken for granted by Latino/a and Spanish American lesbian and gay poets who have adopted her as their patron saint' (Bergmann, p. 232). A lesbian structure of feeling is suggested in a number of ways in Bemberg's film, most obviously in the two scenes – mentioned above – in which we have a declaration of love. In the first the Vicereine looks into sor Juana's eyes, asks her to loosen her bodice for her, and then makes a number of innuendo-laden comments: 'qué bellas eres cuando te apasionas' (how beautiful you are when you become passionate) and 'no se puede negar la naturaleza' (you can't deny nature). Both comments – coupled with her body language and sensual glances – suggest that the Vicereine has fallen in love with sor Juana. It is important to underline, though, as Omar Rodríguez has suggested, that the initiative is portrayed as being the Vicereine's rather than sor Juana's (Rodríguez, p. 145). The second more forthright scene occurs when the Vicereine, after her husband has allowed her to ignore the Archbishop's prohibition to stay out of her library, asks her to take off her veil: 'quítate el velo. Es una orden' (take off your veil. That's an order), after which she plants a delicate kiss on her lips. As Rosa Sarabia suggests, not only the Vicereine but the viewer is thereby constructed as a voyeur of sor Juana's beauty (Sarabia, p. 125); as Bemberg herself once suggested in an interview, there are so many 'splendid women' portrayed on the big screen that it would not be surprising if 'we all ended up being lesbians' ('Somos la mitad del mundo', p. 17). Given that the Vicereine is at one stage given the fictitious name of María Luisa by the Viceroy just as they are about to leave for Madrid, it is perhaps not to stretch the point too much to see the Vicereine as a projection of Bemberg herself who wished to 'de-nun' sor Juana. The gushing words uttered by the Vicereine ('¿Cómo es Juana, con ella misma, cuando está sola, cuando nadie la mira?'; What is Juana like, with herself, on her own, when nobody sees her?, and – after the veil is removed – 'esta Juana es mía, solamente mía'; this Juana is mine, mine only) could almost be the words of the artist, seeking in Pygmalion fashion to create a new image of womanhood for the modern day. In an interview Bemberg has suggested that she chose Assumpta Serna to play sor Juana not only because of her beauty and poise but because she would give the role a contemporary feel, which is what she wanted: 'Uno se olvida de que este personaje es una monja porque ella supo darle un toque de actualidad' (Bemberg, 'Somos la mitad del mundo', p. 15).

But perhaps just as intriguing as these scenes in which innuendo speaks volumes, are those scenes in which the poems for which sor Juana is famous are recited in voice-over, and are framed within a new context, thereby transforming them into examples of *littérature à clé*, with the key being the lesbian sub-text. Perhaps the best example of this occurs when the sonnet 'Detente, sombra de mi bien esquivo . . .', a love poem traditionally seen as a stylistic exercise (de la Campa, p. 260), but now provided – given the view the camera provides of the Vicereine just to the right of the frame – with the sense of being a love poem to the Vicereine. This is also the meaning given to the poems by the small committee set up by the Archbishop to determine what to do with sor Juana. Though given a lead by Octavio Paz, Bemberg pursues some imaginative juxtapositions which breathe a new, ambiguous light into what were seen as rhetorical exercises. It does not matter so much whether the interpretation is an historically justifiable one (Paz, for example, sees the love poems more in terms of feudal submission than of eroticism; see Ramírez, p. 60), what is more important is how the sub-theme works within the film as a whole. It certainly allows sor Juana's transgression to be understood more clearly by a modern audience.

Camerawork and Setting

The setting of the film is very sparse and minimalist, and the colours used are contrastive. The Archbishop often appears surrounded by darkness, while sor Juana and the convent are often surrounded by light, thereby echoing the atmosphere of a baroque painting. As Bemberg said to Félix Monti when they were filming *Yo, la peor de todas*: 'Félix, remember Zurbarán's light' (King, Whitaker and Bosch, *An Argentine Passion*, p. 48). One critic has noted that, 'through long, static, shots, confined staging, and minimized tracking, Bemberg creates a visual metaphor for the pervasive repression and claustrophobia of the times, as Sor Juana struggles to defy social convention and pursue an independent life as an intellectual and artist' (*Strictly Film School Review*). The film was not filmed on location, and instead Bemberg used a film set. This gave a rather spacey, artificial feel to the convent, an ambiance that Bemberg no doubt required since she wanted to give the film not so much an historical feel as the sense of a story about female oppression which transcended a particular historical setting. The blues and greens and greys used to convey the convent give it, indeed, almost an art décor feel.

Works Cited

Anonymous, 'María Luisa Bemberg', *The Daily Telegraph* (9 June 1995), p. 27.

Bemberg, María Luisa , 'Somos la mitad del mundo', *Cine Cubano*, 132 (July–August 1991), 11–17.

Bemberg, María Luisa, 'Being an Artist in Latin America', lecture notes of presentation given in 1992 at the University of Warwick. Kindly supplied by Professor Jason Wilson.

Bergmann, Emilie, 'Abjection and Ambiguity: Lesbian Desire in Bemberg's *Yo, la peor de todas*', in *Hispanisms and Homosexualities*, eds Sylvia Molloy and Robert McKee Irwin (Durham: Duke University Press, 1998), pp. 229–47.

De la Campa, Antonio, and Raquel Chang-Rodríguez (eds), *Poesía hispanoamericana colonial: antología* (Madrid: Alhambra, 1985).

Graham-Yooll, Andrew, 'María Luisa Bemberg', *The Independent* (24 May 1995).

Hart, Stephen, *White Ink: Essays on Twentieth-Century Feminine Fiction in Spain and Latin America* (London: Tamesis, 1993).

King, John, *Magical Reels: A History of Cinema in Latin America* (London: Verso, 1990).

'María Luisa Bemberg', www.filmref.com/directors/dirpages/bemberg.html. (consulted on 6 January 2004)

Miller, Denise, 'María Luisa Bemberg's Interpretation of Octavio Paz's *Sor Juana*', in *An Argentine Passion: María Luisa Bemberg and her Films*, eds John King, Sheila Whitaker, Rosa Bosch (London: Verso, 2000), pp. 137–73.

Paz, Octavio, *Sor Juana o las trampas de la fe* (México: Fondo de Cultura Económica, 1984).

Ramírez, Susan E., '*I, The Worst of All*: The Literary Life of Sor Juana Inés de la Cruz', in *Based on a True Story: Latin American History at the Movies*, ed. Donald F. Stevens (Wilmington, Delaware: Scholarly Resources, 1997), pp. 47–62.

Rodríguez, Omar A., 'Poder, institución y género en *Yo, la peor de todas*', *Revista Canadiense de Estudios Hispánicos*, XXVII, 1 (2002), 139–56.

Sarabia, Rosa, 'Sor Juana o las trampas de la restitución', *Revista Canadiense de Estudios Hispánicos*, XXVII, 1 (2002), 119–38.

Shaw, Deborah, *Contemporary Cinema of Latin America: 10 Key Films* (London: Continuum, 2003), pp. 9–20.

'Yo, la peor de todas', *Strictly Film School*, http://www.filmref.com/directors/dirpages/bemberg.html (consulted on 6 January 2004)

18

LA FRONTERA (THE FRONTIER, 1991), DIRECTED BY RICARDO LARRAÍN

Cast

Ramiro Orellana, played by Patricio Contreras
Maite, played by Gloria Lasso
Diver's assistant, played by Eugenio Morales
Diver, played by Aldo Bernales
Hilda, played by Griselda Núñez
Father Patricio, played by Héctor Noguera
Secretary, played by Sergio Scmied
Detective, played by Aníbal Reyna
Elsa, played by Elsa Poblete

Crew

Director: Ricardo Larraín
Screenplay: Jorge Goldemberg and Ricardo Larraín
Producer: Eduardo Larraín
Executive Producers: Eduardo Larraín, Ricardo Larraín
Photography: Héctor Ríos
Costume Designer: Susan Bertram
Production Designer: Jane Stewart
Editor: Claudio Martínez
Sound: Miguel Hormazabal
Music: Jaime de Aguirre
Art Director: Juan Carlos Castillo
Production Director: Mara Sánchez
Head of Production: Alvaro Corvera

Awards

OCIC Award, Chile, 1991
Silver Bear, Berlin Film Festival, 1992
Goya Award, Spain, 1992
Golden Sun, Biarritz Festival, 1992
Best Film, Trieste Festival, 1992
Coral Award, Havana Film Festival, 1992

Plot

The film opens with a maths teacher, Ramiro Orellana, being escorted by two policemen to a remote part of Southern Chile. The car goes over a lake on a raft; we see a very drunk man travelling across who – we learn later – is the diver's assistant. The two men hand over the 'relegado' to the 'authorities' in the town; they explain that – because of his subversive activities (he signed a petition denouncing the disappearance of a colleague) – Ramiro has been sentenced to 'internal exile' in a remote part of Chile. The two men also hand over the log-book which Ramiro must sign on a regular basis. The superintendent and his assistant clearly do not know what they are doing though they accept their new assignment without complaint. Ramiro has a letter from the Archbishop but the local priest is not in town so the superintendent leaves him out in the rain. Ramiro meets a local woman, Maite, who gets the key to the sacristy and lets Ramiro in. Ramiro goes to the local bar and, while he is there, the diver's assistant dies from alcoholism. His coffin is, later on, brought into the church. The priest arrives and explains the residency rules to Ramiro. The priest conducts the funeral of the diver's assistant. Ramiro accompanies Maite to the ruins by the sea of the house where she used to live with her father, Ignacio, before the tidal wave came; he is beginning to fall in love with her. Ramiro gets a fever – and the superintendent is concerned that he is now unable to sign the log-book – but the local 'curandera' cures him. The diver explains his theory of the hole at the bottom of the ocean to Ramiro, and then invites him to be his new assistant; Ramiro accepts. Ramiro sees Maite's father, Ignacio, going off to 'visit Spain', by which he means gazing trance-like at the sea near the house they used to live in. Ramiro goes out on his first expedition with the diver. Ramiro talks with Ignacio who explains he is a Spanish refugee who came to Chile to escape Franco's dictatorship. Ramiro's ex-wife and son visit, but they are not allowed to meet, and must shout to each other over the lake. Ramiro accuses his friend of going off with his ex-wife. Ramiro goes with Maite once more to the ruined house she used to live in, and they make love on a rock; they are interrupted, however, by the arrival of the superintendent and his assistant who have been looking for him. Ramiro goes diving, and he discovers a statue which used to be in the town square, the 'Abrazo de Maipú'. Ramiro receives news that his 'exile' is over and he is free to return to Santiago, but he decides to stay. The 'curandera' warns Ramiro to leave because of the imminent tidal wave, but he ignores her. The tidal wave arrives, and floods Ignacio's house, drowning him. Ramiro pleads with Maite to leave with him, but she refuses and stays with her father, nursing his dead body. The townsfolk flee to the local graveyard; Mapuche and Christian prayers are chanted in unison in an attempt to avert disaster. A news team arrives from Santiago; they interview Ramiro and – on camera – he repeats his denunciation of the disappearance of his colleague.

Analytical Overview

La frontera has been described by one critic as 'post-Pinochet Chile's most accomplished and successful film to date, breaking attendance records for a Chilean film since the Popular Unity period of the early 1970s' (Barnard, p. 241). It explores a theme which is intrinsic to the culture of the area of Latin America now called Chile, namely, capture on the frontier. Ranging from Alonso de Ercilla y Zúñiga's three volume verse epic on the struggle between the Spanish conquistadors and the Araucanian Indians in Southern Chile, *La Araucana* (1569, 1578, and 1589; Hart, pp. 32–3) to Francisco Núñez de Pineda y Bascuñán's account of how he was held captive by the Indian chieftain, Maulicán, from May to November of 1629, *Cautiverio feliz* (1863), Chilean literature has the frontier as one of its most intrinsic themes (Operé). *La frontera* is based on the actual mechanism whereby individuals who disagreed with Pinochet's regime – instituted in 1973 and continuing up until 1990 – were sent away to a remote part of the country, and thereby in effect an internal 'exile'. People were sent to the most inhospitable places, the Dawson Islands in the Magellan Straits, Pisagua, and Quiriquina Island in Talcahuano Bay (Shaw, p. 88). As Miguel Littín remembers, these remote areas of Southern Chile became famous in the popular imagination in the months after the coup: 'Talcahuano, sede de la escuela naval de suboficiales, es el principal puerto militar de Chile y su astillero más activo. Se hizo célebre en los días siguientes al golpe por el triste privilegio de ser el punto de concentración obligado de los prisioneros políticos que iban a ser llevados al infierno de la isla Dawson' (García Márquez, p. 74). The film, though, as the rear crawl credits suggest, was filmed in Puerto Saavedra in Southern Chile. It is important to note that Ramiro in the film is not an 'exiliado' – this is the case in the film of Ramiro Orellana's ex-wife and her new partner – but a 'relegado'. The message of the film is subtle in this sense, since it does not focus on the brutality of state oppression, on torture, murder, on the 'desaparecidos', the people who were 'disappeared' during the Pinochet regime during the infamous Operation Condor (Verdugo). It does not show us the bodies which were found in mass graves in rural cemeteries, the bodies which were found in disused mine shafts – an example of this type of literature/film is *La casa de los espíritus* and *De amor y sombra* by Isabel Allende, which recount the actual events of the coup, and the repression which occurred afterwards (Davies, pp. 39–57). The latter type of work focuses on torture, and is direct in its critique of political oppression – the torture and mutilation which has been documented in a number of studies (O'Shaughnessy). Larraín's film, however, concentrates on a more subtle type of torture, one which concerns the everyday life of a 'relegado' living in remote village in southern Chile, and the basic problems he encounters in his everyday life. It also has a light touch, in that the film has a number of humorous incidents which balance the seriousness of the political message. But these humorous incidents are not there simply to alleviate an otherwise painful political message; as we shall see they are part of the point. *La frontera* is essentially about the misuse of state power, the way in which the individual is 'ground down' by a faceless bureaucracy, and the mindboggling absurdity of the whole situation. The endlessly absurd rules that the two officials make up in order to make Ramiro's life difficult are shown to be comic, yet it is a tragicomedy, since these are rules which are designed to humiliate the individual. We laugh at them, but this allows the absurdity of the situation to be expressed even more nakedly.

Abuse of Power

The two officials who receive Ramiro follow a very similar routine throughout the film, which is often humorous, in a way which is reminiscent of Laurel and Hardy. The best example is perhaps the scene in which the officials receive their 'prisoner'; it is clear that the superintendent does not really understand what 'relegado' means, since he continually refers to Ramiro as a terrorist. When not understanding a question, he turns to the assistant and repeats the question: '¿entendido?' Clearly neither of them know what is going on, and they cling on to some semblance of power when making up different rules for the control of their 'relegado'. The signing-in book becomes the central focus of the superintendent's life. He demands, for example, that Ramiro write out his name in capital letters: 'aclaración de firma', even though there can be no doubt about his identity, since, as Ramiro himself points out, there are no other 'relegados' anywhere around. This is taken to absurd lengths when Ramiro is on his deathbed and all that the superintendent is concerned about is the signature; so his assistant has to practise his signature until he gets it right. Finally, they simply resort to putting his fingerprint in the book. Another absurd use of power occurs when the superintendent threatens to confiscate the magazines which arrive, and then allows them to be handed over, but instead confiscates the letter. And – the cruellest blow of all – he does not allow Ramiro's ex-wife and his son to get off the raft. This leads – predictably – to an argument between them. The message here being that the separation enforced upon people leads to dysfunctionality with the family unit.

Continuity Editing and Mise-en-scène

The film is characterised by continuity editing; thus the story is presented sequentially with no awkward loose ends not tied up. There are very few unusual film shots. The only one that is slightly unusual occurs when we see Ramiro go into the church, after he is finally allowed to have the keys. Suddenly we see Ramiro from above; the suggestion is that we see him, as it were, as 'God sees him'. There is also at this juncture in the film – aided by the somber, slow-paced music – a sense of unfathomable destiny. Also striking is the use of an atmospheric mise-en-scène; mist and rain, scenes shot at night, mean that we are unaware of what is going on. The viewer struggles to make out forms in the night; like Ramiro, we are struggling to find out how this could have happened. Rather than have the character say: 'what is happening?' we see the character trying to work things out in the dark. The idea is presented visually rather than stated verbally.

Spain and Chile

Ramiro's love-affair with Maite, the daughter of a veteran of the Spanish Civil War of 1936–1939, has a central role in the film. It suggests the solidarity between the 'losers' in that war – the Republicans who lost against General Franco – and the losers in the war against Pinochet. The father, Ignacio, is portrayed as a lost soul; he hangs up newspaper accounts of the war in the basement and he is, in particular, haunted by what happened in the battle of Durango, one of the worst routs of Republicans in the war (Thomas, pp. 616–17; Preston, pp. 139–43). He frequently goes off into his own daydream world when he goes to the beach to sit and look at the ruined church turret swept away by the tidal wave. In a sense this is all that is left after the devastation caused by Fascism. Thus when Ramiro stumbles across him on the beach, all Ignacio will say is: 'no me hable' (don't speak to me). To make matters worse, Maite is infuriated by what he has done, and blames Ramiro for trying to destroy her father's world. Her reaction seems absurd – as absurd, indeed, as Ignacio's absurd ritual of putting on his coat before saying 'me voy a España' (we see this at various times throughout the film, but only later discover where he is going) – but in an absurd, nebulous world the father's reaction is as sensible as any other. Maite is also involved in trying to protect the idyllic nature of her past, the house she grew up in, and since destroyed by the 'maremoto', and which she calls – ironically – the 'atracción turística' (tourist attraction) of the town. This is where she takes Ramiro when she is showing him her inner life, and where – finally – she and Ramiro make love, an event which is interrupted by the superintendent and his assistant when they realise that Ramiro has not been back to sign. Pablo Neruda (1904–1973) is mentioned eulogistically by Ignacio, and this allusion manages to bring the two political worlds together. A Nobel Laureate and a fierce supporter of Salvador Allende, Neruda wrote some of his most famous poems about the Spanish Civil War, *España en el corazón* (1937), and he is reputed to have died of a broken heart when he heard that Pinochet had taken over the country by *coup d'état*. The allusion to his left-wing views provides a continuity with the Chile that the viewers have been experiencing for the last thirty years. History is, in the process, given a harder contemporary edge.

The Tidal Wave

Water is central to the film's symbolism. As Deborah Shaw points out, Ramiro, 'like the land he now inhabits, is in a fluid state of being' (Shaw, p. 89).The tidal wave has an important role to play in the creation of the film's message. It is a disaster which destroyed the community many years before and has a realistic quality to it, but it is also clear, as the film goes on, that it operates in the film at a symbolic level as well. In the same way that, for example, the cockerel in Gabriel García Márquez's *El coronel no tiene quien le escriba* functions not only as a real cockerel but also on a symbolic level as well – meaning left-wing ideology, Agustín, the dignity of the people, and so on and so forth (Box, pp. 58–66). The important point here is that an image can exist on two levels, that is, as an actual event, but also as a vehicle expressing another reality.

Early on in the film, it is clear that the tidal wave is associated with the mythical and/or biblical flood of the Old Testament. When the diver describes

his outlandish theory that the tidal wave was produced by the water from a sub-
terranean world coming up from the depths and erupting into this world, we look
at the landscape, and we see the rainbow there. The biblical metaphor, thus,
alludes to God's promise in the Book of Genesis that He would never again
attempt to destroy mankind. There is also a reference to the Mapuche myth, since
the diver is reading about how 'Tentén-vilu, the goddess of the land who fights
to overcome Coicoi-vilu, the sea serpent who caused the waters of the sea to rise
in order to destroy all living creatures on land' (Shaw, p. 96). It is clear, though,
that the tidal wave stands for something else. In the important speech in which
Ignacio repeats the Republican war-cry of 'No pasarán' (they will not get
through), he ends gloomily, saying that: 'pero pasaron' (but they did get
through), and then explicitly compares the tidal wave to what happened during
the Civil War and also, more recently, in Chile. The tidal wave, thus, is being
compared to the uncontrollable forces of Fascism which erupted into the world,
blowing everything in its path out of the way, and leaving havoc wherever it
went. The tidal wave functions simultaneously as the Fascism of the 1930s in
Spain as well as the Fascism of the 1970s in Chile and, in a neat type of symbolism, it is fitting (though not necessarily verisimilous) that Ignacio should be
the first victim of the second literal tidal wave which floods the town. Ignacio
thereby becomes a victim of propitiation, and his death re-enacts the evil which
has befallen Chile and which first erupted in Spain some forty years before.
Aqueous symbolism is, indeed, enhanced throughout the film by Héctor Ríos's
skilfully atmospheric filming; as a result, 'an enchanting blue gloom pervades
the film' (Barnard, p. 242).

The Mapuche

As the blurb to the film suggests, the area in which the film is set is a zone somewhere between the Indian and the Spanish worlds, 'the historical border between
Mapuche Indian territory and lands of the Spanish conquerors. This is a rough
place where cultures meet, natural disasters look and reality, myth and legend
mix.' The main representative of the Mapuche culture is Hilda, the 'curandera',
who cures Ramiro when he first falls ill; she works with herbs and leaves, and is
presented as someone close to the earth and nature. Her role is a beneficient, positive one. She also cures his hand which has been burnt, and we are not told how
this happened, but it may have been by torture. She also is a seer in that she
knows that the tidal wave is about to return, and tells the priest that it is about to
happen. It is significant that she is the only one to know this; the priest simply
dismisses her ideas as those of a pagan. Yet, at the end of the film, when the
community are united in their grief, it is not fortuitous that both Christian prayers
and Mapuche prayers of supplication are used simultaneously to appease the
gods, as if to embody a sense of transculturation. The Christian prayer used is
the Ave María: 'Ave María, madre de Dios, ruega por nosotros ahora y en la hora
de nuestra muerte, amén.' The Mapuche prayer is more eloquent and asks for
forgiveness from the gods – who are masculine as well as feminine – as a result

5. *La frontera*: The 'Family' Photo

of man's blindness. Deborah Shaw has argued that there is 'a negative representation of Christianity in the film' (Shaw, p. 92), but it is more plausible to see
these final scenes in terms of a rare moment of ideological syncretism between
the two religions. Both Mapuche and Christian are united in seeing the tidal wave
as a punishment visited upon the people, like one of the plagues from the Old
Testament.

The tidal wave, as we can see, suggests the contiguity of the human and the
divine worlds. It is very much a layered, ambiguous symbol in the film for, as
we already know, the tidal wave operates as a representation of the unstoppabil-
ity and destructiveness of Fascism. In this way, rather curiously, the tidal wave
functions at once as a symbol of God's wrath as well as the devastation caused
by human agency inspired by political evil. The tidal wave – since it is also
described by the diver – also becomes an image of the unconscious mind, since
it is a world which exists beneath the surface, rather like the reservoir of the id
which exists beneath the ego. A central image in *La frontera* which offers counterpoint to that of the tidal wave is the statue of the founders of Chile which is
rescued at the end and becomes a point of anagnorisis, in that the statue is also
that of the 'Abrazo de Maipú'; the bringing together of the two cultures – the
Spanish and the Mapuche – rather than the destruction that Fascism has brought
about. This is in contrast to the official culture which is represented by the absurd
posing of the two detectives in front of the national flag for the 'family' snap.

The idea here is that the true history of Chile – its authentic roots – has been buried under the tidal wave of fascism.

The Diver and Politics

The diver is an idealistic character who studies the sea hoping to discover the secret of the tidal waves which threaten to destroy the village. He is the other visionary in the film, like the Mapuche Indian, because he is the only person in the village who is trying to avert the catastrophe. As it turns out, his theory is a wayward almost surreal one, since he is looking for the hole at the bottom of the ocean. The message of the film appears to be that coming close to the truth is dangerous: first of all it can lead to madness, like the diver's assistant who is first seen reeling around drunk on the raft, and then dying suddenly in the bar. His death is important because the assistant has to keep the air going or else this will lead to death. Again Ramiro becomes a central part of the search for the answer, yet even he is unable to avert it when it arrives, and the tidal wave devastates the village.

Since *La frontera* came out when Pinochet still possessed great political power (he had stepped down from the presidency in 1990 as the result of a plebiscite but was still head of the Armed Forces), it needed to make its point in a symbolic way or else it could have led to the film director's arrest. So it presents the drama and agony of modern-day Chile from a softer angle than a documentary on torture would have done. And yet, because it had to use symbolism to express its message, it therefore produces a more subtle work of art which, nevertheless, ends with a clear message of denunciation. Ramiro is filmed repeating his denunciation to the press at the conclusion of the film – the very words which got him into trouble in the first place.

Works Cited

Barnard, Timothy, 'La frontera', in *South American Cinema: A Critical Filmography 1915–1994*, eds Timothy Barnard and Peter Rist (Austin: University of Texas Press, 1996), pp. 241–2.

Box, Ben, *García Márquez: El coronel no tiene quien le escriba* (London: Grant and Cutler, 2000).

Davies, Lloyd, *Allende: La casa de los espíritus* (London: Grant and Cutler, 2000).

García Márquez, Gabriel, *La aventura de Miguel Littín clandestino en Chile* (Madrid: El País, 1986).

Hart, Stephen, *A Companion to Spanish-American Literature* (London: Tamesis, 2001).

Operé, Fernando, *Historias de la frontera: el cautiverio en la América hispánica* (México: Fondo de Cultura Económica, 2001).

O'Shaughnessy, Hugh, *Pinochet: The Politics of Torture* (New York: New York University Press, 2000).

Preston, Paul, *The Spanish Civil War 1936–1939* (London: Weidenfeld, 1986).

Shaw, Deborah, *Contemporary Cinema of Latin America: 10 Key Films* (London: Continuum, 2003), pp. 88–100.

Thomas, Hugh, *The Spanish Civil War* (Harmondsworth: Penguin, 1979).

Verdugo, Patricia, *Pinochet and the Caravan of Death* (Miami: University of Miami Press, 2001).

19

EL VIAJE (1991) THE VOYAGE, DIRECTED BY FERNANDO SOLANAS

Cast

Martín, played by Walter Quiróz
Vidala (mysterious silent girl), played by Soledad Alfaro
Celador Salas, played by Ricardo Bartis
Violeta (girlfriend in Ushuai), played by Cristian Becerra
Wayta (Peruvian girlfriend), played by Liliana Flores
Helena (Martín's mother), played by Dominique Sanda
Nicolás (Martín's father), played by Marc Berman
Paizinho, played by Chiquinho Brandao
Tito the Hopegiver, played by Carlos Carella
Américo inconcluso, played by Kike Mendive
Martín's musician friend, played by Fito Páez

Crew

Director: Fernando Solanas
Producers: Envar El Kadri, Fernando Solanas
Executive Producers: Assunção Hernandes, Djamila Olivesi, Luis Figueroa, Grazi Rade
Screenplay: Fernando Solanas
Cinematography: Félix Monti
Sound: Aníbal Libenson
Art Director: Fernando Solanas
Editors: Alberto Borella, Jacqueline Meppiel
Music: Egberto Gismonti, Astor Piazzolis, Fernando Solanas
Assistant Director: Horacio Guisado
Produced by: Cinesur (Argentina) and Les Films du Sud (France), in association with Films A 2 (France), Televisión Española (Spain), TVE S.A. (Spain), Channel Four (UK), Instituto Mexicano de Cine, IMCINE (Mexico), Ministère de la Culture et des Grands Travaux (France)

Award

Grand Prix Technique de la Commission Supérieure Technique, International Film Festival, Cannes, 1992

Plot

In the establishing scenes of the film, a 17-year-old Argentine boy, Martín, sees a number of buildings crash to the ground on what looks like a lake of ice. Set in Ushuia, in Tierra del Fuego, at the southern tip of Argentina, we witness the daily routine of a school – a Colegio Nacional Modelo – but it soon becomes clear this is no ordinary school: it starts snowing indoors, enormous framed paintings pictures of Argentina's famous statesmen of the past – Sarmiento, etc. – keep crashing to the floor, and – to cap it all – the horse from San Martín's statue is stolen. We cut to a depiction of Martín's home life; we learn that his father left when he was young – leaving him a book of advice and also a cartoon strip based on his travels. It is clear that Martín does not get on at all with his step-father. He goes to see his girlfriend. The world – amazingly – starts tipping backwards and forwards like a boat. The musician leaves to go to Buenos Aires. The school brings a new statue of San Martín on his horse but it flies away. Martín has a fight with his step-father, then finds that his girlfriend has been forced to have an abortion. He decides to leave in search of his father. He takes his bicycle on his travels, first passing by the Magellan Straits, then visiting Patagonia. He is subsequently picked up by a mad Caribbean driver called Américo Inconcluso (one of the characters from his father's comic strips). Martín sees a beautiful girl and offers to give her a lift – she accepts but says nothing, and then gets onto a bus. In order to get to Buenos Aires he must take a ride from a sailor in a boat; Buenos Aires and all the surrounding countryside are submerged under water. He sees President Frog emerging from the Casa Rosada, encouraging everyone that they will be OK, and that the country will 'float'. He arrives at his grandmother's house (which is likewise under two feet of water) and he has tea; afterwards they take the grandfather in his coffin to the Recoletos cemetery in a boat. Martín sees his friend, the musician, going past on a boat, and he then sees the buildings fall down (a repeat of the establishing shot of the movie). He finds Tito the Drummer – another character from his father's comic strip – who explains that his music is based on the human heartbeat. Martín subsequently crosses the border into Peru; he is robbed, but looked after by a family with more of a human streak. Martín is impressed by Machu Picchu, but then he notices the Foreign Debt van drive past him. He sleeps in the Sacred Temple in Cuzco. Martín continues his travels, arriving in Brazil by train, and then catching a boat in the Amazon – he is hoping to find his father at the gold mine where he heard that he had been working (these scenes were filmed in the Serra Pelada mine in Brazil). Martín starts working at the gold mine; he watches a news programme on TV in which everyone is trussed up. He learns that his father has gone to Mexico and makes his way there. He is attacked, flees and is saved by the Cuban man, Américo Inconcluso. Martin witnesses a meeting of the Organisation of Nations on their Knees. He gets on a bus and – finally – sees his father who is driving a truck carrying the Plumed Serpent.

Analytical Overview

Given that this movie was released in 1992, it must – at first glance – be seen as Solanas's take on the Quincentenary events 'celebrating' the discovery of

America. Via the journey of a seventeen-year-old young man, Solanas is offering a mythical search into the cultural identity of Latin America. So, in order to avoid the limitation of this film being simply an Argentine 'reading' of the history of Latin America Solanas makes sure to include scenes and sequences from other representative segments of Latin America – the Straits of Magellan, Patagonia, Buenos Aires, rural life in the Andes, Machu Picchu, Cuzco and the Holy Temple, the Amazon, a gold mine in Brazil, and finally Mexico. (The Caribbean is, arguably, 'covered' by virtue of the virtuoso appearance of the Cuban truck driver, who picks Martín up on two different occasions.) To strengthen this impression, Martín travels by bicycle from the southern tip to the northern tip of the continent of Latin America. Martín's journey is, in a sense, a search for Latin America's soul. Like Solanas's earlier movies, *El viaje* explores those empty gaps in the national psyche, what David William Foster calls 'the spaces in which the individual becomes lost because of the absence of codes with which a relationship of identity can be established' (Foster, p. 93).

The answer he gets from this search – though rewarding in the sense that he finally finds his father – is a rather sobering one, for it shows Latin America submerged under a flood of foreign debt (which is shown graphically by the fact that Argentina is flooded), so poor that it can only give out matches one at a time (as occurs when Martín wants to buy a box of matches in Andean Peru), or 'tied up' by its commitments to other more powerful countries (as suggested by the news programme in Brazil in which the President, his advisors and the TV reporters are all, literally, trussed up). This message – though not exactly a new one, dependency theory has, after all, been with us for a while now – is expressed in a novel way, using the rhetoric of tragicomedy.

Humour and the Absurd

It is quite likely that *El viaje* will catch the unsuspecting viewer off his or her guard. The title, the cast – even the director's reputation – suggests that this film will recount in a naturalistic way the journey undertaken around Latin America. Indeed, the establishing scenes of *El viaje* suggest that, though set at the 'end of the world' in Ushuia in Tierra del Fuego, will tell a 'straightforward' story of endurance. But, soon it becomes apparent that this is no ordinary school – it snows indoors, and enormous portraits keep falling off the walls – and, indeed, that it is an allegory of Argentina, unprotected from the 'ills' of the outside world, and a country which is in crisis, and in which a faith in national destiny is beginning to crumble. The individuals whose enormous portraits are on the wall are former presidents and intellectuals such as Faustino Domingo Sarmiento, author of *Civilización y barbarie* (1845), a crucial political text which advocated the espousal of western (that is, North-American and European) values at the expense of Amerindian values. Another individual whose 'demise' is lamented by the headmaster is Mariano Moreno, a reference to the man whose ideas led to the proclamation of independence in the southern part of the Viceroyalty of Peru, an area which would one day become Argentina. Yet these events are not – in themselves – seen as remarkable by either the pupils or teaching staff of the school; they simply deal with them in the same way that Gregory in Franz Kafka's *Metamorphosis* deals with the fact that he has changed into an insect. The allegorical level of the film is also underlined when – in a bizarre sequence redolent of Samuel Beckett's Theatre of the Absurd (Williams, pp. 343–50; Esslin, pp. 29–87) – the weather forecaster predicts the world will 'tilt', and then it truly does, as if the world had as much stability as a boat on the high seas. Once more, this event is not interpreted as in itself strange, which forces the viewer to re-evaluate his or her own notion of what is real and what is imaginary, but then leads to an awareness that the sequence is a graphic depiction of economic instability. Since nobody thinks it strange – and even the weather forecaster predicts it will happen, thereby lending the event a degree of verisimilitude – it has the internal logic of an event from a magical-realist novel.

Other events show a sense in which the film director has 'thought through' the consequences of the situation. Thus the best example of the use of an absurdist motif is the notion of Argentina being under water. The consequences of this bizarre situation are followed through: many people have started selling 'plots of water' rather than plots of land, while some (including Martín's grandmother) refuse to speculate on their property and to sell up, which leads to family arguments. Martín has tea with his grandmother under two feet of water, and she advises him to drop nothing since it will be lost for ever. (This last comment – understandable in empiric terms – alludes to a sense of how the country's debt mountain swallows up anything it touches, including its citizens' personal belongings.) The follow-through is also evident in the scene in which Martín's grandfather's body is taken to be laid to rest in the family plot at Recoletos cemetery, and he is taken there not in a hearse, but in a coffin which floats behind the boat. The Argentine President is Dr Rana (Dr Frog), and we see him (by virtue of some effective cinematographics) outside the Casa Rosada in the Plaza de Mayo, the central square of Buenos Aires) wearing huge white flippers. The irony of this image is that, unlike the rest of Argentina's citizens who will gradually sink beneath the water, as an amphibious frog, he will naturally survive. This is a very cogent and humorous image suggesting how – as many Argentines will tell you – the man in the street always sinks whereas politicians always find a way of surviving. As Solanas has pointed out in an interview: Dr Frog is 'the symbol of a governing class (. . .) frivolous and contemptuous of the people, advised by experts who plan the ruin of our democratic societies, but they offer apparently seductive recipes' (Horacio González, p. 2). Though absurd and humorous, the idea is an effective expression of popular wisdom about the two-faced nature of politicians.

Social Critique

As we have seen, the Absurd – and the humour which is elicited by the portrayal of absurd events – provides a clever means of social commentary on contemporary events. It is clearly in the sequences devoted to Argentina that the social satire bites hardest, and especially those devoted to Buenos Aires. It is important to recall that Solanas's film was released in 1992, that is, just one year after the Argentine 'peso' was pegged to the U.S. dollar, a disastrous move the consequences of which are only now becoming obvious. (The Argentine economy went into meltdown in 1999, and there are no signs that the destruction wreaked by pegging the 'peso' to the dollar, which effectively allowed the government to borrow at unsustainable levels, will be solved in the foreseeable future.) *El viaje* was, therefore, a prescient film. It would be false, however, simply to interpret the flooding which Argentina is depicted as suffering in the film as representing – in a one-for-one way – the external debt. Given that it is a symbol, the flooding can also function as an image simultaneously alluding to other 'ills' as well. The ferryman, Someone rows, who picks Martín up and takes him through Buenos Aires to his grandmother's house (surely an allusion to Charon who transports travellers across the River Styx in the mythology of classical antiquity) mentions that the floods have been here since 1973, and that they came from Chile – the reference to Pinochet's *coup d'état* which occurred on 11 September of that year is unmistakable. (The image of flooding as a representation of the ills of military dictatorship is also evident in another film of about this era, *La frontera*, by Ricardo Larraín; see chapter 18.) Solanas has therefore – in choosing a visual image which is multi-layered – been able in *El viaje* to allude to the various ills plaguing the Southern Cone which range from military dictatorships to serious economic problems.

But there are other junctures in the film in which social critique is evident. Tito the Drummer, for example, is a (perhaps over-obvious) symbol of the people. When finally waylaid by Martín, he explains that his music is the heartbeat of the people. Drums form a part of any popular demonstration in Buenos Aires's streets, and his representation as an agent of social resistance is therefore easily grasped. Solanas expands this naturalistic image to encompass not only the more poetic sense of the people's 'heartbeat', but also includes a Borgesian allusion. Since he calls himself 'Tito el memorioso', the attentive viewer is put in mind of the eponymous narrator of Jorge Luis Borges's short story, 'Funes el memorioso' from *Ficciones* (1944); though simply a philosophical conundrum in Borges's story, Tito 'el memorioso' becomes the voice-piece of the memory of the people – the vanquished and the social oppressed in particular – whose story is deliberately cast into oblivion by the authorities (as epitomised by the fate of the 'disappeared' in Argentina during the Dirty War of 1975–1983).

Another event which draws attention to the central theme of External Debt is the External Debt truck which arrives in the Andes and then demands contributions from the peasants through its loudspeakers. This is a clever scene, since we can only laugh at something so absurd, yet there is no denying that the idea has a deeper truth. The External Debt **is** paid by the citizens of Third World countries, and falls most heavily on those least able to pay. The Brazilian sequence explores a similar idea as that in the Argentine section of the film. Though not as suggestive or subtle as the latter, the Brazilian sequence has a high level of slapstick comedy, particular those scenes in which the President of Brazil is seen trussed up, and advising all Brazilians to 'tighten up their belts by a few more notches'. The complacency of the media in this process is suggested by the way in which we see two TV commentators fastening up their belts, smiling at the viewers as they do so. Though using a humorous scene, Solanas is making a serious point about the complicity of the mass media with the government in Brazil. Slapstick comedy is also provided by the sequence about the conference attended by representatives of 'Naciones Arrodilladas' (Nations on their Knees), an allusion to sycophancy which operates at the meeting of the United Nations. The implication is that some of the countries which attend have no choice but to kowtow to the more affluent nations. That Solanas's critique has a hard edge to it is suggested by that the fact he was a victim of grievous bodily harm as a result of his anti-government views. As Philip Strick points out: 'Fernando Solanas's outspoken contempt for Carlos Menem's administration in Argentina nearly cost him his life – an assassination attempt confined him to a wheelchair for most of the post-production on *The Voyage*' (Strick, p. 54).

The Symbolism of the Search

El viaje is at once a Bildungsroman as well as a movie about a search; in Solanas's own words, the film is 'a long meditation on the journey of self-discovery, the learning journey of an adolescent' (Horacio González, p. 2). True to the Bildungsroman the young man finally achieves some enlightenment at the conclusion, since he finds his father, and – the film suggests – has his various questions answered. (Though there is the possibility, given the rest of the film, that this is a spoof Bildungsroman.) The search for the father-figure can be interpreted on a number of levels. That it is a search for national identity is clear from the fact that the search begins at the point that San Martín's statue is whisked away into the skies. As Strick points out, 'it seems more than coincidental that Martín himself appears named after the founding father of Argentine independence, José de San Martín, whose statue Solanas dismissively blows away on the wind, an unreliable construction of cardboard' (Strick, p. 9). Martín's search, though, is not purely for the nineteenth-century individual who liberated the southern part of American continent; like his friends, Martín has little time – as we see in the opening sequences of the film – for the history lessons about Argentina's independence, for the ritual glorification of names such as Puerreydón and Moreno. That this film is patently not about that kind of search is made abundantly clear by the fact that all the portraits in the portrait gallery are periodically crashing noisily to the ground; the House of the Nation (based in real life on the Warnes Building, started in 1955 as a children's hospital which was never finished, and torn down in 1991 because of political and legal problems) is in a dilapidated state. As Ismail Xavier suggests, *El viaje* attempts to 'reach encompasssing views of contemporary experience or of politics in certain regions through overt allegorical strategies' (Xavier, p. 350).

Martín's search is for a trans-national Latin American cultural identity, as suggested by the fact that his journey takes him through Argentina, Peru, Brazil,

the Caribbean and Mexico. Its trans-national character is underlined by the fact
that the film uses Quechua, Portuguese, (Welsh) English, and highly differenti-
ated varieties of Spanish (Argentine, Andean and Cuban) at different points. It
is striking that – having rejected all the examples of external European and
western influence in Latin America – Martín should embrace his father and
therefore become part of the latter's search: Martín's father is driving a truck
which is carrying an enormous image of the Aztec God, Quetzalcoatl, the
Plumed Serpent, thereby in a sense becoming cyclical (Pérez Murillo and
Fernández Fernández, p. 360). The main moral of the film – it would appear –
is that Latin America should search for its cultural destiny not in espousing
western values but by delving into its Amerindian past, epitomised by
Quetzalcoatl.

   Though his search is above all for a cultural identity, it is accompanied by
the sub-plot of love. Women – though they all different – play an important
role in Martín's quest. The first love of his life – the girl he makes love to in
Ushuia – is the most important. His only feeling of happiness – expressed as
love and a oneness with nature – occurs when his girlfriend tells him she is
pregnant with his child. But this euphoria is destroyed when his girlfriend's
father forces her to have an abortion, and then bans him from coming to the
house. There are others – the woman he makes love to in the hammock in
Brazil, the young girl he kisses in the Sacred Temple in Cuzco – but the most
enigmatic is the girl that he sees twice but who refuses to talk to him: first when
he lets her ride on his bike, and later when he sees her in a dilapidated house
in Buenos Aires just before she gets onto a boat. The various women that he
meets form an enigmatic sub-text within the film, ensuring its haunting quality. Deborah Shaw has pointed out, though, that the search is couched in masculinist terms, and that the film, furthermore, 'fails to adequately represent the
female characters' (Shaw, p. 109).

The Metatextual Level

A metatextual level is provided in *El viaje* by the characters whom Martín meets
on his voyage, and who are recognisably from the comic strip that his father left
for him when he went off to 'find himself' in Mexico. In what is in some respects
the anagnorisis scene of the novel, Martín meets Tito the Drummer who – though
straight from his father's comic strip – is a real person who explains the role he
plays in social resistance movements. Américo Inconcluso is also a very important figure in this respect; in an interview Solanas described him as a 'grotesque,
pathetic and poetic' character, for whom he coined the term 'grothetic' (Horacio
González, interview, p. 2). Soon after Martín has got into his cab, he says:
'You're in my father's comic strip', which is countered by the former's comment:
'I invented your father's comic strip.' The important point here is that the film is
playing with levels of reality, leaving unsolved the question as to whether the
people Martín is meeting during his travels are real or inventions of his father's
fantasy.

Works Cited

Esslin, Martin, *The Theatre of the Absurd* (Harmondsworth: Penguin, 1977).

Foster, David William, *Contemporary Argentine Cinema* (Minnesota: University of Missouri Press, 1992).

González, Horacio, 'Interview with Fernando Solanas' (May 1992), Video cover [Tartan Videos], pp. 1–2.

Hart, Stephen, 'Solanas', in *An Encyclopedia of Latin American Culture*, ed. Peter Standish (Detroit: Manley Publishers, 1995), pp. 254–5.

King, John, *Magical Reels: A History of Cinema in Latin America* (London: Verso, 1990).

Pérez Murillo, María Dolores, and David Fernández Fernández (eds), *La memoria filmada: América Latina a través de su cine* (Madrid: IELPA, 2002).

Shaw, Deborah, *Contemporary Cinema of Latin America: 10 Key Films* (London: Continuum, 2003), pp. 105–20.

Strick, Philip, 'El viaje', *Sight and Sound* (September 1993), 54–5.

Williams, Raymond, *Drama from Ibsen to Brecht* (Harmondsworth: Penguin, 1978).

Xavier, Ismail, 'Historical Allegory', in *A Companion to Film Theory*, eds Toby Miller and Robert Stam (Oxford: Blackwell, 2004), pp. 333–62.

20

FRESA Y CHOCOLATE (STRAWBERRY AND CHOCOLATE, 1993), DIRECTED BY TOMÁS GUTIÉRREZ ALEA

Cast

Diego, played by Jorge Perugorría
David, played by Vladimir Cruz
Nancy, played by Mirta Ibarra
Germán, played by Joel Angelino

Crew

Director: Tomás Gutiérrez Alea and Juan Carlos Tabío
Director's assistant: Mayra Segura
Screenplay: Senel Paz
Photography: Mario García Joya
Cameras: Mario García Joya and Ernesto Granados
Music: José María Vitier
Sound: Germinal Hernández
Editing: Miriam Talavera, Osvaldo Donatién
Set: Fernando Pérez O'Reilly
Costume Design: Miriam Dueñas
Make-up: Graciela Crossas
Producer: Miguel Mendoza

Awards

Silver Bear, XXIV International Film Festival, Berlin, 1993
First Prize, Director (Tomás Gutiérrez Alea), Best Actor (Jorge Perugorría), Best
Female Backing Role (Mirta Ibarra), International Film Festival, Havana, 1993
Goya Award, Best Foreign Film in Spanish, Film Academy, Spain, 1995
Nominee, Best Foreign Film, Film Academy, Hollywood, 1995

Plot

A young man, David Alvarez, takes a young woman, Vivian, to a brothel for sex.
She complains he's like all men and interested in only one thing, which shames
him, and he agrees to wait until they are married. The young girl gets married, but

not to David; she gets married to an older man. While having his lunch David is chatted up by an older man, Diego, who invites him back to his apartment where he tries to seduce him. Vivian tells David that she would like an affair with him, but he refuses. David tells his friend, Miguel, a stalwart member of the Young Communist Youth Movement, about Diego, and Miguel tries to persuade him to shop Diego. Nancy, the member of the local Vigilante group – and also a prostitute – living in the same building block, slashes her wrists, and Diego takes her to hospital. David gives blood for Nancy's operation. David goes to see Diego to find out about the art exhibition he is organising. Diego then finds out that Germán's exhibition – because of its anti-revolutionary content – has been banned. He has a furious argument with Germán, and the latter ends up smashing all his art exhibits. Diego sends a letter complaining about the decision to ban the exhibition, an unwise act since – as we find out later – he loses his job. David gives some of his poems to Diego to look at; Diego pulls them to pieces, saying they are simply propaganda. Diego holds a Lezama Lima meal for David, and David sleeps with Nancy. Diego decides he has no choice but to leave Cuba. The film ends with David giving Diego a hug before he leaves for the United States.

Analytical Overview

Fresa y chocolate caused quite a stir when it first came out in Cuba since it treated a hitherto taboo subject – homosexuality. In Cuba the film was so popular that 'impatient crowds broke down a cinema's doors to see it' (Davies, p. 177); it showed continuously in Havana for eight months (Chanan, p. 11), and 'became the first Cuban film to be nominated for an Oscar as Best Foreign Film; the year before it won first prize at the Berlin Film Festival' (Chanan, p. 9). The film is based on Senel Paz's novel, *El lobo, el bosque y el hombre nuevo* (The Wolf, the Woods, and the New Man), published in 1991, the year after it had been awarded the prestigious Juan Rulfo Prize. Alea read the novel, saw its filmic potential, and he asked Paz to write a script based on it (Schroeder, p. 109). As Schroeder points out, the film adds two new elements to the original plot: (i) the character of Nancy (according to Mirta Ibarra, who played Nancy in the film, the idea to include her part came from Senel Paz himself; Davies, p. 179), and (ii) Germán's exhibition (Schroeder, p. 110), but there are other departures from the original. Just as interesting are the more subtle differences. As one might expect, events which are merely recounted in the novella – either in David's monologue or which arise in conversation with Diego – are fleshed out as visual narrative in the film. Thus, while, in *El lobo, el bosque y el hombre nuevo*, David simply mentions that he is no longer in a relationship with Vivian (Paz, p. 9, p. 11) this event is given more concrete visual form in *Fresa y chocolate* via the depiction of David's disastrous visit to a brothel with Vivian, his witnessing of her marriage to a safer bet, and her offer to him – after she has got married – that they continue to be lovers. Likewise the reason for Diego's decision to go into exile which arises in conversation in the novella ('Es por la exposición de Germán. (. . .) Reconozco que me excedí en la defensa de las obras'; Paz, p. 49) is expanded in the film to become a central cog in the plot: we witness the fraught argument between Germán and Diego, and we see Diego write the letter, both of which are scenes which have been added to the screenplay.

There are other differences between novella and film, however, which go beyond simple techniques of dramatisation involved in the scriptwriting process. Unlike the film, the novella describes, in graphic detail, Diego's first sexual experience with a basketball player in the shower (Paz, pp. 23–5), it depicts Diego's attempts to create a sexual intimacy with David ('Cuéntame algo, viejo. Tu primera experiencia sexual, a qué edad empezaste a venir, cómo son tus sueños eróticos (. . .). ¿Y por qué (. . .) ahora que somos como hermanos, no permites que te vea desnudo?'; Paz, pp. 41–2), and it has a lengthy description about the different types of gay men (the 'homosexuales', who are socially responsible individuals, the 'maricones' who balance their social responsibilities with their sexual orientation, the 'locas' who are sexually obsessed, the 'locas de carroza' who are camp and deliberately defy social convention, and the 'picha-dulce' who are extremely lascivious; Paz, pp. 33–7). These gay elements are erased from the film and, as mentioned above, a new sexual cog is placed in the machine – the heterosexual relationship between David and Nancy. Just as important, perhaps, the figure of authority to whom David initially reports Diego's suspicious activities, Ismael, is presented negatively as an ironic, condescending individual (Paz, p. 31).

There are other indications that the subversiveness of the novella's political message has been downplayed. *El lobo, el bosque y el hombre nuevo* ends with David voicing quite defiantly his message of acceptance of Diego's perspective: 'y entonces le dije (. . .) que al próximo Diego que se atravesara en mi camino lo defendería a capa y espada, aunque nadie me comprendiera (. . .) porque si entendía bien las cosas, eso era luchar por un mundo mejor para ti, pionero, y para mí' (Paz, p. 59). The fact that Diego has been presented as a pioneer is not lost on the reader, given the highly fraught relationship between Cuban exiles and Cuban nationals residing in Cuba. David's symbolic acceptance of Diego's Weltanschauung is rammed home by the last sentence of the novella – 'Porque había chocolate, pero pedí fresa' (p. 59) – in which he re-enacts Diego's original act of defiance in the restaurant when they first met ('habiendo chocolate, había pedido fresa'; Paz, p. 10). In the film, of course, this central image finds its way into the new title, with the original title of the novella (*The Wolf, the Wood and the New Man*) being discarded. The new title is much better and encapsulates the flavour of the film, but it does thereby downplay the political message of the original title, where the wood logically stands for Cuba, the new man for Diego and his new disciple, David, and – although it is not made explicit – the wolf must surely be interpreted to represent Ismael and, by extension, Fidel Castro. In the film these rather uncomfortable associations are removed and the discipleship between Diego and David is transmuted into a (touching) hug – the still which was used to promote the film. Some critics, such as Emilio Bejel (p. 70), have expressed unease about the way the film is resolved in a heterosexual direction; others, such as Enrico Mario Santí, have seen the resolution of the film more in

6. *Fresa y Chocolate*: Diego and David Hug

terms of a political 'reconciliation' (Mario Santí). It is clear, nevertheless, that the anti-regime message of *El lobo, el bosque y el hombre nuevo* – both in terms of its portrayal of the figure of authority, as well as its depiction of gay sexuality – has been toned down in the film version, this despite the fact that Senel Paz sees himself as a non-political writer, as he stressed in an interview (Resik, p. 88).

Cuba as a Split Identity

The main idea behind the film is the sense in which there are two types of Cuba which are being compared to each other. It is as if Cuba were at a crossroads, and needed to decide what its future holds. The film came out in 1993 at precisely the time when Cuba was beginning to experience the beginning of a deep and lasting crisis, as a result of the fall of the Berlin Wall (1989), Perestroika (in the early 1990s), and the decision taken by the Soviet Union to pull its funding of the Cuban Republic after 1992. The crisis really began to bite in 1993 and 1994 (at which point Fidel Castro decided to lure tourism to Cuba in order to remedy the national deficit), and so Gutiérrez Alea's film was very opportune. Despite its veneer of gentle humour, *Fresa y chocolate* is an anguished film which addresses the collapse of Cuba's national identity in the context of the post-Cold War era.

Two opposing styles of being are presented in the film, and they border on the caricaturesque. On the one hand we have David, the young member of the Communist Party, a believer in the aims of the Revolution, convinced that the United States is ready to pounce on Cuba at the first opportunity, a university student who is an idealist though not particularly aware of what is going on in the rest of the world (as his lack of knowledge about products such as whisky, and his ignorance of literary figures such as Mario Vargas Llosa and John Donne suggest), a believer in dialectical Marxism, a heterosexual looking for true love. On the other hand we have Diego, a tortured artist, a thinker, a man who is disillusioned with the Communist regime, fascinated by the foreign and the exotic, a man who likes drinking tea from India in the English way, out of French cups, or drinking Scotch, while reading Russian novels, and who is religious, as well as a fierce individualist, and – to boot – gay.

The main idea behind the film concerns the way in which these two apparently very contradictory notions of Cubanness are eventually brought together – here epitomised by the hug between Diego and David at the end of the film. Both Diego and David in a sense come nearer to each other politically, though this political rapprochement is represented in terms of a physical attraction. Everyone, it seems, is in love with David. Diego, as the older, gay man, has completely fallen for David's innocent ways and his good looks. Nancy is also in love with him, and even prays to the African deities to allow her to keep him for just one year. Vivian offers him love, and sex, even though she has recently got married. Even Miguel wants to keep him for himself and the Communist Party, and even accuses him of being a faggot when he senses that he has begun to lose him towards the end of the film. His emotions are more like those of a spurned lover than a work colleague. In this sense we can argue that David in a sense represents Cuba, and all of these different aspects of Cuba – the artistic gay, the conventional young woman who plays safe, the ageing prostitute, and the Communist youth – are 'in love' with David, and want him for their own, exclusively.

Symbolism

The most important piece of symbolism is that of the use of physical love to stand for different political ideologies, suggesting that people live different life options, which include politics, with the central body, as suggested above, being David's. David is a symbol of the body politic of Cuba in the post-Perestroika era. The other important symbolic image which weaves its way through the filmic text is that of food, which is captured in the film's title, thereby reminding viewers of its centrality to the film's message. At the beginning of the film we see Diego trying to seduce David by showing him what he can 'afford' to eat. (In fact it is never clear where he gets his money from.) A chocolate and strawberry ice-cream for Cuba in the early 1990s is a symbol of the profligacy of the west; not one but two ice-creams, and this in a country where ice-cream is too expensive for most people to eat. Notice that, at the time, David is eating frugally – a bowl of soup. This image continues when Diego offers David tea, whisky, and finally the Lezama Lima meal, a symbol of decadence: Lezama Lima was an obscure, Symbolist poet, the opposite of the more political, overt, and anti-art for art's sake posture of a writer such as José Martí, whose work has been canonized extensively in modern-day Cuba.

Indeed, the meal itself is based on that depicted in chapter 7 of Lezama Lima's *Paradiso* (1966) (Paz, p. 44). This is, in a sense, one of the more subtle pointers in the film: the meal stands for the narcissistic art-for-art's-sake of Lezama Lima rather than the political utilitarian stance favoured by Martí (who was promoted by Castro as a paradigmatic symbol of Cuba's revolutionary identity) – whose warning is read by Diego as he puts his letter in the letter box, thereby sealing his fate.

Gayness

It is no secret that Gutiérrez Alea was gay. At the same time it has never been a secret that Gutiérrez Alea was proud of his revolutionary credentials. Fidel Castro was happy to promote Gutiérrez Alea as a central plank of his ideological outreach in the 1960s, when he came to have a central role in the establishment and day-to-day running of the Cuban Film Institute. So, we are bound to ask – knowing the anti-gay credentials of Castro – if Gutiérrez Alea in this film was making an anti-Castro statement. This was certainly the view taken by the author of the film preview which appeared in *Variety*, which read as follows: 'Filled with malicious swipes against the Castro regime, *Fresa y chocolate* is a provocative but very humane comedy about sexual opposites and, with proper handling, could attract the *Wedding Banquet* crowd in cinemas worldwide' (quoted in Smith, p. 81). Castro, indeed, was asked if he liked the film but he did not comment (West, p. 19). On one level, then, the film can be interpreted as an apology for the freedoms of the West. Diego's interest in John Donne and Mario Vargas Llosa, his taste for tea and whisky, are not presented as reprehensible in the film; indeed, it is David's naïveté that is more susceptible of criticism. But it is important to realise that Gutiérrez Alea, throughout his career, has always been asking hard questions of the regime, and indeed has never shied away from criticising certain reprehensible aspects of that regime, although it has always been in the sense of constructive criticism rather than outright attack. As Stephen Wilkinson suggests, the film 'seems to be making the point that Cuba and Revolution are very much the less for having lost the contribution that figures like Diego could make' (Wilkinson, p. 22).

It is important to underline that the perspective engendered by the film, and particularly its dénouement, is distinctively Cuban. Thus, when Diego emigrates at the conclusion of the film we are not left with a sense of liberation (which is how this film might have ended had it been written by one of the hard-line Miami Cuban-Americans). Rather we are left with a sense of failure, a yearning that Cuba can be changed to allow people like Diego to stay, rather than a joyful acceptance of emigration. As Catherine Davies suggests, Diego is 'clearly the catalyst for change and represents the views of many young Cubans today; he is therefore recognised within the collective trauma, and, as in all successful therapies, once recognised and understood, once brought under the control of language, he is no longer of any use' (Davies, p. 179). David has learned an important lesson, but he will continue to live in Cuba, perhaps with Nancy, perhaps with someone else. Indeed, the perspective in this scene, as throughout the film, as Deborah Shaw has pointed out, 'is that of David' (Shaw, p. 22). It is for this reason that we cannot call *Fresa y chocolate* an anti-Castro film. Rather it is an honest look at many of the almost unbearable strains that Cuba was suffering during the first half of the 1990s, and, to some extent, still is. It is also important to point out that it is not a pro-gay film. Alea agreed with Senel Paz, the screenplay writer, that 'el tema de la película no es tanto el homosexualismo como la intolerancia' (Évora, p. 53).

An analysis of the key events of the film suggests that the roadmap to gay love is consistently blocked. Though much more sophisticated than David, Diego is presented in the first scene in exaggeratedly queer terms; sucking on his strawberry and chocolate, while looking longingly at David, he epitomises campness. His homosexuality is also presented at various junctures as if it were a displaced feminity with which at times it is fused; like Nancy, Diego is emotional, and places his faith in religious icons (which, it should be noted, are transculturated icons, based on the fusion of the Afro-Cuban maternal deity, Ochum, and the Catholic Virgen del Cobre [Copper Virgin]; Pérez Murillo and Fernández Fernández, p. 265). Lastly, and here the gay agenda – if ever there was one – is upturned, the Lezama Lima banquet leads to David's seduction, not by Diego, but instead by Nancy. Diego, as the film suggests, is complicit in this arrangement, despite the love he ostensibly feels for David. Gay sexuality has been replaced by feminine sexuality. In an important essay on the film, Paul Julian Smith has argued that, 'as the film develops, the female characters prove to share a slippery, supplementary status: at once additions to and substitutes for the "red queen" Diego' (Smith, p. 89). It is in this sense that homosexuality is reduced to a phantom presence which is always off-stage. As Smith further indicates, 'by narrativizing explicitly, if discreetly, the oppression of homosexuals in Cuba, the films stages a domesticated mise-en-scene in which the unspeakable horrors of the other scene (out of shot, behind the door) are allowed to emerge into visibility, but only on condition that they do not trouble the heterosexual spectator' (Smith, p. 88). The heterosexual normativisation of homosexuality appears to be elicited triumphantly by the final, sexless hug of the film between Diego and David. But there is one discordant note in this apparently seamless heterosexualisation of gay sexuality, and this is the scene in the shower in which Miguel – presented as the macho, homophobic communist – who, in a gesture which seems very much out of character, pats David on the buttocks. Though this is the only point at which a same-sex gesture is hinted at, it is nevertheless significant that it should be initiated by the character whose actions and words up until this point suggest he is ruled by homosexual panic. This surely must be seen as a deliberate wink at the viewer as well as a humorously ironic jibe at sexual intolerance. Smith has argued that the 'pervasive naturalism' of the film's cinematic language, though at first puzzling, should be seen as a direct result of its timidity in addressing the concept of gay love: the 'mediocrity of *Fresa y chocolate*'s technique (its preference for medium shots, reverse angles and continuity editing) is thus consistent with its ideological project in which the (unexamined) pro-filmic object of homosexuality must be bound within the frame and cannot be allowed to transform existing modes of perception or simply accompany the camera on a journey whose aim is not mapped out in advance' (p. 89; for further discussion of this point, see Smith's more forthright criticism of the film in his *Sight and Sound* review, 'The Language of Strawberry').

The assimilation of gayness within the feminine – Eduardo González has referred to the 'feminization' of the plot that occurs in this film (González, p. 73) – is clearly important for the way *Fresa y chocolate* is ultimately interpreted. As Catherine Davies suggests, 'the film encourages the Cuban audience (men and women) to identity with a suicidal, confused woman, the female embodiment of a nation about to self-destruct. Cuba is presented as the reformed whore, saved by the Communist prude who has been taught a lesson in pleasure, aesthetics and, above all, Cubanidad (national cultural identity) by a non-assimilable gay' (Davies, p. 179). It is clear, given the various ways in which *Fresa y chocolate* can be interpreted, that it offers the viewer a probing insight into the ambiguous tensions which were dividing Cuba in the early 1990s.

Works Cited

Bejel, Emilio, '*Strawberry and Chocolate*: Coming out of the Cuban Closet', *The South Atlantic Quarterly*, 96.1 (1997), 65–82.

Chanan, Michael, 'Cuban Cinema in the 1990s', in *Changing Reels: Latin American Cinema Against the Odds*, ed. Bob Rix (Leeds: Trinity and All Saints College, 1998), pp. 1–15.

Davies, Catherine, 'Recent Cuban Fiction Films: Identification, Interpretation, Disorder', *Bulletin of Latin American Research*, 15.2 (1996), 177–92.

Évora, José Antonio, *Tomás Gutiérrez Alea* (Madrid: Cátedra, 1996).

González, Eduardo, 'La rama dorada y el árbol deshojado: reflexiones sobre *Fresa y chocolate* y sus antecedentes', *Estudios Iberoamérica y el cine*, in eds Francisco Lasarte & Guido Podestá (Amsterdam: Rodopi, 1996), pp. 65–78.

Paz, Senel, *El lobo, el bosque y el hombre nuevo* (Mexico City: Ediciones Era, 1991).

Pérez Murillo, María Dolores, and David Fernández Fernández (eds), *La memoria filmada: América Latina a través de su cine* (Madrid: IELPA, 2002).

Resik, Magda, 'Interview with Senel Paz', *The South Atlantic Quarterly*, 96.1 (1997), 83–93.

Santí, Enrico Mario, '*Fresa y chocolate*: The Rhetoric of Cuban Reconciliation', *Modern Language Notes*, 113 (1998), 407–25.

Schroeder, Paul A., *Tomás Gutiérrez Alea: The Dialectics of a Filmmaker* (London: Routledge, 2002).

Shaw, Deborah, *Contemporary Cinema of Latin America: 10 Key Films* (London: Continuum, 2003), pp. 20–30.

Smith, Paul Julian, 'The Language of Strawberry', *Sight and Sound*, 4.12 (1994), 31–3.

—— '*Fresa y chocolate*: Cinema as Guided Tour', in *Visions Machines* (London: Verso, 1996), pp. 81–98.

West, Dennis, 'Strawberry and Chocolate, Ice Cream and Tolerance: Interviews with Tomás Gutiérrez Alea and Juan Carlos Tabío', *Cineaste*, 21.1–2 (1995), 16–20.

Wilkinson, Stephen, 'Homosexuality and the Repression of Intellectuals in *Fresa y chocolate* and *Máscaras*', *Bulletin of Latin American Research*, 18.1 (1999), 17–33.

21

COMO AGUA PARA CHOCOLATE
(LIKE WATER FOR CHOCOLATE, 1993), DIRECTED BY ALFONSO ARAU, BASED ON THE NOVEL OF THE SAME NAME BY LAURA ESQUIVEL

Main Cast

Tita, played by Lumi Cavazos
Doña María Elena, played by Regina Tome
Pedro Muzquiz, played by Rodolfo Arias
Chencha, played by Pilar Aranda
John, played by Mario Iván Martínez

Crew

Screenplay: Laura Esquivel
Music: Leo Brower
Setting: Denisse Pizzini, Marco Antonio Arteaga, and Mauricio Aguinaco
Editing: Carlos Bolado, Francisco Chiu
Photography: Emmanuel Lubeski, Steve Berstein
Producer: Alfonso Arau
Director: Alfonso Arau

Awards

Winner, eleven awards (all categories), Mexican Academy of Motion Pictures, 1993
Nominee, Golden Globe, 1993
Nominee, British Academy Award, 1993

Plot

Esperanza, Tita's niece, recalls the birth of her aunt, Tita, to doña Elena on the kitchen table in Rio Grande in 1895. Doña Elena's husband, Juan, dies of a heart attack when he discovers his daughter, Gertrudis, is not really his. Pedro Muzquiz asks to marry Tita but doña Elena refuses, and offers him her older sister, Rosaura, whom he accepts. Tita's tears fall into the batter of the wedding cake, and Pedro and Rosaura's wedding ends in chaos, tears and mass vomiting.

Gertrudis runs off with a *villista* during the Mexican Revolution. Rosaura gives birth to a child, Roberto. A North-American doctor, Dr John Brown, falls in love with Tita and offers her marriage. Rosaura and Pedro go to San Antonio where the child dies. Tita is nursed back to health by Chencha. Tita accepts Dr Brown's offer of marriage. Back in Mexico Chencha is raped by some revolutionaries and doña Elena is killed. Rosaura has a second child, Esperanza (the narrator). Pedro and Tita become amorous. Doña Elena's ghost comes back and curses her. Pedro is severely burnt out of doña Elena's desire for revenge from beyond the grave. Tita and Rosaura argue about Pedro. 1934: Esperanza, Rosaura's daughter, is getting married to Alex Brown, Dr Brown's son. Flashback to Rosaura's gruesome death (by flatulence). Pedro and Tita finally consummate their love. Pedro dies, and the bedroom explodes into flames. Esperanza explains how the story of her aunt's love was found among the ashes.

Analytical Overview: The Novel

Set on an isolated ranch in northern Mexico near the Texas border, *Like Water for Chocolate* (1989, trans. 1993), has the Mexican Revolution (1911–1919) as the main historical backdrop to the story. The authoritarian Mamá Elena offers Pedro Muzquiz Rosaura, her eldest daughter, in marriage rather than her younger daughter, Tita, whom Pedro really loves, but who is destined to look after Elena until the latter dies. Pedro agrees to marry Rosaura just to be close to Tita. Gertrudis, the second of the three daughters, runs off to join the Revolution. Pedro's and Tita's love is finally allowed to blossom after Rosaura dies (she suffers from bad breath and an appalling case of flatulence) and her daughter, Esperanza, leaves home in order to marry the son of a wealthy American doctor, John Brown. The novel is structured like a soap, and is reminiscent of the Mexican 'telenovela' in its reference to the next episode once one has finished. When asked in an interview why people read novels, Laura Esquivel said it was when 'there is some truth, something real and, above all, something emotional' (Smith), and this certainly applies to *Like Water for Chocolate*. Kristine Ibsen has argued that, although on the surface the novel appears to mimic popular forms such as the telenovela, it also 'appropriates' and 'challenges' the genre at the same time, a point which is also applicable to the film (Ibsen).

One of the strengths of the novel, indeed, is that it touches on such a variety of contemporary themes and issues. It shows the ways in which private and social spaces inter-relate and sometimes collide (as when Gertrudis runs off with an officer in Villa's army). It delves into the thorny issues of U.S.-Mexico relations, particularly in the Platonic love-affair between Tita and John Brown. It has delightfully humorous episodes, as when an illiterate soldier, Treviño, tries to cook, or when John Brown and Tita dine with Brown's deaf aunt. A major focus is given to the tensions within the family unit, which include repression (Elena's prohibition of Tita's desire to marry), and jealousy (Rosaura and Tita spend most of the novel fighting over the same man, Pedro). One of the more intriguing things about the novel is the skeleton in the cupboard, namely, the fact that Gertrudis's

7. *Como agua para chocolate*: Tita's Gaze

father is a mulatto and not Elena's husband (whom we witness dying of a heart attack early on in the film when he learns the truth about Gertrudis).

Like Water for Chocolate is, in essence, a feminine counter-version of the Mexican Revolution, offering a kitchen-eye's view of those turbulent years, which is at odds with the masculinist rhetoric of the history books with their emphasis on battles and the struggle for civic power. As Esquivel has pointed out in an interview: 'the kitchen, to me, is the most important part of the house. It is a source of knowledge that generates life and pleasure' (Smith). The most striking characteristic of the novel, as its title suggests, is the use of food as a metaphor for the human emotions. There are various examples of this: Tita's tears which drop into the cake being prepared for Rosaura and Pedro's wedding meal produce a fit of vomiting in the guests, and Tita's blood mixed up with rose petals, when added to the quails, produces an aphrodisiac reaction in those who consume it, an idea which is repeated in the last chapter of the novel when Tita makes 'chile en nogada' (one of the many 'old family recipes' in the novel; see interview) and unleashes an orgy of the senses. While the link between food and sex is a traditional one, *Like Water for Chocolate* manages to extend this association in unexpected ways. Perhaps the best illustration of this occurs when Tita has to sing to the beans to make them cook. In a house, so popular knowledge suggests, where there have been arguments, the food is 'annoyed' and therefore will not allow itself to be cooked. Most intriguing of all is the way in which the emotions are depicted as emanating from the body like a cloud, influencing everything in their path. Such is the cloud of rose perfume which emanates from Gertrudis's body and attracts Juan, the *villista*, to her, at which point, following a Romantic stereotype, they sail off into the sunset on a horse, copulating as they go, as well as the anger which invades Tita when she has a tiff with Pedro. Love is, of course, central to this novel. As Esquivel has suggested in an interview: 'For me, love is the most important force. It moves the universe' (Smith). Yet, it should be said that the love being referred to here is a sexual love; 'like water for chocolate', 'in Mexican slang (. . .) often implies the height of as-yet-unfulfilled sexual longing, particularly in women' (Tenenbaum, p. 158).

Esquivel has mentioned that her two most important influences were García Márquez and Juan Rulfo (Smith). So it is not surprising to note the strong affiliation that her work presents with magic realism. Her novel is, true to the magic-realist formula, full of ghosts. Tita sees John Brown's Indian grandmother, when recovering from an illness, and she is haunted by the spirit of her mother, Mamá Elena. Often Esquivel will present fantastic events as if they were part of everyday life, including those already mentioned such as tears in food producing botulism, or food producing sexual frenzy, or others such as Tita suddenly lactating and therefore being able to feed her nephew, and people dying of love (this is essentially what happened to Tita and Pedro at the conclusion of the novel). Perhaps the best example of magic realism occurs in the opening scene of the book. Tita is born in floods of tears, which leads (once they have evaporated) to mounds of salt being deposited in the kitchen. Rather than declaring the event a 'miracle' they simply decide to use the salt in their cooking. They now have a seemingly endless supply. In a simple scene, the magical is rendered real. Written from a feminine perspective, – its thesis is essentially that women are closer to food, love and life – *Like Water For Chocolate* was able to give a clever, feminine, and humorous, twist to the genre of magic realism (for further discussion, see below).

From Novel to Film

The first point to make is that the film does not diverge in any significant way from the novel, as Claude Potvin has pointed out (Potvin, p. 56). The dialogue is retained almost intact, the ordering of the narrative events is retained, and there are only minor changes. Unlike in film versions of literary classics such as Robert Louis Stevenson's *The Strange Case of Dr Jeckyll and Mr Hyde* and Bram Stoker's *Dracula*, where the differences between novel and film are quite substantial (see Lehman and Luhr, pp. 198–217), in Alfonso Arau's version of his then wife's novel, the changes are minimal. This is in some ways because the original novel is written like a screenplay. It has short cinematic background information, focuses very much on dialogue and has a smooth, forward-propelled plot containing clearly-drawn characters. As Carlos Arau has pointed out, indeed, his aim was to put Laura Esquivel's novel on the screen rather than – in the manner of an *auteur* – produce a new cinematic version of the original novel. His decision was a good one. The film *Como agua para chocolate* was a box-office hit in Mexico (it was screened continuously in Mexico City in six movie theatres for six months; Shaw, p. 37). In the seven months following its February 1993 release alone, it had grossed $6.1 million, which was the most ever by a Latin American film (Tenenbaum, p. 157). It was also an international hit as well, grossing $21.6 million in the U.S. (Shaw, p. 37).

While it was a great hit with audiences in Latin America, the United States and Europe, it was not always such a hit with the reviewers. As the Mexican critic Tomás Pérez Turrent rather memorably put it, 'the response to the film by the world public was "chocolate" while the response of the critics was "water"' (quoted in Wu, p. 184). Deborah Shaw, for example, has argued that *Como agua para chocolate* 'reinvents the past in such a way as to negate social history' (Shaw, p. 39). It harks back, she suggests, to a pre-feminist, pre-classist era. For his part, John Kraniauskas has suggested that the film 'retreats from the masculinized terrain of hig politics and the battlefield and concentrates our attention on the so-called private sphere of a household run by woman' (Kraniauskas, p. 42). Harmony Wu has observed that the ideology underlying the film is conservative, since, 'even in a magically reimagined past, the white patriarchy dominates' (Wu, p. 190). Why has there been so much controversy about this film? we may ask. The answer surely lies in the expectations that each viewer brings to the film, and which will have much to do with the sense of where Latin American cinema is going. If a critic favours the *cinema novo* of the 1960s, as well as the more politicised films of the 1970s and 1980s then *Como agua para chocolate* will seem like a sell-out to the values and techniques of the Hollywood blockbuster. But, surely, it can be argued that, by the end of the 1980s, the European-style Neo-Realism and French New Wave innovative film had run its course, and the only way forward was to look elsewhere for a film idiom to use. Perhaps it is better to see it as a first step before the creation of a new Latin American filmic tradition, one which is able to assimilate European cinema as much as Hollywood, but which is always able to offer an autochthonous vision. This it mainly does through its portrayal of reality as magical.

Magical Realism

The secret of magical realism is to depict reality objectively but with a magical dimension. The paradigm of magical-realist art is the photograph of a ghost, that is, an art which simulates the crispness of the camera lens with the thrill of the supernatural. Magic may be defined as that which goes beyond the bounds of human understanding, relating to the supernatural, and has almost universal application. Realism, on the other hand, refers to a specific European nineteenth-century literary movement, specifically a type of writing which gives the impression of recording or reflecting faithfully an actual way of life. Magical realism as an art term was first applied to the *Neue Sachlichkeit* (New Objectivity) group of German artists of the 1920s who depicted reality objectively but showed how it had a deeper, metaphysical dimension as well. It was this combination of a crisp, sharply defined phenomenal world with a metaphysical dimension which was, some forty years later, to emerge as the hallmark of Latin America's version of magical realism, in works such as Alejo Carpentier's *The Kingdom of This World*, Gabriel García Márquez's *One Hundred Years of Solitude* (1967), Isabel Allende's *The House of the Spirits* (1982), and Laura Esquivel's *Like Water for Chocolate* (1991) (Hart). This lineage was certainly picked up by the critics. As Janet Maslin, writing for the *New York Times*, suggested of *Like Water for Chocolate*: 'It relies so enchantingly upon fate, magic, and a taste for the supernatural that it suggests Gabriel García Márquez in a cookbook-writing mode' (quoted in Tenenbaum, p. 157). The important point to make, though, is that in Latin America's version of magical realism the conflict between the magical and the real became not just an artistic problem but became the building block for the search for cultural identity. Latin America culture is an oxymoronic fusion of western and pre-Columbian societies, and that is why magic realism, with its paradoxical juxtaposition of two ways of looking at the world, provides such an appealing vehicle for depicting Latin American reality.

Symbolism

The symbolism such as there is in the film derives from the novel, and some examples should be highlighted. The most significant example of symbolism concerns that between food and sexuality, hardly an original motif, but one which is explored with great skill in the film. Related is the parallelism explored between digestive disorders and hatred, epitomised in the trials and tribulations suffered by Rosaura. The best example of symbolism is that between sadness and salt, as expressed through the central image of the tear. The film opens with a close-up of an onion, and this motif is explored through the tears that the foetus Tita is heard to shed in the womb, the salt in the amniotic fluids which gush over the kitchen table when she is born, the salt which is used in the meals – a set of associations which is parallelled in the subsequent scene when Tita's tears drop into the batter from which the wedding cake will be made. Food – the film is telling us – like life, can make us cry or bring us joy. In this way, as Lillo and Sarfati-Arnaud point out, the film produces a greater sense of depth and complexity within domestic space (Lillo and Sarfati-Arnaud, p. 487).

Fairytale and Myth

The most important fairytale structure which is used in the film is that of Cinderella (Giannotti, pp. 117–20). Like the younger sister in that famous fairytale, Tita is destined to a life of misery and hardship in the home, while her two older sisters are allowed to express themselves in terms of love and sex (Gertrudis runs off with a *Villista*, and Rosaura gets the man that Tita is in love with). As in the fairytale, Tita does have a fairy godmother, and this role is taken by Chencha, the Indian maid. Also echoing the fairytale, after a life of hardship, Tita does finally receive the glass slipper, yet – and here the Romantic credentials of the film are most in evidence – the point at which she finds love is also the juncture when she finds death. This, a classic example of the *Todlieb* of Romantic literature, is used to tidy up the conclusion of the film. The Amerindian cultures are introduced into the film via a number of sources. John Brown's grandmother is mentioned as being a member of the Kikapoo tribe (Giannotti, pp. 60–1), and the Indian substratum is introduced into the film, mainly via the motif of healing. Chencha heals Tita when she loses her mind as a result of the death of her nephew, Roberto. Tita uses Indian folklore in order to build a new skin on Pedro's wound after he suffers horrific burns as a result of doña Elena's desire for revenge. The interesting point about the use of Amerindian culture in the novel is that it suggests a deeper complementarity between North and South American cultures than is normally the case – the standard cultural formulation often suggests how different the United States is from Mexico in racial terms. Here that racism has been turned on its head.

Cinematic Techniques

Though, as stated above, this film follows the novel very closely, a number of cinematic techniques used in the film deserve mentioning. It is clear, for example, that the close-up is used for the portrayal of doña Elena's ghost in order to stress her psychologically threatening presence, as opposed to the long shot used to portray Nacha's ghost, which offers a homely, non-threatening feel to the supernatural. The point here is that the shot itself can tell us something about how the supernatural is being viewed in each case. The portrayal of magical-real events – surely an endurance test for any film director given the visual nature of his medium – varies in success rate. Whereas the portrayal of the magical events which occur when food is involved are presented successfully in cinematic terms (i.e. such as the wedding feast scene in which the guests are overtaken by a desire to cry or vomit, or the reaction at the table when Tita's quails are eaten), those involving fire (such as when Gertrudis's shower bursts into flames, or when Tita and Pedro finally make love at the conclusion of the film) are less believable, or, put another way, less visually convincing. Some shots – such as the panning shot during the wedding feast – though part of any film director's repertoire, are used skilfully and flexibly in the film.

Works Cited

Giannotti, Janet, *A Companion Text for 'Like Water for Chocolate'* (Ann Arbor: University of Michigan Press, 1999).

Hart, Stephen, *Reading Magic Realism from Latin America* (London: Bloomsbury, 2001). ISBN: 0747556202. Internet book.

Ibsen, Kristine, 'On Recipes, Reading and Revolution: Postboom Comedy in *Como agua para chocolate*', *Hispanic Review*, 63 (1995), 133–46.

Kraniauskas, John, '*Como agua para chocolate*', *Sight and Sound*, 2.10 (1993), 42–3.

Lehman, Peter, and William Luhr, *Thinking About Movies: Watching, Questioning, Enjoying* (Oxford: Blackwell, 2003).

Lillo, Gaston & Monique Sarfati-Arnaud, '*Como agua para chocolate*: determinaciones de la lectura en el contexto posmoderno', *Revista Canadiense de Estudios Hispánicos*, XX.1 (1994), 479–90.

Potvin, Claude, '*Como agua para chocolate*: ¿parodia o cliché', *Revista Canadiense de Estudios Hispánicos*, XX.1 (1995), 55–67.

Shaw, Deborah, *Contemporary Cinema of Latin America: 10 Key Films* (London: Continuum, 2003), pp. 36–51.

Smith, Joan, 'Interview', www.salon.com/oct96/interview961104.html (consulted on 9 January 2004).

Tenenbaum, Barbara A., 'Why Tita Didn't Marry the Doctor, or Mexican History in *Like Water Chocolate*', in *Based on a True Story: Latin American History at the Movies*, ed. Donald F. Stevens (Wilmington, Delaware: Scholarly Resources, 1997), pp. 157–72.

Wu, Harmony W., 'Consuming Tacos and Enchiladas: Gender and the Nation in *Como agua para chocolate*', in *Visible Nations: Latin American Cinema and Video*, ed. Chon A. Noriega (Minneapolis: University of Minnesota Press, 2000), pp. 174–92.

22

CENTRAL DO BRASIL (CENTRAL STATION, 1998), DIRECTED BY WALTER SALLES

Cast

Dora, played by Fernanda Montenegro
Josué, played by Vinícius De Oliveira
Ana (Josué's mother), played by Soia Lira
Irene, played by Marília Pêra
Pedrão, played by Otávio Augusto
Moisés (Josué's half-brother), played by Caio Junqueira
Isaías (Josué's half-brother), played by Matheus Nachtergaele

Crew

Production Designers: Cassio Amarante, Carla Caffe
Cinematographer: Walter Carvalho
Editors: Isabelle Rathery, Felipe Lacerda
Music: Antonio Pinto, Jacques Morelenbaum
Screenwriters: João Emanuel Carneiro, Marcos Bernstein
Associate Producers: Paulo Brito, Jack Gajos
Executive Producers: Lillian Birnbaum, Thomas Garvin, Donald Ranvaud
Producers: Martine de Clermont-Tonnerre, Arthur Cohn
Director: Walter Salles

Awards

Golden Bear, Berlin International Film Festival, 1999
Silver Condor, Best Foreign Film, Argentinian Film Critics Association, 2000
BAFTA film award, Best Film not in the English Language, 1999
Winner, Golden Globe, Best Foreign Language Film, 1999
Nominee, Best Actress in a Leading Role (Fernanda Montenegro), Academy of Motion Picture Arts and Sciences, Hollywood, 1999
Winner, Best Screenplay, Sundance Institute International Award ($310,000)

Plot

Film opens with Dora, the letter writer, writing letters for various people in Central Station in Rio de Janeiro. Ana, Josué's mother, arrives, accompanied by

Josué, and asks to write a letter to her absent husband, Jesus, in Estrela do Norte in the backlands of central Brasil. The letter is direct and forceful. We follow Dora, after her day's work has finished, going home; she is a spinster who has a close friend, also a spinster, who helps Dora decide what to do with the letters. Despite her promise to her clients that she will post the letters, sometimes Dora simply tears them up and sometimes she stores them away in a drawer. Dora is presented as a cynical, unfeeling individual, made so by a life of hard knocks. Ana returns the next day and writes a kinder letter to her absent husband. Soon after writing the letter, Ana is run over by a bus. Josué, now an orphan, begins living in Central Station. He asks Dora to write another letter to his father, Jesus, but she refuses to do so because he has no money. She takes him to a 'home', from where she believes he will be taken to the United States to be adopted. She buys a television with the proceeds of her transaction – 1,000 dollars – but her friend becomes suspicious. She says that Josué will probably be killed and his organs sold on the black market. Taking fright, Dora goes back to the house and rescues Josué. After her initial reluctance, she decides to use the letter and help Josué find his long-lost father. After Josué gets drunk on the journey, Dora tires of him and tries to pay a bus driver to take him to Josué's house. But he gets off. Then they meet an Evangelist who befriends them but, while Dora goes into the toilet to put some lipstick on, he beats a hasty retreat. When they finally arrive at the address, Josué initially thinks he has found his father, but they are told that he has moved. Completely down on their luck, Josué has a brainwave: he advertises Dora's ability to write letters to the saints. They finally arrive in Estrela do Norte, described as the end of the world. At the new address, they hear the same story; the father has moved on. By a stroke of chance, they meet Josué's two half-brothers, Isaías and Moisés. They do not know where their father is, but they ask Ana to read the last letter written by him. It is addressed to Ana, and expresses his hope that, one day, they will all live together. Dora puts the two letters – one from Jesus to Ana, and the other from Ana to Jesus – both of which were never received by their destinees, and leaves the family home. On her way back to Rio de Janeiro she writes her last letter to Josué, saying he will be better off with his brothers.

Analytical Overview

Produced on a high budget of $2.9 million (Shaw, p. 162), *Central do Brasil* soon proved to be well worth the investment. It was a huge hit as much in Brazil – on its release in 1998 there it drew greater audiences than *Titanic* and *Godzilla* – as much as internationally; by the spring of 1999 the film had been seen by 1.3 million spectators and had grossed over $17 million (Shaw, p. 162). The film is a very human drama with a robust, engaging storyline and strong acting performances by Fernanda Montenegro as Dora and Vinícius de Oliveira as the nine-year-old boy, Josué. Its continuity editing suggests that the story will be the most vibrant element in the film, and this proves to be the case. It is, of course, a personal drama, but the film also re-enacts a common theme in Latin American literature

8. *Central do Brasil*: Josué Behind Barbed Wire

and film, namely, the search for the absent father, formulated as much in Juan Rulfo's *Pedro Páramo* and Gabriel García Márquez's *Cien años de soledad* (1967, One Hundred Years of Solitude) as much as in the Mexican and Brazilian soap operas that dominate the airwaves in Latin America. The search for the absent father, which is as much a search for cultural as well as personal identity, as in many of the literary classics which address this theme, ends in failure. At the end of *Central do Brasil*, the expectation is split between Moisés, the pessimistic brother, who does not expect their father to return, and Isaías, who does. Given the religious connotations of their names – and the fact that the latter third of the film is suffused with evocations of various Christian religious rites, it seems clear that the film is also alluding, if subtly, to the conflict in the gospels as to whether Christ will return epitomised by the good and the bad thief. A common theme in Brazilian cinema, the town Estrela do Norte is also characterised as a human version of hell on earth. As the ticket inspector at the Bus Station points out, it takes a long time to get out of town because 'este é o fim do mundo' (this is the end of the world).

Religious Motifs

It is quite clear that the plot and the thematics of the film are shaped around a set of crucial religious motifs. The most obvious is the set of associations conjured up by the names of the main characters. It is surely not coincidental that Josué's father's name is Jesus; this suggests that the motif of the pilgrimage – which was

based on an actual event (Shaw, p. 165) – is being used to highlight the significance of Josué's search. It is not that the religious motif indicates that Josué's
search is for Christ, for this would be to devalue the film, converting its very
human story into an allegory which would be over-determined. Rather it
appears that the motif of pilgrimage appears in order to demonstrate just how
important this search is for Josué. It is clear that this film cannot be translated
into allegory so easily, and this is because of the other significant names of the
main characters. All of the three brothers have the names of Old Testament
prophets, Josué (Joshua), Isaías (Isaiah) and Moisés (Moses). The Old Testament
prophets are often associated – at least in the Christian lore – with the prophe-
sies about the future coming of the Messiah, and this is so in the case of two
brothers; Josué has come from Rio de Janeiro searching for his father, and
Isaías, right up to the end, is holding out hope that their father will come back.
One of the brothers, however, Moisés, is sceptical about the possibility of the
return of their father.

There are other motifs which build on this religious theme. The Evangelical
lorry-driver at first strikes the audience as possibly offering a site of 'salvation'
for Dora and Josué. He offers them food, protects them from being persecuted
when Josué and then Dora steal some food from the Evangelist's shop. But, just
when it seems that Dora and he have arrived at some agreement – the beer they
have together is, it seems, part of a body-language pact – he beats a hasty retreat,
and Dora is left (in a delicately choreographed scene) to cry behind the window
pane. Just as popular Protestantism does not seem to offer the father figure, so
popular Catholicism seems, similarly, to be wanting. Josué runs off from Dora
into the crowds during the climax of the pilgrimage and Dora's presence there
could not be more awkward, more out of place. A rather hardboiled urban type,
given to cynicism, she is hopelessly thrown when the crowd of worshippers rise
and therefore prevent her from following Josué. And when she arrives at the holy
of holies – the shrine which the pilgrims are moving towards – the incense, the
candles, the chants, the noise, exacerbated by her hunger and stress – all become
too much for her, and she faints – her head making a distinctly realistic noise as
it hits the floor. Dora here re-enacts the death of Ana at the begining of the film;
unlike Ana, though, Dora comes to, and is saved by Josué.

While Protestantism and Catholicism offer 'false' fathers, so too do the families that Dora and Josué visit. The first house they visit, to some extent, produces
the worst let-down because the man has already reacted warmly to Josué in a
kindly way ('is he a good boy?' he asks; 'yes', Dora answers, 'he's a good boy'),
but then they discover that Jesus is the former owner of the house. As occurs on
three separate occasions, Josué's subsequent sadness is depicted by a rear-angle
long shot (with a similar mise-en-scène in each case) as he runs off alone, head
held low and shoulders hunched. This scene of disillusionment is repeated later
on when the finally reach the father's house and meet Josué's two brothers, Isaías
and Moisés. Jesus has disappeared without a trace and, despite the optimistic
expression of hope by Isaías and Josué, the overwhelming suggestion is that he
will never return. Thus Dora decides to put the two letters – one from Jesus to

Ana, the other from Ana to Jesus – on the cupboard underneath the picture, a tragic image of non-communication, since both have died while looking for the other, and both sent letters which were not received by the other. Their letters placed together under the picture is the nearest they got to togetherness.

It is in this sense that we can argue that *Central do Brasil* is a very sparse and highly focused film; the sub-plots such as they are – the brief liaison with the Evangelist lorry-driver, the disastrous interruption of the pilgrimage – are symbolic tributaries which relate back to the core theme of the search for the lost father. It is a bitter-sweet film, bitter because Josué ultimately does not find his father, and because Dora does not find a man, but sweet because Josué has found his brothers and will live with them now, and because Dora has found something new in her life, the love of somebody else. By leaving him, she shows true love, not the inter-fering love of someone who is thinking of him/herself more than the loved one. She has also gone through a spiritual change. While at the beginning of the film she is a cynic who exploits others, witnesses the death of others (Ana and the thief, for example, with indifference), and will even sell a child for self-gain, by the end of the film her heart has been broken by love, and she is now more human, more maternal. Her change of heart is suggested by the fact that – whereas before she would throw away the letters she dictated or put them into the 'purgatory' of the top drawer – at the conclusion of the film, she decides to send them. The sugges-tion is that her work has taken on a transcendent dimension – now, with Josué's help, she writes letters to saints rather than to absent or lost people.

The Capital Versus the Provinces

It is clear right from the beginning of the film that a contrast is being set up between the ideology of the city and that of the provinces; life in Rio de Janeiro is characterised by perpetual movement. Dora works in Central Station and much is made of the endless pairs of legs walking past her stall in a site which is, in Salles's own words, a 'Darwinist place' (quoted in Shaw, p. 166); the brutalising effect of her commuting trips from Central Station home is underlined, and the inescapability of the urban rush is emphasised by the fact that, even when she gets home, an open window shows that the train is never far away. Dora sym-bolises the 'loss of identity' characteristic of the urban environment of the eight-ies and nineties where 'the only criterion was efficiency', causing the individual to 'ignore others' (Salles's words; quoted by Shaw, p. 167). In this restless urban environment, travel becomes a central metaphor, sometimes used in incongruous ways. The metaphor that Dora uses to describe the difference between the bore-dom of marriage and the excitement of an extramarital affair (a bus journey com-pared to a trip in a taxi) works well in the context of the film, but it seems a little forced that the image that should plague Dora's mind during her sleepless night should be that of wheels turning and sounding like knives being sharpened. Whatever one thinks of these images, they indicate that the recourse to the metaphor of travel is relentless and inescapable throughout the film; some would see this as one of the film's strengths.

One important aspect of the film – underlined by its title, *Central do Brasil* – is the fact that Dora is in a central place in Brazil. Dora's job as a letter writer functions also as a metaphor of what Angel Rama has called the 'lettered city', the space inhabited by the educated (Dora is a school teacher), white elite (Dora is white and she lives in an apartment) who dominate the rest of Brazil, using their literacy as the agency of their material and symbolic power. The letter, indeed, has a very important symbolic role in the film, since it is a vehicle expressing the absence of the loved one (Pérez Murillo and Fernández Fernández, p. 353). There is no doubt that, at the beginning of the film, Dora is presented in negative terms since she uses her literacy in order to trick her customers into handing over money for a service she will not provide (she either rips up letters or keeps them in the top drawer; she never sends them, as her conversation with Irene suggests). As Nina Caplan points out: 'As a letter writer, she interprets rather than instructs: if knowledge is her currency, she has exchanged generosity for avarice' (Caplan, p. 39). Dora is the lettered city which exploits the provinces of Brazil. This is why her journey outwards from the centre into the outback of La bahia is – in symbolical terms – so important, for it forces her to open her eyes to the life of the interior of Brazil. Her journey inward to Brazil is also a psychological journey inward; though on a more minor scale than some nineteenth-century novels such as Flaubert's *L'Éducation sentimentale*, *Central do Brasil* is also a Bildungsroman of Dora's life.

The Spinning Top

The spinning top is symbolic of the various stages of this awakening for both characters. When Dora and Josué first meet, they are involved in a tug of war over the spinning top – an omen, indeed, of how their lives will soon unfold. Dora is not prepared to allow Josué to play with the spinning top which she keeps on her desk, but – though we don't see how or when – Josué manages to steal the top. This theft will have tragic circumstances – echoing the death of the thief who stole from one of the stalls – for it is because he turns backwards to retrieve the top while crossing the road that he leaves his mother, Ana, stranded in the middle of the road, thereby unintentionally causing her death. (This scene, as mentioned above, is repeated in Estrela do Norte, but this time, Josué – who is himself also redeemed – saves his 'mother', Dora, when she faints during the pilgrims' ceremony; he is there to comfort her when she wakes up.) The spinning top re-appears towards the end of the film when Dora and Josué go to visit the brothers' carpentry shop, itself an important motif as Shaw points out: 'The professions of the two older boys are also significant: Moisés is a builder and Isaías a carpenter, jobs that can be seen to symbolise the rebuilding of the country' (Shaw, p. 174). The object Isaías makes for Josué is a spinning top, thereby suggesting – in a symbolic way – that the pain of separation from the mother because of her death has been replaced by the sense of belonging to a family now that he has found his long-lost brothers; as Caplan suggests, the top is 'no longer a toy but a symbolic token of initiation into the community' (Caplan, p. 39). The spinning-top thus functions as a tool suggesting how times have changed from one set of circumstances to another – tragedy has been transformed into reconciliation.

Works Cited

'Awards: Hollywood' www.awardsdatabase.oscars.org.
'Awards: BAFTA' www.imdb.com/Sections/Awards/BAFTA_Awards/2000.
'Awards: Sundance' www.sundance.org.
Kaplan, Nina, 'Central Station', *Sight and Sound* (March 1999), 38–9.
King, John, *Magical Reels: A History of Cinema in Latin America* (London: Verso, 1990).
Pérez Murillo, María Dolores, and David Fernández Fernández (eds), *La memoria filmada: América Latina a través de su cine* (Madrid: IELPA, 2002).
Shaw, Deborah, *Contemporary Cinema of Latin America: 10 Key Films* (London: Continuum, 2003), pp. 158–74.

23

AMORES PERROS (LOVE'S A BITCH, 2000), DIRECTED BY ALEJANDRO GONZÁLEZ IÑÁRRITU

Cast

Octavio, played by Gael García Bernal
Susana, played by Vanessa Bauche
Daniel, played by Alvaro Guerrero
Valeria, played by Goya Toledo
Jorge, played by Humberto Busto
Luis Miranda Solares, played by Jorge Salinas
Ramiro, played by Marco Pérez
Gustavo Garfias, played by Rodrigo Murray
Leonardo, played by Jose Sefamí
El Chivito, played by Emilio Echeverría
Andrés, played by Ricardo Dalmacci

Crew

Executive Producers: Martha Sosa Elizondo, Francisco González Compeán
Photography: Rodrigo Prieto
Production Designer: Brigitte Broch
Wardrobe: Gabriela Diaque
Casting Director: Manuel Teil
Original Music: Gustavo Santaolalla
Production Director: Tita Lombardo
Editors: Alejandro González Iñárritu, Luis Carballar, Fernando Pérez Unda
Audio Design: Zeta Audio by Martín Hernández
Musical Supervisor: Lynn Fainchtein
Associate Producers: Raúl Alvaro Ferrer, Guillermo Arriaga Jordan, Pelayo Gutiérrez, Mónica Lozano

Awards

BAFTA winner, The Orange British Academy Film Award, Best Film not in the English Language, 2000
Winner, Critics' Week, International Film Festival, Cannes, 2000
Winner, Film Festival, Bogotá, 2000

Winner, Chicago International Film Festival, 2000
Winner, São Paolo International Film Festival, 2000
Nominee, Best Foreign Film, Academy of Motion Picture Arts and Sciences,
Hollywood, 2000

Plot

The film opens with a car chase, Octavio and his friend are being pursued by a
gang in a truck wielding a gun, and have a dog bleeding to death on the back seat.
Car crash; the woman in the other car is screaming to get out. Cuts to a dog fight
in which Jarocho's dog wins, and then to the house in which Susana and Ramiro
live with Ramiro's mother and Ramiro's brother, Octavio. Susana accidentally lets
the dog out, Cofi, and it kills Jarocho's dog. Jarocho asks for Alejandro's dog in
exchange, but he refuses. Chivito pulls out a gun and shoots someone in the back
sitting in a restaurant. Daniel and his wife, Julieta, come home; the phone rings but
nobody's there. Susana tells Octavio that she is pregnant with Ramiro's child;
Octavio confesses his love for his sister-in-law, Susana. Ramiro and his friend rob
a pharmacy. It soon becomes clear that what we are seeing is not cross-cutting so
much as flashbacks to different scenes from different people's lives. We reconstruct
Octavio's life as he begins to win money with his dog, Cofi, and tries to persuade
Susana to run off with him. We become part of Ramiro's life as he carries on rob-
bing pharmacies while working in a supermarket, and eventually gets beaten up by
a gang paid off by Octavio. As a result of that, he flees with Susana, and takes
Octavio's money with him. We also follow the life of Chivito, the old tramp, who
attends his wife's funeral, and then tries to get to know his daughter whom he has
not seen for many years. We also catch a few glimpses of Daniel and his wife,
Julieta, whose marriage is on the rocks. Another person soon comes into the action,
and this is the glamorous model, Valeria Amaya, who is first seen on the TV
programme, *Gente de hoy*. Since we follow her to her new apartment, we realise
that she is the other woman in Daniel's life. In the middle section of the film we
witness how Jarocho and Octavio bring their dogs together for a fight, and –
because his dog is losing – Jarocho shoots Cofi; Octavio retaliates by stabbing
Jarocho in the stomach. We re-see the car chase and now see that the woman driving the other car was Valeria. At this point Valeria and Daniel's lives come to form
the central focus of the film and we see their trials and tribulations as their dog,
Richie, falls down the hole in the floorboards, and is lost for months. In the meantime, Valeria's leg has to be amputated. At this point the film takes a new tack and
we follow the life of El Chivito as he attempts to meet up with his daughter, Maru,
as well as his job as a hired assassin; his assignment is to kill Gustavo Garfias's
half-brother and business associate, Luis Miranda Solares. We see the car crash
once more, but this time from Chivo's point of view as he is about to assassinate
Luis, and instead saves Octavio's dog, Cofi, whom be re-names Negro. There is
a sub-plot, however, in that Cofi kills all of Chivito's dogs. We see Ramiro's bank
raid which goes disastrously wrong, and he gets shot dead. At his funeral, Octavio
asks Susana to run away with him, but she refuses. Chivito captures Luis Solares

and keeps him prisoner in his house, but he twists the plan by also capturing his half-brother who organised the hit. He leaves both of them together to fight over the gun, and goes to his daughter's apartment, leaving a tearful message on her answer machine, and then walking off into the sunset.

Analytical Overview

A very sophisticated film which, on a budget of $2.4 million, took ten weeks to shoot from April to June 1999 (Smith, p. 12), it is not surprising that *Amores perros* has won so many prizes, scooping the best film prize at a number of international film festivals (BAFTA, Cannes, Flanders, Chicago, Bogotá, Valdivia, São Paolo, Tokyo). The film clearly took a number of critics by surprise, and it became the first ever Latin American film to sweep the board at various film festivals as a result of its own merits, rather than attaining the (always second-best) award of Best Foreign Language film at the Hollywood Oscars. It made $8 million in Mexico in box office and DVD and video sales, as well as an extra $5.4 million in the United States alone (Shaw, p. 51) and $20 million worldwide (Smith, p. 13). Opening in the UK in May 2001, it took $680,000 in just five weeks (Smith, p. 13). For more reasons than one *Amores perros* was a Mexican film which broke the mould. It did not receive government support; it was jointly financed by two private companies, Altavista (86%) and Zeta Films (14%), the latter González Iñárritu's own production company (Smith, pp. 11–12). It also offered a very different view of Mexico. As González Iñárritu has pointed out in an interview: 'I am not a Mexican with a moustache and a sombrero and a bottle of tequila (. . .) Nor am I a corrupt cop or a drug trafficker. There are millions like me. And this is the world I live in and the one I want to show' (Patterson, p. 11). With *Amores perros* Latin American cinema finally came of age. As John Patterson suggests, this film is 'the first sign of a Mexican movie renaissance' (Patterson, p. 11). González Iñárritu offered a totally new view of Mexico. As he put it in the Cannes pressbook:

> Mexico City is an anthropological experiment, and I feel I'm part of it. I'm just one of the twenty-one million people in the world's largest and most populated city. In the past, no person had ever lived (survived, more likely) in a city with such rates of population, violence and corruption: however – incredible and paradoxical as it may seem – it is a beautiful, fascinating city, and that is precisely what *Amores perros* is to me: a product of this contradiction, a small reflection of the baroque and complex mosaic that is Mexico City.
> (quoted in Smith, pp. 50–1)

Los amores perros was also unique in that it launched the lead actor, Gael García Bernal, – who was only twenty years old when the film was released – into unprecedented stardom. He is highly in demand in Latin America, Spain and Hollywood because of his good looks and excellent acting abilities.

9. *Amores perros*: Haunted Octavio

The first draft of the 170-page script was put together by Guillermo Arriaga, González Iñárritu, Martha Sosa and Francisco González Compeán and was described as follows:

> The film will be structured around three loosely connected stories linked by a car accident; it will use documentary-style camerawork, with the film stock processed with silver retention to create stronger contrasts and texture in colour; the dog fights will not be explicit and the dogs will be handled with extreme care; the cast will largely consist of unknowns; and there will be a strong soundtrack.   (quoted in Smith, p. 11)

There are a number of features of the film which marked it as a new departure in the until then rather staid trajectory of Latin American cinema. If nothing else, the rear crawl credit indicates just how far Latin American film has come since the early days of 'imperfect cinema' with its miniscule budgets and minimal crew. González Iñárritu is clearly a *cinéaste* with a sense of his own artistry; *Amores perros* is the first film of the director's planned trilogy, the second film being *21 Grams* (2004) and the third as yet unknown. With the third film, as he explained in a recent interview, he will be able to 'create a triptych and close the triangle' (Intxausti, p. 29). What nobody could avoid was the arresting way reality was thrown at the reader from the very opening sequence of the film. A stock technique of Hollywood cinema, the car chase (which is 'indebted to *Reservoir Dogs*', Arroyo, p. 39) became in Iñárritu's hands a very gritty sequence, enhanced by a number of new elements. Firstly we do not know who the drivers are in either car; secondly (and again the viewer does not know why) there is a big black dog bleeding on the back seat; and thirdly – and perhaps most importantly – the crash which concludes the sequence is anything but seamless. The shot of the beautiful woman trying desperately to get out of the car is a haunting, horrible image. And, as the film develops, it all just gets worse and worse. Peter Bradshaw makes the point well: 'The opening car-chase sequence of this movie delivers the kind of unapologetic rocket-fuelled excitement not experienced since the days of Tarantino in the early 1990s. Three inhabitants of a car are being chased through Mexico City by a gun-wielding gang in a truck. One of them, Cofi, whimpering and shuddering with pain, has taken a bullet; Luis is pressing his hand up against the wound to staunch the flow of blood. The problem is that Cofi is a dog' (Bradshaw, p. 12).

One other element which struck viewers was its amoralism. Refusing to sound a self-righteous tone, *Amores perros* launched into a portrayal of unbridled violence, incest, company corruption, and lives built around crime, in a way that most viewers found breathtaking. Its depiction of dog-fighting, indeed, nearly got it in trouble with the British censors; the British Board of Film Classification was at one stage considering statutory cuts (Johnston, p. 2). For many years the expectation had been that Latin American films would take on serious social or philosophical issues and deliver a message to a blasé world. *Amores perros* broke the mould in more ways than one, showing a *tranche de vie* as it is, and not moralising about it. Iñárritu explained his philosophy of filmmaking in the following terms in an interview: 'Tal vez mis películas sean duras, pero son reales. La realidad no se puede maquillar, sería incapaz de adulterarla para hacer las cosas más fáciles al espectador. Siempre he pensado que tengo que contar las cosas como son y no como nos imaginamos que deberían ser para hacerlo más fácil' (Intxausti, p. 29).

Symbolism

The most important symbolic level explored in the film concerns the notion of the interconnections between the human and the animal kingdoms, between men and dogs. The parallel is inescapable. Just as Ramiro and Octavio fight each other to the death – as Garfias and Solares will do, though off-screen – so the dogs fight each other. The only solution to the dog fight or the man fight, it appears, is death. In all but one of the dog fights, one of the dogs is carted off dead; likewise Ramiro dies. The men are fighting for money, food and sex and, as the film suggests, their fighting can be just as vicious, since it can involve using deception to get one's way. In both of the Cain and Abel narratives, for example (see below), one of the parties tries to get rid of the other by paying off a third party. Intriguingly enough, however, as the pattern of events suggests, in each case this underhand strategy goes wrong. The comparison between dog and man is a far-reaching rather than localised one. As Geoffrey Kantaris has pointed out, 'the business of dog-fighting becomes in itself a powerful allegory for the economic violence inherent within globalized capitalism' (Kantaris, p. 187).

The interchangability of man and dog leads to some strange events and circumstances. Chivito, for example, though he simply smiles when he reads the news of the death of the businessman he killed, is mortified when his dogs die, shedding desperate tears in particular when Gringuita dies in his truck. When he comes across the car accident, he does not miss the chance to pocket the loose cash on the seat – suggesting he is unconcerned by the carnage he witnesses – and yet he is extraordinarily keen to nurse Cofi back to health. Chivito loves animals more than human beings.

The love that Ramiro and Octavio have for Susana is a red-blooded, animal lust; we hear the loud sexual noises which Ramiro and Susana make, which drive Octavio to distraction – such that he knocks on their door, saying that Susana's mother is on the phone, and then tries to pull her dress down. The animal violence of this desire is emphasised when we shock cut from the sequence portraying Ramiro getting beaten up to the sexual scene when Octavio seduces Susana; the sight and sound of Ramiro hitting the floor is echoed visually and audially by a medium shot of Susana's body hitting the bed in preparation for Ramiro's sexual onslaught; the scene is 'shot in the style of a music video, with images accompanied by the Spanish band Nacha Pop's "Lucha de gigantes" (Battle of the Giants)' (Shaw, p. 65; for more on the soundtrack, see Smith, pp. 69–72).

The love experienced by Daniel and Valeria is portrayed as a genteel, middle-class affair which gradually degenerates into misfortune and yet, even here, the central metaphor for that love is a dog, though it is Richie, a small domesticated puppy, rather than a bullhound or a boxer. Richie functions as a subtle indicator of the health of Daniel and Valeria's love. In the original script Valeria was described as having aborted Daniel's child, though this detail was subsequently edited out; this suggests that Richie functions in the film as an image of the lost child (Smith, p. 34). Its rather bizarre disappearance down the floorboards (if interpreted in naturalistic terms) becomes symbolic of the way in which their love is beginning to disappear somewhere; their love nest becomes a chimera as Daniel finally starts smashing up the floor. This ruination of the foundation of his world is also related to his economic demise; he says – during the enormous row that they have just before Valeria develops thrombosis – that he is experiencing financial problems. Intriguingly Daniel does find Richie under the floorboards, and cuddles him in his arms. Since this is just before Valeria returns home after her leg has been removed – and they both look through the window at the now empty bill board which once carried her gorgeous image – we can interpret the re-encounter as a pyrrhic victory at most. The final scene of Daniel and Valeria together suggests that their lives are now practically over.

Cain and Abel

The Abel and Cain story from Book of Genesis of the Old Testament is implicit in the main narrative of *Amores perros*. In particular it appears in two of the micro-narratives: the relationship between Octavio and Ramiro, and that between

Gustavo Garfias and Luis Miranda Solares. In this context it is important to recall that the film's original working title was *Perro negro/perro blanco* (Smith, p. 32), which points to rather drastic contrasts pursued throughout the narrative. The extremely divisive relationship between Octavio and Ramiro is evident from very early on in the film. In the very first sequence taking place within the family home, Ramiro verbally abuses his wife, Susana, and Octavio defends her. As soon becomes clear – and here the biblical parallel is apparent – Octavio is jealous of his brother, because he is in love with Susana. In their subsequent conversation which takes place at the breakfast table the aggression is just beneath the surface; Octavio threatens to spill the beans about his armed robberies, and Ramiro tells him to mind his own business. Octavio attempts to buy Susana's love by giving her his winnings from the dog fights. The rivalry soon escalates into violence; Octavio headbutts Ramiro while he is at work, Ramiro retaliates by hitting him with a metal bar in the shower, and Octavio then decides to have Fat-so's gang jump Ramiro, kidnap him and work him over. As if this were not stark enough a portrayal of hatred between brothers, the director decided to have Octavio trying to persuade Susana to run away with him during Ramiro's funeral wake. Iñárritu's view of human relationships is clearly a dog-eat-dog one.

The Cain and Abel relationship between Ramiro and Octavio is also echoed by that between Gustavo Garfias and his half-brother and business associate, Luis Miranda Solares. Whereas Octavio and Ramiro are fighting over a woman, Garfias and Solares are fighting over money. Here the rivalry is presented in a more didactic way; thus Chivito actually calls them Cain and Abel when he brings both men to his house, and asks them to attempt to settle their differences. He places the gun midway between the two of them; we do not see what happens next. Whereas in the original screenplay the ending was more pessimistic, since two 'shots' are heard to ring out as Chivito leaves the house (Smith, p. 74), the issue is deliberately left hanging in the air in the final cut version of the film.

The sequence concerned is also more didactic – one of the very few mildly didactic features of the film – in the sense that it records why Chivito decided to complete his assignment in such an unorthodox way. While his original plan was to shoot Solares when the latter is seated in a restaurant, he subsequently changes his mind – as he explains to a bemused Solares whom he has chained to a post – because of the dog. What he means by this is that he was about to kill Cofi in revenge for the latter having killed all of his dogs – *inter alia*, Flor, Frijol, and Gringuita – but he decided, just before he pulled the trigger, not to. As a hired assassin and former terrorist/freedom-fighter, this moment became a defining one for the shape that his life would take. In the same way that he decided not to continue the cycle of violence – i.e. by not killing Cofi – he followed through by not killing Solares. His hope – and it may be a naïve one – is that the brothers should attempt to patch up their differences. His tearful phone message to his daughter suggests a similar idea; as a terrorist/freedom-fighter he justified killing others for a greater (abstract) cause. But it is only now that he has realised that the most important bond is within the family unit. This is what he has learned, and this, in effect, makes Chivito the message-bearer of the film.

The Synoptic Vision of the Car Crash

The dynamic, edgy portrayal of the car crash was achieved by a new technique pioneered by the director of photography, Rodrigo Prieto, who used skip bleach in post-production in order to enhance the contrast of colour and tone within the frame. As he explained in an interview:

> The contrast in general is enhanced with skip bleach, but so is the contrast of the grain. [The process] desaturates certain lines and colours, such as skin tones, but the reds and blues [are] even enhanced (. . .). We wanted the film to feel realistic, but with an edge. We were after the power of imperfection [and wanted to] use 'mistakes' to enhance the urgency and impredictability of life in a place like Mexico City.   (quoted in Smith, p. 77)

By making the whites in the frame that much whiter, Prieto was, in effect, producing a quasi-hallucinogenic effect, dazzling the viewer, thereby inducing a sensation in the viewer's mind that the phenomenal world is that much more vivid, much more 'in-your-face'. Perhaps even more noteworthy about the car crash in *Amores perros*, though, is the way in which its impact is gradually built up in the viewer's mind. Rather than adopting a chronological approach, or using the time-honoured technique of the flashback (which, in any case, adopts a chronological methodology) the film is structured around the car crash which we see on three separate occasions and from three different points of view. González Iñárritu did not, of course, invent this technique (one of the first examples of a story told from three different angles is Akira Kurosawa's *Rashomon* (1950); see Aumont, p. 88), but the Mexican film director produces a powerful vision of an action-packed event with great dexterity. As one critic has pointed out, 'the collision itself occurs at a cross roads, signifying the life-changing aspect of the event' (Shaw, p. 55). Just as important, the momentum of the horror of the crash gradually builds up in the viewer's mind. As Laura Podalsky has suggested: 'The circularity or looping nature of the narrative infuses the spectator with an ongoing sense of dread; having seen the tragic car crash once, then twice, then a third time, the film conditions the spectator to be wary, to assume that another encounter with violence is just around the corner, or just around the edges of the next frame' (Podalsky, p. 285). The first time we witness the impact, the film immediately afterwards sets off into a reconstructive mode, and we track backwards into the past (in the manner of a cross-cutting flashback) highlighting those events which led up to the crash. The first car accident sequence drops us *in medias res* during the car chase, presented from Octavio's mindscreen if not POV – with many of the shots given within the car, and the focus being Octavio's POV as the car ploughs into Valeria's car as it jumps the red lights. The second time we witness the crash we do so from the perspective granted by Daniel and Valeria's lives. We see Valeria leave the TV studios with Andrés Salgados who leads her to her new apartment purchased by her lover, Daniel, and we follow her as she decides to go and buy a bottle of champagne to celebrate their new life together. It is her mindscreen rather than her POV that the viewer is encouraged to adopt; that is, we are in her car rather than in her eyes. The final and definitive sequence is the fullest; in a brilliantly choreographed shot we see the crash occurring over Chivito's shoulder, we follow Chivito as he approaches the two cars – essentially adopting his mindscreen – comes first to Octavio's car and then Valeria's, and finally, in Chivito's POV, we perceive the dog being carted unceremoniously away and dumped on the freeway, and we see him pick it up, and surreptitiously take it off to his lair. Each of the three sequences of the crash are tightly co-ordinated; in sequence 1, for example, we see a beautiful blond woman (Valeria, though we don't yet know her name) struggling to get out of the hit car; in sequence 2, we see Valeria's car drive past an old tramp (Chivito, who was at the time planning to take out Solares but was interrupted before he did it). These details are then re-confirmed by the fuller, wide-lens depiction of the crash in sequence 3.

Works Cited

Arroyo, José, 'Amores perros', *Sight and Sound* (May 2001), 39–40.

Aumont, Jacques, Alain Bergala, Michel Mairie and Marc Vernet, *Aesthetics of Film*, translated by Richard Neupert (Austin, TX: University of Texas Press, 1992).

'Awards' www.imdb.com/Sections/Awards/BAFTA_Awards/2000 (consulted on 22 December 2003).

Bradshaw, Peter, 'The Collar of Money', *The Guardian* (18 May 2001), pp. 12–13.

Intxausti, Aurora, 'Una deslumbrante metáfora sobre la muerte: González Iñárritu presenta en Madrid *21 gramos*, que se estrenará en España el 30 de enero', *El País* (13 December 2003), p. 29.

Johnson, Trevor, 'Dog Fights, car crashes, love – that's life down Mexico way', *The Independent on Sunday* (6 May 2001), p. 2.

Kantaris, Geoffrey, 'The Young and the Damned: Street Visions in Latin American Cinema', in *Contemporary Latin American Cultural Studies*, eds Stephen Hart and Richard Young (London: Arnold, 2003), pp. 177–89.

Patterson, John, 'Aztec Cameras', *The Guardian* (18 May 2001), p. 11.

Pérez Soler, Bernardo, 'Pup Fiction', *Sight and Sound* (May 2001), pp. 29–30.

Podalsky, Laura, 'Affecting Legacies: Historical Memory and Contemporary Structures of Feeling in *Madagascar* and *Amores perros*', *Screen*, 44.3 (Autumn 2003), 277–94.

Shaw, Deborah, *Contemporary Cinema of Latin America: 10 Key Films* (London: Continuum, 2003), pp. 51–66.

Smith, Paul Julian, *Amores perros* (London: British Film Institute, 2002).

24

Y TU MAMÁ TAMBIÉN (AND YOUR MOTHER TOO, 2001), DIRECTED BY ALFONSO CUARÓN

Cast

Julio Zapata, played by Gael García Bernal
Tenoch Iturbide, played by Diego Luna
Luisa Cortés, played by Maribel Verdú
Ana Morelos, played by Ana López Morelos
Alejandro 'Jano' Montes de Oca, played by Juan Carlos Remolina
Manuel Huerta, played by Nathan Grinberg
María Eugenia Calles de Huerta, played by Verónica Langer
Cecilia Huerta, played by María Aura
Nicole Bazaine, played by Giselle Audirac
Esteban Morelos, played by Arturo Ríos
Diego 'Saba' Madero, played by Andrés Almedia
Silvia Allende de Iturbide, played by Diana Bracho
Miguel Iturbide, played by Emilio Echeverría
Enriqueta 'Queta' Allende, played by Marta Aura
Leodegaria 'Leo' Victoria, played by Liboria Rodríguez

Crew

Casting: Manuel Teil
Costume Designer: Gabriela Diaque
Music Supervisor: Liza Richardson, Annette Fradera
Edited by: Alfonso Cuarón, Alex Rodríguez
Art Director: Miguel Álvarez
Line Producer: Sandra Solares
Director of Photography: Emmanuel Lubezki
Executive Producers: Sergio Agüero, David Linde, Amty Kaufman
Producer: Jorge Vergara
Screenplay: Carlos Cuarón
Director: Alfonso Cuarón

Awards

Winner, Mastroianni Award, Venice Film Festival, 2001
Winner, Best Screenplay awarded to Alfonso Cuarón and Carlos Cuarón, Venice Film Festival, 2001

Best New Actors awarded to Gael García Bernal and Diego Luna, Venice Film
Festival, 2001
Nominee, Hollywood Oscars
Nominee, Best film not in the English language, BAFTA, 2003

Plot

The film opens with the scene of Julio and Ana making love. (It is only later that
we realise that Julio is making love not to his girlfriend but his best friend's girlfriend.) Since Ana is going to Italy, Julio makes her promise that she will not
sleep with any foreign men while there. Julio is then seen at Cecilia's house, and
he has sex with her hurriedly before he goes to see her off at the airport. Julio and
Tenoch bid farewell to their respective girlfriends (Cecilia and Ana) at the airport.
The voice-over explains the background of the main characters, the career of their
parents, and so on. Before each sound-over we hear a short silent pause, announc-
ing its appearance. Julio and his friend, Tenoch, are driving in the car, and they
hit a traffic jam caused, the voice-over informs us, by the death of a building
worker, Marcelino Escutia, in a car crash. Julio and Tenoch attend a wedding
where they meet Tenoch's cousin, Jano, who is a writer and married to Luisa,
whom they invite to the beach called Boca del Cielo (Heaven's Mouth). Luisa
goes to the doctor to get some tests. Jano rings Luisa and confesses that he has
been unfaithful. Luisa decides to take up Julio and Tenoch's offer and go the
beach with them. Tenoch borrows the car from his sister, picks up Luisa and off
they go on their adventure. As they drive along they start talking about sex. The
car breaks down, and they stay in a motel, where Luisa seduces Tenoch; Julio
watches from the hall. That night Julio confesses to Tenoch that he slept with
Tenoch's girlfriend, Ana. Tenoch becomes furious. The next day, while they are
driving, Luisa seduces Julio in the back seat, and Tenoch walks off, furious. Then
Tenoch tells Julio that he has slept with the latter's girlfriend, Cecilia, and now it
is Julio's turn to become furious. Luisa has had enough of them and gets out of
the car. They persuade her to get back in, drive further along the road, and finally
arrive – it seems – quite by chance at the beach. They dive into the sea. A fisher-
man called Chuy and his wife offer them food, and then offer to take them to a
beach called Boca del Cielo. They go there – an idyllic setting – but when they
return to their tent, they find it has been destroyed by a herd of pigs. Luisa rings
Jano to say that she has left him for good, and to wish him well. While drinking
in a bar, Julio tells Tenoch that he slept with the latter's mother: 'y tu mamá también', an expression whose centrality is suggested by the fact that this became the
title of the film. The subsequent sexual ménage-à-trois scene culminates in Julio
and Tenoch kissing each other. They wake up the next morning, feel disgusted
(Tenoch goes outside and is violently sick), and then decide that they have to
leave and go home. Luisa says she will stay longer. Tenoch and Julio have an
uneventful journey back to Mexico City, break up with their girlfriends, Ana and
Cecilia, and lose touch. They have coffee a year later, and Tenoch tells Julio that
Luisa died of cancer a month after they left. Julio pays the bill.

10. *Y tu mamá también*: Ménage-à-trois

Analytical Overview

Following the trend set by *Amores perros*, *Y tu mamá también* was privately financed, ironically enough by a nutritional supplements corporation (Smith, pp. 85–6). Winning first prize for the film (the Marcelo Mastroianni Award), as well as awards for the screenplay and for the two lead male actors at the 2001 Venice Film Festival ('Awards') – though it failed to gain an Oscar after nomination at the 2000 Hollywood Ceremony ('Hollywood 2002') – Cuarón's film appears at first take to focus unremittingly on the psychology of men. What makes them tick, as *Y tu mamá también* suggests, is sex, but also the power over others that having sex with somebody gives the individual. Thus it is no coincidence that Julio tells Tenoch he has been sleeping with the latter's girlfriend (something we, as viewers, actually witnessed in the establishing scenes of the film), in order to get his own back on Tenoch whom he saw sleeping with Luisa. By telling Tenoch he has slept with his woman he feels that he has re-asserted his power in their own relationship. From this point onwards the one-up-man-ship starts in earnest. The following day, while they are driving Julio himself has sex with Luisa, right in front of Tenoch. Tenoch leaves the car, furious. If this were a tennis match, the score would now be 30–15 to Julio. In order to get his own back, Tenoch tells Julio that he has slept with the latter's girlfriend, something which surprises not only Julio but also the viewer, since we had not been privy to this side of Tenoch's life. Julio also reacts as a furious 'macho cornudo'. 30–30. At this point Julio releases his winning card, which is that he has also slept with Tenoch's mother. In the rather grotesque power games being played out here, this signifies that Julio becomes the 'father' to Tenoch. They are both too drunk to care, and it is at this point that the final bombshell is released: that these two macho young men are also homoerotic. Psychoanalytic theory argues that when two men are in love with the same woman they are in effect in love with each other. This is suggested to be the case in Cuarón's film in the anagnorisis scene when they kiss each other, an episode for which the viewer has not been prepared. The fact that *Y tu mamá también* is not only a road movie but that it also introduces the sub-theme of male bonding suggests that Cuarón is alluding subtly to the work of Wim Wenders (in whose films – especially *Kings of the Road*, *The American Friend*, *Paris, Texas* and *Wings of Desire* – these two themes are central; see Buckland, pp. 69–70).

Luisa knew all along that Julio and Tenoch were not really interested in her, but were far more absorbed by the power relationships occurring between each other. This is indicated early on when she leaves the car in disgust, saying that they are simply like dogs fighting over their territory, and what they would like to do most is have sex with each other. This comment – made when she is so annoyed at the way they are fighting – turns out to be very prescient, since this is exactly what they do later on. The culmination of the sex scene with Luisa ends in the two men kissing each other. Luisa was right; their *machista* attitude was masking a homoerotic structure of feeling.

Oedipus and Homoeroticism

Julio and Tenoch are clearly two narcissistic men, very much in love with the image of themselves. Their love for Luisa is revealed, in the scene three-quarters of the way through the film, in which they kiss, to be a displaced version of their own homoeroticism. What makes this sexual stew even more intriguing is that, from the very opening scene of the film, the two men are presented as if they were brothers; certainly their closeness at the beginning of the film suggests this. It is in this sense that we can interpret Julio's act of sleeping with his best friend's mother as a displaced version of the breaking of the Oedipal taboo. It is in effect a gay version of the Oedipal complex. The important point being underlined here is that the sexual drive is so strong that it breaks down cultural taboos. The opening scene of the film introduces the notion of sexual cross-over, since what we are witnessing is Julio making love with his best friend's girlfriend. The cross-over is here within one generation (i.e. men of roughly the same age 'swap' their lovers). The voice-over which accompanies the description of Julio's sexual antics implies that this cross-over also occurs between generations. It mentions that Ana's mother is French and does not mind Julio staying over, and therefore implicitly raises the question of the ways in which male lovers are 'swapped' between generations, i.e. between mothers and daughters. *Y tu mamá también* is, thus, not only about the sexual mores in operation in modern Mexico, but also makes some probing comments about the sexual interplay between generations, a practice which culture terms and defines as taboo. The film in a sense re-enacts a journey which pushes the envelope of the taboo gradually further and further from conventional, 'straight' normative sexuality. It begins with pre-marital sex (Julio and Ana), evokes the practice of 'swapping' sexual partners (Julio and Ana), probes the taboo involved with stealing another man's woman (Julio steals Luisa), as well as stealing a woman with whom there is a family connection (Tenoch steals his cousin's wife). If that were not enough, the film then proceeds to break the taboo of two men sharing one sexual partner (Julio and Tenoch share Luisa), and then graduates to the devastating revelation that a man will also sleep with his best friend's mother (Julio sleeps with Tenoch's mother), before concluding on the final taboo of gay love between two men. The successive stages of this process of gradually breaking down social taboos is carefully choreographed, and demonstrates that this film is as much about the psychology of sex as about the 'liaisons dangereuses' that define human relationships. Yet *Y tu mamá también* is also a specifically Mexican reading of Laclos's insight into the destructiveness of sexual relationships, for it evokes Octavio Paz's sense of the Mexican subject as 'hijo de la chingada' expressed in his classic essay *El laberinto de la soledad* (1950), and, indeed, revels in the humiliation associated with the sexual exploitation of another man's woman. This immediately alerts the viewer that the portrayal of the journey proper as well as the sexual journey are to be understood as metaphors of the search for Mexican identity. As the film suggests – through its deconstruction of various levels of social taboo and sexual gender, and indeed, portrayal of a bewildering array of sexual 'cross-overs' – that identity is shown finally to be essentially fluid and elusive.

It is, of course, possible that the fact that Luisa is Spanish is not coincidental. Octavio Paz, in *El laberinto de la soledad*, as mentioned above, and Carlos Fuentes in his play *Todos los gatos son pardos*, have focused on the rape of La Malinche, an Indian woman, by Cortés, a Spanish man, as the primal scene in which Mexican identity was formed (for a discussion of Fuentes's play, see Hart, pp. 29–37). By having two Mexican men sexually exploit a Spanish woman, we might argue that this film attempts to 'reverse' the trauma of Conquest by exchanging the nationalities of the two parties involved in the primal scene. There are other motifs within the film which suggest that Cuarón is playing with this notion. Chroniclers of Mexican history have often interpreted the growth of Mexican nationhood in terms of the Fall, the idea being that the Eden of the New World was somehow corrupted by the arrival of the Europeans. In *Y tu mamá también* there are a number of coy references to heaven, beginning with the sense of the search for Eden, and the (though tongue-in-cheek) name of the beach they are searching for: Boca del Cielo (Heaven's Mouth). It is also clear that Luisa, Julio and Tenoch are, in their own ways, searching for a sexual heaven. If taken independently these motifs might not add up to much, but when taken together they suggest that Cuarón is alluding – albeit ironically – to the search for paradise. He is careful to point out that – during the journey – Julio goes through the region once inhabited by his maid before she came to live in Mexico City, and this indicates that the journey may also be construed as a journey backwards in time. The journey, thus, is multi-layered, evoking not only the sense of a personal journey backwards in time for certain individuals but also a tracking backwards into the history of a culture; in this case we are being drawn back to what might be called the 'dawn of Mexican time'.

Given the above, it is therefore doubly ironic that the anagnorisis should involve not the discovery of a natural heaven (an Edenic beach, perhaps), or a happy heterosexual heaven (marriage saves the day), but rather the notion that the two main protagonists are gay. By evoking various topoi relating to the identity of the nation and to personal identity, *Y tu mamá también* evokes not only an incestuous union (as occurs within the stiflingly close *ménage-à-trois*, in which Tenoch is sleeping with his cousin's wife), and thereby evokes one of the master tropes of Latin American literature, as Efraín Kristal has pointed out (Kristal), but also prompts a gay reading of Mexican male identity. To compound matters still further, the film refuses to evoke these themes in a self-righteously important tone, but instead laughs them off. All sexual taboos are shrugged off with an ironic smile. It's nothing, the film seems to be telling us, to get worked up about.

Symbolism and the Voice-Over

Though clearly a film which relies for its intensity on the ability to capture the reality of a *tranche de vie*, *Y tu mamá también* also has a number of images which, by a process of accretion, build up a symbolic sub-text within the film. The beach, Boca del Cielo, works on two levels of suggestion – firstly as an image of the heaven of sexuality to which Luisa invites both Tenoch and Julio, but also as an image of the death to which Luisa is gradually drawing nearer, though no-one but her knows this. Her husband's nickname, Jano, is a reference to the Latin god, Janus, who could tell the past and the future. In the film, though, the ability to predict the future and decipher the past is transferred to the voice-over, while Jano simply comes over as a two-faced snake in the grass. The water which appears obsessively throughout the film is symbolic of the death to which all the characters are drawn, especially of course Luisa – for whom this journey is a path towards death. So, while Luisa is running away from her husband Jano, she is being drawn towards the god Janus, who sits at the entrance to Hades.

The voice-over has a very specific function in the film. It provides a great deal of information about the characters – their early years, what their parents are like – and echoes the omniscient narrator of the nineteenth-century novel. While at the beginning of the film it emphasises what happened in the past, towards the end of the film it also begins to predict what will happen in the future, an example being what will happen to the pigs which attacked their tent, right down to the most specific details of how many there were (23), how many would be sacrificed the following spring (14) and how many would spread a disease (3). The voice-over has a God-like resonance within the film which contrasts sharply with the only too human behaviour of the protagonists whose lives we see developing before our eyes.

Death and Water Imagery

Death hangs like a brooding force over the whole film from beginning to end in that – although we are not provided with this information (strangely the voice-over is, though omniscient, also selective in the information it provides for the audience) Luisa has been given a death sentence by her doctor. The tests showed that she has only six months to live. Other details also fit into this pattern of random death experienced by 'others'. The first example concerns the building worker whose dead body causes the traffic jam early in the film. The second concerns the cross on the roadside which the voice-over explains as put there to commemorate a gruesome car crash which happened on that stretch of the road five years before. The third example of death which is alluded to concerns the story of Luisa's first love, who died at the age of seventeen. The more subtle allusion to death, however, occurs in the various water scenes, beginning with the first swim in the swimming pool, the second occurring when they swim underwater, and the third when Luisa asks Chuy to try to imagine that she is dead, and the camera immediately switches to an underwater shot of Luisa's legs, indicating that the underwater scenes are to be understood as references to death. This means that the viewer is encouraged to track back mentally to those scenes in which the two young men compete against each other in order to stay under water the longest. In each case they are returning to a womb-like death, which is provided later on by Luisa, the femme fatale cum mother figure. The intriguing connection being pursued here is that of the female body as death. When Julio and Tenoch masturbate on the swimming boards we catch a glimpse of their sperm dropping into the water from beneath the surface, and it is not coincidental that they should have mentioned Luisa's name before ejaculating. This image is repeated later on when both men ejaculate into Luisa's womb. As we discover later, Luisa was dying, and the ejaculation into her womb was therefore appropriately imaged by the dropping of their semen into the swimming pool, since water – in Cuarón's private symbolic landscape – stands for death. The fact that Luisa is to all intents and purposes dead suggests that Cuarón is making an observation about the ways in which macho sexuality petrifies and finally kills the female body.

Works Cited

'Awards', www.imdb.com/Sections/Awards/Venice_Film_Festival/2001.

Buckland, Warren, *Film Studies* (London: Hodder and Stoughton, 1998).

Hart, Stephen, *The Other Scene: Psychoanalytic Readings in Modern Spanish and Latin-American Literature* (Boulder, CO: Society of Spanish and Spanish-American Studies, 1992).

'Hollywood 2002', www.oscars.org/academyawards/index.html.

King, John, *Magical Reels: A History of Cinema in Latin America* (London: Verso, 1990).

Kristal, Efraín, 'The Incest Motif in Narratives of the United States and Spanish America', in *Internationalität nationaler Literaturen: Beiträge zum ersten*

Symposium des Göttinger Sonderforschungbereichs 529, ed. Udo Schöning (Berlin: Wallstein, 2002), pp. 390–403.

Mora, Carl J., *Mexican Cinema* (Texas: Texas University Press, 1985).

Paz, Octavio, *El laberinto de la soledad* (Mexico City: Joaquín Mortiz, 1950).

Smith, Paul Julian, *Amores perros* (London: BFI, 2003).

25

CIDADE DE DEUS (CITY OF GOD, 2002), DIRECTED BY FERNANDO MEIRELLES

Cast

Buscapé (Rocket), as a boy, played by Alexandre Rodrigues
Buscapé (Rocket), as a man, played by Luis Otávio
Zé Pequeno (Li'l Zé), played by Leandro Fermino da Hora
Dadinho (Li'l Dice), played by Douglas Silva
Bené (Benny), as a child, played by Michel de Souza
Bené (Benny), as a man, played by Phellipe Haagensen
Cabeleira (Shaggy), played by Jonathan Haagensen
Mané Galinha (Goose), played by Seu Jorge
Barbatinho, as a boy, played by Emerson Gomes
Barbatinho, as a man, played by Edson Oliveira
Cabecão (Knockout Ned), played by Mauricio Marques
Sandro Cenoura (Carrot), played by Matheus Nachtergaele
Tio Sam (Uncle Sam), played by Charles Parventi
Thiago, played by Daniel Zettel
Angélica, played by Alice Braga

Crew

Producers: Andrea Barata Ribeiro, Maurico Andrade Ramos
Co-producers: Hank Levine, Daniel Filho, Marc Beauchamps, Vincent Maraval
Executive producers: Walter Salles, Donald K. Ranvaud
Line producers: Bel Berlincx, Elsa Tolomelli
Original Music: Antonio Pinto, Ed Côrtes
Art Director: Tulé Peake
Editor: Daniel Rezende
Cinematographer: Cesar Charlone
Scriptwriter: Braulo Mantovani
Co-director: Katia Lund
Director: Fernando Meirelles

Awards

Winner, Gran Coral, Best Fiction Film, New Latin American Film Festival, Havana, 2002

Official Selection, International Film Festival, Cannes, 2002
Winner, BAFTA Award, Best Editing, 2003
Nominee, BAFTA, 2003, Best Film not in the English Language
Official nominee on behalf of Brazil, Oscar, Academy of Motion Picture Arts and
Sciences, Hollywood

Plot

The establishing shots of the film place us within the slums of Cidade de Deus
(City of God) in Rio de Janeiro. A chicken is being prepared for a street barbecue, and the other chicken escapes. The gang members go in pursuit of the
chicken, until they meet Rocket; Li'l Zé (formerly Li'l Dice), the gang leader,
asks him to catch the chicken. Rocket, the photographer, is then caught between
the gang and the police. The camera swivels back to Rocket's childhood and tells
his story, starting with his childhood in the 'favela' City of God. His older
brother, Goose, and his two friends, Chipper and Shaggy, rob a truck. Li'l Dice,
a young boy, tells them to rob a brothel, which they do, while Li'l Dice keeps
watch. While Chipper, Goose and Shaggy simply steal, Li'l Dice (as we find out
later) goes in and shoots all the customers. The police hunt them down. but
Shaggy hides with Berenice, his girlfriend, and Goose starts selling fish. Goose
has an affair with Shorty's wife, and, when Shorty catches them *in flagrante
delicto*, he takes a nasty revenge, by burying his wife alive. **The Seventies**.
Rocket falls in love with Angélica, and buys himself a camera. **The Story of the
Apartment**. The Apartment is the drugs den of City of God, and passes through
various hands until it is taken over by Li'l Zé. Li'l Zé attends a shamanistic
–ceremony in which he changes his name, decides to kill off all the competition,
and then becomes the local drug baron. We find out that, as a young boy, he had
killed Goose. Li'l Zé's right hand man is Benny, who becomes the cool guy.
Competition grows between Li'l Zé and Carrot who controls the other half of
City of God. Li'l Zé wounds one of the kids who are creating a disturbance, and
kills another. **A Sucker's Life**. Rocket gets a job in a supermarket, but is thrown
out. **Flirting with Crime**. Rocket and his friend try to become hoods but they
find it too hard. A man kills his girlfriend, and the body is found. **Benny's
Farewell**. Li'l Zé tries to get a girl at a disco, but is too ugly. He humiliates the
girl's boyfriend by forcing him – at gunpoint – to strip. In the ensuing chaos,
Benny is shot and killed. Li'l Zé rapes Knockout Ned's girlfriend, kills his
brother and uncle, and then shoots his house to pieces. **The Story of Knockout
Ned**. The slum becomes more and more violent. Rocket wants to become a photographer, and his hero is Rogerio Reis. Knockout Ned decides to link up with
Carrot in order to get his revenge on Li'l Zé. Gang warfare between Li'l Zé and
Carrot's gangs. Rocket takes a picture of Li'l Zé's gang, and it gets on the front
page. Marina, a journalist at the paper, invites Rocket round for a meal and they
have sex. Li'l Zé makes his fatal mistake by not paying up for the guns he is
getting from a gunrunner, little knowing that he has double-crossed the police
who are involved in racketeering. The police decide to get him. We return to the

chicken sequence. Follow through until we find Rocket between the police and Li'l Zé's gang. Carrot's gang arrives, and battle commences. The police clean up afterwards, and take off Carrot and Li'l Zé. In a secluded building, the police frisk Li'l Zé, and seize his money. Li'l Zé is subsequently shot to death by a gang of kids who want his patch. Rocket is taking pictures all the time, and exposes police corruption. Sequence of the gang of new kids on the block discussing how they will become hoods. Rocket is now a photographer, and has become Wilson Rodrigues.

Analytical Overview

Seen by more than 2,000,000 Brazilians in the first two months after release (Xavier, p. 28), *Cidade de Deus* soon afterwards became an international box-office hit, justifying its high (by Brazilian standards) budget of $3,500,000 (Nagib), and subsequently scooping various prizes, at Havana (Tiemey, p. 334), and BAFTA ('Awards'). The important point to remember here, though, is that the multi-million-dollar budget was based on the funding for the project (the year-long training of actors, the extended shoot) rather than, as in Hollywood, on attaching a high-impact movie-star name to the film who can launch it inter-nationally. (Typically a substantial percentage of a $3,000,000–5,000,000 Hollywood film will be spent on attaching an internationally-known face to a film; Simens.) *Cidade de Deus* had no professional actors in the cast (for more information see below). The film is based on the novel of the same name by Paulo Lins (*Cidade de Deus: Romance*), which came out in 1997, and which was re-issued in a reduced edition in 2002. The novel is based on a true story of the life of a number of gang members living in the City of God, a violent shanty town on the outskirts of Rio de Janeiro. More than a novel, Paulo Lins's work can be described as a 'testimonio', that is, a fictionalised version of a real-life story based on real-life characters; perhaps even more intriguing, as its author has confessed in an interview, *Cidade de Deus: Romance* is deeply poetic ('I thought that if I didn't put a poetic charge into the work nobody would be able to read so much horror'; Arias, p. 2). Lins's work springs from a long tradition of *favela* literature dating back to Carolina Maria de Jesus's *Quarto de despejo* (1940) (Williams). Testimonial literature of this kind typically seeks to offer a vision of the subaltern sections of society to a literate audience, and this sense of the work providing an authentic vision of life on the other side of the tracks is carried successfully over into the film. The birth of the novel and the film within the Latin American tradition of 'testimonio' is confirmed throughout by the use of the voice-over, which is used extensively in the film in order to fill in the gaps between the spectacular action shots which make up the major part of the film. The life which is portrayed within the film, as in the novel, is a dog-eat-dog existence, one in which, as Rocket says in the establishing sequence, 'Fight and you'll never survive. Run and you'll never escape.'

It is important to underline, however, that the sense of reality within the film is an effect rather than an intrinsic characteristic of the subject matter. Not for nothing did *City of God* win a BAFTA Award for Best Editing in 2003 ('Awards'). Though the film used non-professional actors, they were trained in the art of acting over an extended period of time. The street scenes were not 'real' in the sense of being filmed 'live', but were instead vast elaborate stage sets. A small detail perhaps but, for one of night scenes, a black body was painted red, and the image of the body further touched up during post-production (Nagib). Even the use of voice-over – normally seen as part of the film director's repertoire of naturalist techniques – has a staged feel about it in the film. Meirelles had clearly decided to use the voice-over in order to avoid using up precious film time 'explaining' the life-history of the characters or the set of events leading up to the present. The use of the voice-over gives Meirelles more time to experiment with the visual image of his film. As Paul Julian Smith points out, we are 'treated to slow and fast motion, expressionist coloured filters, even *Matrix*-style circling around combatants. The sequences set in the 1970s break into split screen' (Smith, p. 39; for more on the use of split screen, which was probably inspired by Brian De Palma's works, see Lehman and Luhr, p. 55).

The Image of the Subaltern

It would be difficult to think of a story which had less hallmarks of what has traditionally come to be known as the subaltern class, a violent, voiceless, illiterate group of murderers living in a shanty town near Rio de Janeiro. This illiteracy is emphasised throughout the film by the vigorous repetition of the colloquial vocative form 'rapa' (boy) rather than 'rapaz'; the oxytone suggests the abruptness of a life cut short, while the repetition of the sounds 'ra' and 'pa' simultaneously echoes the sound of machine gun fire, and resounds with the violent ethos of U.S. 'rap' music (Nagib). Indeed the music used throughout the film is a transculturated amalgam of U.S. and Brazilian music (samba, 70s disco music, and rap are all components of the final mix), stressing a dialogical continuity between local and international musical discourses (Treece). Most of the actors who appear in the film are non-professional; 'the children and teenagers were selected largely from Rio's *favelas* (some come from the theatre group Nós do morro / We from the hillside) and were trained by Fátima Toledo and Katia Lund for a year' (Xavier, p. 29). Li'l Zé epitomises the subaltern in that his conduct transgresses all norms of social propriety. What this film does address is the way in which the lives of the subaltern classes are manipulated by the mediatic, governmental, and law-enforcing powers within society. An underlying current within *Cidade de Deus* is the hypocritical ways in which the authorities react. The police, as we soon find out, are quite happy to allow the killing in the City of God to carry on as long as it does not escalate out of control, and affect their 'clients', the middle classes. It is – ironically enough – only as a result of Li'l Zé's refusal to pay for his guns that the police decide to act, because they have been providing him with the guns in the first place.

The most complex relationship between the media and a site of authority occurs when the gangs intersect with the media. Rocket first becomes aware of the media by the number of pictures which are taken of Shaggy's body when he is shot to death by the police. He subsequently becomes the 'official' photographer of his group of friends during the seventies when they live out their teenage dreams on the beach, but this is not enough for him to get the girl he wants (Angélica). His first attempts at employment – i.e. in the supermarket, and subsequently as a trigger-shy gangster – do not come to anything, and it is only when he takes a photograph of Li'l Zé's gang that he achieves a degree of fame. His photograph is put on the front page of the newspapers and, in a cute allusion to Hollywoodesque rhetoric, he gets the girl (Marina the journalist – a white, middle-class woman who would normally be way out of his league – invites him round to dinner, and sleeps with him). The film is very clear on this point: as a result of his ability to take photographs – that is, produce images which are appetising to the middle-class press – Rocket escapes his roots in the City of God. It is a world, as he says at the beginning of the film, which, if you fight, you will never survive, and which, if you run from it, 'you'll never escape', but Rocket has, in effect, proved that you can escape, since he becomes – as the closing sequence of the film makes clear – a professional photographer: no longer Rocket, he is 'Nelson Rodrigues, fotógrafo'. As Ismail Xavier points out, Rocket 'refuses to engage in the gang wars, substituting a camera for a gun, culture for violence' (Xavier, p. 28).

Ironic Religious Symbolism

There are a number of elements in the film which suggest a pattern of meaning is being built up which portrays religious symbolism ironically. The most obvious, of course, is the name, 'Cidade de Deus', an ironic inverted image of St Augustine's description of The City of God, a world in which peace, love and harmony reign. In this very earthly City of God, war, hatred and chaos are the order of the day. The shamanistic ceremony which Li'l Dice takes part in is also important in this regard. It is essentially his baptism into a new religion of hate. In an ironic reversal of the Christian ceremony of baptism, he is provided with a new name – Li'l Zé – and immediately begins his devilish work, destroying in one day all of his rivals by murdering them, and taking over the apartment which operates as a drugs den. During the ceremony in which the red lights are designed to capture the stereotypical notion of the 'fires of hell', Li'l Zé receives an amulet, which will protect him as long, the shaman tells him, that he doesn't fornicate while wearing it. It is because he eventually ignores this warning — specifically when he rapes Knockout Ned's girlfriend (we do not know if he is wearing the amulet at the time, but internal logic suggests he is) – that his days are numbered. Knockout Ned, after all, eventually takes his revenge by joining forces with Carrot. It is not by chance that the first time we see Li'l Zé's image of seeming invincibility changed – he limps off with Tule – as a result of Knockout Ned's attack on the gang. It is at this point that his power retreats from him, and the audience senses that his days are numbered. Pointing in a similar direction, it is at the point that the two gangs decide to fight to the death that they begin to recite the Lord's Prayer. Their subsequent action is in contradiction of the prayer they have been reciting, suggesting once more that the film is building up a set of ironic resonances with the Bible.

The Voice-Over

The function of the voice-over in the film is similar to that in a number of other recent Latin American films (*Y tu mamá también*), and it could almost be signalled as a characteristic of modern Latin American cinema, a feature which differentiates it from standard Hollywood film which tends to minimalise the voice-over, seeing it as the director's cop-out (Simens). When over-used, of course, it can become a safety-net for the bad director, but in *Cidade de Deus* it provides an excellent means of shifting between stories. The opening sequence of the film, indeed, offers a good example of what becomes a standard technique – the flashback initiated by the voice-over, and the subtitle, indicating – in the manner of a novel – what will be coming next. *Cidade de Deus*, because it does not attempt to mask what it's doing, comes over as more authentic as a result. The voice-over also allows the film director to introduce a note of suspenseful anticipation into the narrative. One of the best examples of this occurs when Rocket and his friend consider stealing from the bus, and get a bit of friendly advice instead from Knockout Ned. As the voice-over suggests: 'Ned did not have to protect himself that day, but one day he would.' The prolepsis introduced here allows for a neat tying into the future event, which loses none of its dynamism as a result, and is eagerly anticipated by the viewer. It is, though, a technique more readily associated with the novel form rather than the film; but Meirelles is not afraid to use it, and indeed creates a filmic style which uses the language of film and that of the 'testimonio' osmotically.

Flashback

The flashback is, of course, a supremely filmic technique which has little place in the novel, and Meirelles uses it successfully in this film, above all because he explores the range of temporal vision it offers to an extraordinary degree. The viewer, for example, is often unaware of at which juncture in the film a new flashback sequence will begin, and this gives an almost picaresque feel to the movie, as if we as viewers are following the story as it unravels before our eyes. The best example of this occurs in the brilliant opening sequence of the film. We see – in a sequence of abrupt close-ups cross-cut delicately between the hen being prepared for the meal and the hen who nervously surveys the events, realising what the future holds – the street barbecue being organised by Li'l Zé, and then follow the hen as it concocts its great escape along the back streets of the City of God. As Paul Julian Smith point outs: 'The quick cutting of the first scene (a blade sharpened, a drum beaten, a chicken careering through the slums) announces bravura filmmaking' (Smith, p. 39). Finally landing in front of a young boy, the chicken is about to be captured, when suddenly the police arrive, and we switch – in a brilliant revolving camera take – from the sight of the police to the sight of Li'l Zé's gang, at which point the camera swivels once more and begins to reconstruct the past from Rocket's vantage point. During the flashback sequence initiated from that juncture, we will meet the young boy – Li'l Dice – whom we saw in the opening sequence, and thereby reconstruct the past as it leads back to the point at which the film began. This angular relationship between people and events is – as the film develops – translated into a frontal relationship, and this is particularly evident in the context of the (fraught) relationship between Rocket and Li'l Zé. The other flashbacks operate in a similar way. It is as a result of Li'l Zé meeting Knockout Ned and his girlfriend by chance in a street of the City of God that their fateful meeting occurs, leading to Li'l Zé's decision to rape the girl, and to Knockout Ned's decision to fight back. After they have met, then the film begins once more its flashback sequence. *Cidade de Deus* thereby manages to balance a sense of the fortuitousness of everyday events with a sense of editorial control which is aesthetically pleasing. It is redolent in some ways of the mastery of Gabriel García Márquez in such novels as *Crónica de una muerte anunciada* (Chronicle of a Death Foretold; see Hart, pp. 39–43).

One other point ought to be made about the flashbacks and this concerns the point at which they re-connect with the narrative proper which, as it were, had halted in order for the past sequence to be 'remembered' by the film's consciousness. Typically the event returns to the present of the film, and then continues its onward thrust, thereby in effect merging the two times (the past re-connects with the present, and their respective times become as one). Meirelles tweaks this technique slightly by having the viewer perceive the same event from a different camera angle. When Blackie's apartment is invaded by Li'l Zé, for example, we hear the banging coming from outside; our mindscreen therefore is internal to the apartment. After the flashback has taken place, however – as initiated by the subtitle, 'The Story of the Apartment' – and brings us back to the present, as viewers we now perceive the event from behind Li'l Zé's gang, and this continues during the following sequence, such that now we 'become' Li'l Zé as he enters the apartment. Though not doing so in the same sequence, Meirelles is overturning the 180° degree rule, whereby the viewer is not allowed to see 'behind' the camera (that is, the fourth wall of the film studio where the camera is). While Meirelles is, of course, not the first to experiment with this rule (we find an example of this trick in the opening scenes of Martin Scorsese's 1976 film *Taxi Driver*; see Buckland, p. 39), it could be argued, nevertheless, that the Brazilian director appears to take delight in breaking the 180° rule since he often wants the viewer to 'see' behind the camera, in a way which is reminiscent of the 'revealed 360-degree space' in the work of the Japanese director Yasujiro Ozu (Lehman and Luhr, p. 81).

One other element of the flashback as used by Meirelles ought to be mentioned and this is that, far from allowing for a seamless projection of events, its use often catches the viewer by surprise. Such is the case, for example, with the sequence in which Goose, Rocket's older brother, happens to stumble across Li'l

Dice. He rough-handles Li'l Dice and then walks off-screen. But a later flash-back shows us what happened next – Li'l Dice shot him to death. Rather than showing us everything the flashback is revealed to be a very human registering device. As human beings we can only remember what we saw. A similar tech-nique is used when portraying what happened at the hold-up of the brothel. We see the dead bodies after the gang has left, and our initial reaction will be to think that we missed something. Only later do we realise – in a subsequent, fuller flashback – that Li'l Dice went in afterwards and started shooting everyone. Flashbacks can be deceptive.

Works Cited

Arias, Juan, 'Paulo Lins: "la poesía da miedo a los adultos por su carga de verdad"', *El País* (26 July 2003), p. 2.

'Awards' www.imdb.com/Sections/Awards/BAFTA_Awards/2003 (consulted on 22 December 2003).

Buckland, Warren, *Film Studies* (London: Hodder and Stoughton, 1998).

Hart, Stephen, *García Márquez: Crónica de una muerte anunciada* (London: Grant and Cutler, 1994).

King, John, *Magical Reels: A History of Cinema in Latin America* (London: Verso, 1990).

Lehman, Peter, and William Luhr, *Thinking About Movies: Watching, Questioning, Enjoying* (Oxford: Blackwell, 2003).

Lins, Paulo, *Cidade de Deus: Romance* (São Paolo: Companha das Letras, 1997). Italian translation (1999); French translation (2003); Spanish translation (2003).

——, *Cidade de Deus*, edicão revista (São Paolo: Companha das Letras, 2002).

Nagib, Lúcia, '*City of God* and the Appeal of Realism', paper given on 4 December 2003 at an ILAS conference, 'Brazil Abroad: Reception of Contemporary Brazilian Culture'.

Simens, Dov S-S, 'Two-Day FilmSchool', Raindance, London, 29–30 November 2003.

Smith, Paul Julian, 'City of God', *Sight and Sound* (January 2003), 38–9.

Xavier, Ismail, 'Angels with Dirty Faces', *Sight and Sound* (January 2003), 28–30.

Tiemey, Dolores, 'The 24th International New Latin American Film Festival', *Screen*, 44.3 (Autumn 2003), 333–6.

Treece, David, 'Soundtrack of an Alternative Black Consciousness? *City of God* and Contemporary Afro-Brazilian Music', paper given on 4 December 2003 at an ILAS conference, 'Brazil Abroad: Reception of Contemporary Brazilian Culture'.

Williams, Claire, 'From *Quarto de Despejo* to Favela Chic: The Western Fascination with the Favela', paper given on 4 December 2003 at an ILAS conference, 'Brazil Abroad: Reception of Contemporary Brazilian Culture'.

GUIDE TO FURTHER READING

An excellent basic introduction to some of the seminal concepts in film studies – film aesthetics, structure, the director as auteur, the basic genres – is found in Warren Buckland, *Film Studies* (London: Hodder and Stoughton, 1998). Peter Lehman and William Luhr, *Thinking about Movies: Watching, Questioning, Enjoying* (Oxford: Blackwell, 2003) is a very accessible discussion of the basic concepts used to analyse film. A more theoretical discussion of the mechanics of film is provided by Jacques Aumont, Alain Bergala, Michel Mairie, Marc Vernet, *Aesthetics of Film*, translated and revised by Richard Neupert (Austin: University of Texas Press, 1992); has superb chapters on montage, narration, and the spectator, *inter alia*. A very helpful anthology of all the essential essays on film theory is provided by Leo Braudy and Marshall Cohen, *Film Theory and Criticism: Introductory Readings* (Oxford: OUP, 1999). Robert Stam, *Film Theory: An Introduction* (Oxford: Blackwell, 2003), is not only a lucid overview of the evolution of film studies, it also introduces and analyses modern approaches to film such as 'Third Cinema' and 'Film and the Postcolonial', which are very helpful in an analysis of Latin American film. An accessible and broad-ranging glossary of film terms is provided by Susan Hayward, *Key Concepts in Cinema Studies* (London: Routledge, 1996); some of the entries are like mini essays. A more technical description of the filming process is found in Daniel Arijon, *Grammar of the Film Language* (Beverley Hills, CA: Silman-James Press, 1976); excellent on shot sequence and camera angle. Lucy Fischer, 'Film Editing', in *A Companion to Film Theory*, eds Toby Miller and Robert Stam (Oxford: Blackwell, 2004), pp. 64–83, helpfully splits up the discussion of editing under various headings, including 'Editing and Realism', 'Editing and Authorship', *inter alia*.

John King, *Magical Reels: A History of Cinema in Latin America* (London: Verso, 1990) is the single most important study of Latin American cinema, and is indispensable reading. Re-issued in 2000, it has lost none of its relevance. An accurate overview which analyses the films country by country is found in Guy Hennebelle and Alfonso Gumucio-Dagrón, *Les Cinémas de l'Amérique latine* (Paris: Pierre L'Herminier, 1981); an advantage of this book is it covers the cinema of less-studied countries such as Honduras and Guatemala. Deborah Shaw, *Contemporary Cinema of Latin America: 10 Key Films* (London: Continuum, 2003) is essential reading. *South American Cinema: A Critical Filmography 1915–1994*, eds Timothy Barnard and Peter Rist (Austin: University of Texas Press, 1996), is a wonderfully informative piece of research; has the advantage of having separate information on each film chosen. Basic background information on the cinematic traditions of Latin America can be found in *Dictionary of Twentieth-Century Culture: Hispanic Culture of South America* (Detroit, MI: Gale Research Inc., 1995), and *Dictionary of Twentieth-Century Culture: Hispanic Culture of Mexico, Central America and the Caribbean* (Detroit, MI: Gale Research Inc., 1996), both edited by Peter Standish. For a history of the cinema from an industrial perspective the reader is referred to Jorge A. Schnitman, *Film Industries in Latin America: Dependency and Development* (Norwood, NJ: ABLEX, 1984), though this study is a little dated nowadays. Zuzana M. Pick, *The New Latin American Cinema: A Continental Project* (Austin: University of Texas Press, 1993) is well-researched and authoritative. José Agustín Mahieu, *Panorama del cine iberoamericano* (Madrid: Ediciones de Cultura Hispánica, 1990), offers general observations on the cinema of the various countries without getting into too much detail. A well-informed, thumbnail sketch of the history of Latin American cinema is provided by Paulo Antonio Paranaguá, *O Cinema na América Latina: longe de Deus e perto de Hollywood* (São Paolo: L&PM Editores, 1984). Augusto Martínez Torres and Manuel Pérez Estremera, *Nuevo cine latinoamericano* (Madrid: Anagrama, 1973), has brief chapters on the development of cinema in Argentina, Bolivia, Brazil, Chile, Colombia, Cuba, Mexico, Peru, Uruguay and Venezuela. *Changing Reels: Latin American Cinema Against the Odds*, ed. Bob Rix (Leeds: Trinity and All Saints' College, 2000), is a collection of essays on national traditions as well as various film directors such as Degregori and Subielo. *Mediating Two Worlds: Cinematic Encounters in the Americas*, eds John King, Ana M. López and Manuel Alvarado (London: BFI, 1993), is an excellent collection of essays on Brazilian, Mexican, Cuban and Argentine cinema. The three volumes of *Hojas de cine: testimonios y documentos del nuevo cine latinoamericano* (Mexico City: Fundación Mexicana de Cineastas, 1988), is an indispensable collection of theoretical and historical essays on the New Latin American Cinema movement. *New Latin American Cinema: Volume One: Theory, Practices and Transcontinental Articulations*, ed. Michael T. Martin (Detroit: Wayne State University, 1997), is a helpful collection of some very important theoretical pieces on Latin American cinema ranging from Glauber Rocha's essay on 'an aesthetic of hunger' to Julio García Espinosa's foundational essay on the notion of 'imperfect cinema'. For background on the Viña del Mar festivals Aldo Francia's *Nuevo Cine Latinoamericano en Viña del Mar* (Santiago: CRAN, 1990), is very helpful. *Cinema and Social Change in Latin America: Conversations with Filmmakers*, ed. Julianne Burton (Austin: University of Texas Press, 1986), is an excellent compilation of interviews with, *inter alia*, Sanjinés, Guzmán, Gutiérrez Alea, Solás, and García Espinosa. Some basic information about female film directors is provided by Concha Irazábal Martín in her study, *La otra América: directoras de cine de América Latina y el caribe* (Madrid: HORAS, 2002). *La memoria filmada: América Latina a través de su cine*, eds María Dolores Pérez Murillo and David Fernández Fernández (Madrid: IELPA, 2002), contains a wide selection of essays of varying quality. *Latin American Cinema, Film and History*, ed. E. Bradford Burns (Los Angeles: UCLA Latin American Center, 1975), is an intriguing early appraisal of a selection of films, including two essays on Sanjinés. Taking a leaf out of Burns's book, but doing a much better job at elucidating the interface between film and history, is *Based on a True Story: Latin American History at the Movies*, ed. Donald F. Stevens (Wilmington, Delaware: Scholarly Resources, 1997); highly recommended. *The Cinema of Latin America*, eds Alberto Elena and Marina Díaz López (London: Wallflower, 2003), is a helfpul collection of essays including discussion of, *inter alia*, *Los olvidados*, *Memorias del subdesarrollo* and *Amores perros*. *Visible Nations: Latin American Cinema and Video*, ed. Chon A. Noriega (Minneapolis: University of Minnesota Press, 2000) offers a collection of essays addressing the connections between Latin American film and the new media.

An excellent overview of Argentine cinema is provided by David William Foster in his *Contemporary Argentine Cinema* (Columbia, MI: University of Missouri Press, 1992). *The Garden of Forking Paths: Argentine Cinema*, eds John King and Nissa Torrents (London: BFI, 1988), is a collection of essays which offers an insightful snap-snot of Argentine cinema in the 1980s. Details on more than 2,000 Argentine films are found in Raúl Manrupe and María Alejandra Portela's *Un diccionario de films argentinos (1930–1995)* (Buenos Aires: Corregidor, 2001). A basic overview of Bolivian cinema is provided by Carlos D. Mesa Gisbert in his study, *La aventura del cine bolivianao 1952–1985* (La Paz: Editorial Gisbert, 1985). More recent coverage is provided by José Sánchez-H. in his authoritative *The Art and Politics of Bolivian Cinema* (Lanham: Scarecrow Press, 1999). For Brazilian cinema the reader is referred to Randal Johnson and Robert Stam's *Brazilian Cinema* (East Brunswick, NJ: Associated University Presses, 1982) which combines a general history of the cinema with a helpful selection of manifestoes relating to *cinema novo*, and some insightful analyses of a selection of films; indispensable. Randall Johnson, *The Film Industry in Brazil: Culture and the State* (Pittsburgh: University of Pittsburgh Press, 1987), has separate chapters on *cinema novo* and Embrafilme. The same author provides an authoritative study of Brazilian New Cinema in his *Cinema Novo times 5: Masters of Contemporary Brazilian Film* (Austin: University of Texas Press, 1984). Two other important books on Brazilian cinema are David E. Neves, *Cinema Novo No Brasil* (Petrópolis: Vozes, 1966), and Glauber Rocha, *Revisión crítica del cine brasileño* (Madrid: Fundamentos, 1971). Worth consulting for studies on contemporary films is Lúcia Nagib (ed.), *The New Brazilian Cinema* (London: Tauris, 2003). David William Foster focuses on the portrayal of gender in modern Brazilian film in his ground-breaking study, *Gender and Society in Contemporary Brazilian Cinema* (Austin: University of Texas Press, 1999), though, unfortunately, there are no studies of the films included in this book. For a study of the early years of Chilean cinema, see Alicia Vega, *Re-visión del cine chileno* (Santiago: CENECA, 1979), and Carlos Ossa Coo, *La historia del cine chileno* (Santiago: Quimantu, 1971). Hernando Martínez Pardo, *Historia del cine colombiano* (Bogotá: América Latina, 1978), is a basic history of the early period of Colombian cinema. The classic study on Cuban cinema is Michael Chanan's *The Cuban Image* (London: BFI, 1985); highly recommended. An interesting point of comparison for Cuban film is provided by the study of English-language and French-language films in *Ex-Iles: Essays on Caribbean Cinema*, ed. Mbye Cham (Trenton, NJ: Africa World Press, 1992). For an overview of the cinema of the Dominican Republic see José Luis Saez, *Historia de un sueño importado* (Santo Domingo: Siboney, 1983). Carl J. Mora, *Mexican Cinema: Reflections of a Society 1896–1980* (Berkeley: University of California Press, 1982) is the classic study of Mexican cinema from its origins until the 1980s. An detailed overview including coverage of more recent films is provided by Emilio García Riera, *Breve historia del cine mexicano: primer siglo 1897–1997* (Mexico City: Instituto Mexicano de Cinematografía, 1998). Other important collections of essays on Mexican cinema are *Mexico's Cinema: A Century of Film and Filmmakers*, eds Joanne Hershfield and David R. Maciel (Wilmington, Delaware: Scholarly Resources, 1999), and *Mexican Cinema*, ed. Paulo Antonio Paranaguá, trans. Ana M. López (London: BFI, 1995). David William Foster has a very informative analysis of various filmic portrayals of Mexico City in his *Mexico City in Contemporary Mexican Cinema* (Austin: University of Texas Press, 2002). For a history of Peruvian film the reader is referred to Ricardo Bedoya, *100 años de cine en el Perú: una historia crítica* (Lima: Universidad de Lima, 1992). *Historia y filmografía del cine uruguayo*, ed. Eugenio Hintz (Montevideo: Ediciones de la Plaza, 1988), is mainly on the roots of Uruguayan cinema. Number 33 of the review, *Cuadernos de Cine*, is a collection of essays by leading film directors and theoreticians entitled *El Nuevo Cine Latinoamericano en el Mundo de Hoy* (Mexico City: UNAM, 1988). Volume 13 of the journal, *Iris*, entitled 'Latin American Cinema/Le cinéma latino-américain' (Summer 1991) has essays on Mexican and Brazilian cinema as well as more general essays on Latin American cinema. *Contemporary Latin American Cultural Studies*, edited by Stephen M. Hart and Richard Young (London: Arnold, 2003), has some essays on film, including Geoffrey Kantaris's 'The Young and the Damned: Street Vision in Latin American Cinema' (pp. 177–89), which analyses *Los olvidados*, *Pixote*, and *Amores perros*, Robert Stam's 'Brazilian Cinema: Reflections on Race and Representation' (pp. 203–14), which offers an important overview of the way race is portrayed in Brazilian cinema, and Stephen M. Hart's 'Mama Coca and the Revolution: Jorge Sanjinés's Double Take' (pp. 290–9), which compares *Yawar Mallku* with one of Sanjinés's more recent films.

Two excellent general studies on Buñuel with separate chapters on *Los olvidados* are Gwynne Edwards, *The Discreet Art of Luis Buñuel: A Reading of his Films* (London: Marion Boyars, 1983), and Peter Evans, '*Los olvidados* and the "Uncanny"', in *The Films of Luis Buñuel: Subjectivity and Desire* (Oxford: OUP, 1995), pp. 72–89. *Luis Buñuel: New Readings*, ed. Peter Evans (London: BFI, 2004), contains essays on Buñuel's Mexican period. The best study on Sanjinés's film is Ariel Gamboa, *El cine de Jorge Sanjinés* (Santa Cruz, Bolivia: Landivar, 1999); collects important reviews on his work, as well as significant essays by Sanjinés. *An Argentine Passion: María Luisa Bemberg and her Films*, edited by John King, Sheila Whitaker, and Rosa Bosch (London: Verso, 2000), is a collection of well-written essays on Bemberg's major films. The *Revista*

Canadiense de Estudios Hispánicos brought out a special number on Bemberg entitled 'María Luisa Bemberg: entre lo político y lo personal' (Vol. XXVII, no. 1, Autumn 2002). Janet Giannotti, *A Companion Text for Like Water for Chocolate* (Ann Arbor, MI: The University of Michigan Press, 1999), is rather basic, but has some helpful background information on the film. Paul Julian Smith's *Amores perros* (London: BFI, 2003), is a sophisticated reading of González Iñárritu's blockbuster.

There are a number of helpful websites which are well worth consulting, including the Awards Database of the Academy of Motion Picture Arts and Sciences in Hollywood, which lists all the nominees and Oscar winners for the different categories (www.awardsdatabase.oscars.org), the corresponding web-site for the Cannes International Film Festival (www.festival-cannes.fr/archives), the BAFTA awards (www.imdb.com/Sections/Awards/BAFTA_Awards/2000), the Venice Film Festival (www.imdb.com/Sections/Awards/Venice_Film_Festival), the Berlin Film Festival (www.berlinale.de), the San Sebastián Film Festival (www.sansebastianfestival.ya.com/2003/es/index.htm), the Sundance Film Festival (www.sundance.org), and the Moscow International Film Festival (www.miff.ru/eng/history). A quite handy selection of reviews of various films is offered on the 'rottentomatoes' website (www.rottentomatoes.com) (all last consulted on 6 January 2004).

GLOSSARY

auteur: film director whose work shows a consistency of style and theme and demonstrates originality in its vision of the world

cinematic identification: process whereby the viewer is encouraged to identity with one or two characters in a film, seeing the character's problems, dilemmas, success, as his/her own

continuity editing: the stitching together of various shots in order to create the illusion of a self-contained unity of space and time from these separate fragments

deep focus photography: camerawork which allows several planes (namely, foreground, medium ground, and background) to be kept in focus at the same time

diegetic sound: sound whose origin is located in the story world (see external diegetic sound and internal diegetic sound)

dissolve: one scene dissolving into the next; originally associated with the flashback, it more recently marks an overlapping between two different episodes

documentary: film in which the director observes and makes an objective record of real events; conventionally there are seen to be five types of documentary: expository, observational, interactive, reflexive, and performative

editing: breaking down a scene into a multitude of shots

external diegetic sound: sound which has a physical origin in the story world, such as the sound of a character's voice, the sound of a car going along the road, etc.

eyeline match: coherence between two shots based on a line of vision; for example, if a character in one shot glances at something off-screen, and the next shot provides a close-up of what he was looking at, then we have an eyeline match

internal diegetic sound: sound which originates from inside a character's mind, such as the rendition of a character's thoughts in voice-over

long take: a shot of long duration from one camera which has not been cut by the director; the maximum long take is ten minutes (the length of a camera reel)

mindscreen: camerawork which allows the viewer to adopt the perspective and emphases of a character in a film; these are implicit shots which allow us to adopt the character's perspective but not necessarily his POV mise-en-scène: literally, 'putting on stage', or 'staging', this term covers the filmed events as well as the way in which they are filmed, including set design, lighting, character movement, camera angle, and framing

montage: the juxtaposition of shots, which are sometimes quite different from each other, and which creates symbolic associations; favoured by Sergei Eisenstein

non-diegetic sound: sound which derives from outside the story world, such as the film's music soundtrack

off-screen: a reality which is out of the frame, but to which the characters respond (such as a gunshot, or a person they apparently see but which the viewer doesn't)

omniscient narration: style of filmic presentation whereby the viewer has a God-like awarness of what is going on in the story

POV, or point of view: refers to a type of shot which shows us an object from a specific character's optical vantage point, thereby allowing the viewer to share the character's eyes

realism: a style of filming in which the image must preserve the impression of reality

reaction shot: camera shot which shows how a character reacts to an event rather than what he or she sees; often used in terror films to indicate how a character reacts when first seeing the monster, or alien, etc.

restricted narration: style of filmic presentation whereby the viewer only experiences those parts of the narrative that one particular character experiences; the viewer thereby has limited access to the events depicted on screen

transparency: a style of filming in which the best technique is that which is not noticed, as championed by the French theorist, André Bazin

SELECT BIBLIOGRAPHY

Arijon, Daniel, *Grammar of the Film Language* (Beverley Hills, CA: Silman-James Press, 1976).

Armes, Roy, *French Cinema*, 3rd ed. (London: Secker and Warburg, 1985).

Arroyo, José, 'Amores perros', *Sight and Sound* (May 2001), 39–40.

Aumont, Jacques, and Alain Bergala, Michel Mairie, Marc Vernet, *Aesthetics of Film*, translated and revised by Richard Neupert (Austin: University of Texas Press, 1992).

Barnard, Timothy, 'La frontera', in *South American Cinema: A Critical Filmography 1915–1994*, eds Timothy Barnard and Peter Rist (Austin: University of Texas Press, 1996), pp. 241–2.

——, and Peter Rist (eds), *South American Cinema: A Critical Filmography 1915–1994* (Austin: University of Texas Press, 1996).

Bedoya, Ricardo, *100 años de cine en el Perú: una historia crítica* (Lima: Universidad de Lima, 1992).

Bejel, Emilio, '*Strawberry and Chocolate*: Coming out of the Cuban Closet', *The South Atlantic Quarterly*, 96.1 (1997), 65–82.

Bemberg, María Luisa , 'Somos la mitad del mundo', *Cine Cubano*, 132 (July–August 1991), 11–17.

Bergmann, Emilie, 'Abjection and Ambiguity: Lesbian Desire in Bemberg's *Yo, la peor de todas*', in *Hispanisms and Homosexualities*, eds Sylvia Molloy and Robert McKee Irwin (Durham: Duke University Press, 1998), pp. 229–47.

Birri, Fernando, 'Cinema and Underdevelopment', in *Twenty-Five Years of the New Latin American Cinema*, ed. Michael Chanan (London: BFI, 1983), pp. 9–12.

Bradshaw, Peter, 'The Collar of Money', *The Guardian* (18 May 2001), pp. 12–13.

Branche, Jerome, 'Barbarism and Civilisation: Taking on History *in The Last Supper*', *The Afro-Latino Forum*, 1.1 (1997), 9 pp. Occasional Papers published by the African American Studies and Research Program and the Latin American Studies and Research Program, University of Kentucky, College of Arts and Sciences.

Braudy, Leo, and Marshall Cohen, *Film Theory and Criticism: Introductory Readings* (Oxford: OUP, 1999).

Buckland, Warren, *Film Studies* (London: Hodder and Stoughton, 1998).

Burns, E. Bradford (ed.), *Latin American Cinema, Film and History* (Los Angeles: UCLA Latin American Center, 1975).

Burton, Julianne (ed.), *Cinema and Social Change in Latin America: Conversations with Filmmakers* (Austin: University of Texas Press, 1986).

Cham, Mbye (ed.), *Ex-Iles: Essays on Caribbean Cinema* (Trenton, NJ: Africa World Press, 1992).

Chanan, Michael, *The Cuban Image* (London: BFI, 1985).

——, (ed.), *Twenty-Five Years of the New Latin American Cinema* (London: BFI, 1983).

Chanan, Michael, 'Cuban Cinema in the 1990s', in *Changing Reels: Latin American Cinema Against the Odds*, ed. Bob Rix (Leeds: Trinity and All Saints College, 1998), pp. 1–15.

Chatman, Seymour, 'What Novels Can Do that Films Can't (and Vice-versa)', in Leo Braudy and Marshall Cohen, *Film Theory and Criticism: Introductory Readings* (Oxford: OUP, 1999), pp. 435–51.

Davies, Catherine, 'Recent Cuban Fiction Films: Identification, Interpretation, Disorder', *Bulletin of Latin American Research*, 15.2 (1996), 177–92.

Edwards, Gwynne, *The Discreet Art of Luis Buñuel: A Reading of his Films* (London: Marion Boyars, 1983).

El Nuevo Cine Latinoamericano en el Mundo de Hoy (Mexico City: UNAM, 1988).

Elena, Alberto, and Marina Díaz López (eds), *The Cinema of Latin America* (London: Wallflower, 2003).

Evans, Peter, *The Films of Luis Buñuel: Subjectivity and Desire* (Oxford: OUP, 1995).

——, (ed.), *Luis Buñuel: New Readings* (London: BFI, 2004).

Évora, José Antonio, *Tomás Gutiérrez Alea* (Madrid: Cátedra, 1996).

Fornet, Ambrosio (ed.), *Alea: una retrospectiva crítica* (Havana: Letras Cubanas, 1987).

Foster, David William, *Contemporary Argentine Cinema* (Columbia, MI: University of Missouri Press, 1992).

——, *Gender and Society in Contemporary Brazilian Cinema* (Austin: University of Texas Press, 1999).

——, *Mexico City in Contemporary Mexican Cinema* (Austin: University of Texas Press, 2002).

Francia, Aldo, *Nuevo Cine Latinoamericano en Viña del Mar* (Santiago: CRAN, 1990).

Gamboa, Ariel, *El cine de Jorge Sanjinés* (Santa Cruz, Bolivia: Landivar, 1999).

García Espinosa, Julio, 'For an Imperfect Cinema', in *Twenty-Five Years of the New Latin American Cinema*, ed. Michael Chanan (London: BFI, 1983), pp. 28–33.

García Riera, Emilio, *Breve historia del cine mexicano: primer siglo 1897–1997* (Mexico City: Instituto Mexicano de Cinematografía, 1998).

Geduld, Harry M., and Ronald Gottesman (eds), *Sergei Eisenstein and Upton Sinclair: The Making and Unmaking of ¡Qué viva México!* (Bloomington, IN: Indiana University Press, 1970).

Giannotti, Janet, *A Companion Text for* Like Water for Chocolate (Ann Arbor, MI: The University of Michigan Press, 1999).

González, Eduardo, 'La rama dorada y el árbol deshojado: reflexiones sobre *Fresa y chocolate* y sus antecedentes', in *Estudios Iberoamérica y el cine*, ed. Francisco Lasarte & Guido Podestá (Amsterdam: Rodopi, 1996), pp. 65–78.

Gutiérrez Alea, Tomás, *Dialéctica del espectador* (Havana: Unión de Escritores y Artistas de Cuba, 1982).

——, 'The Viewer's Dialectic', in *New Latin American Cinema: Volume One: Theory, Practices and Transcontinental Articulations*, ed. Michael T. Martin (Detroit: Wayne State University, 1997), pp. 108–31.

Hart, Stephen M., *A Companion to Spanish-American Literature* (London: Tamesis, 1999).

——, *Reading Magic Realism from Latin America* (London: Bloomsbury, 2001). ISBN: 0747556202. Internet book.

——, 'The Art of Invasion in Jorge Sanjinés's *Para recibir el canto del pájaro*', *Journal of Hispanic Research*, 3.1 (2002), 71–81.

Hart, Stephen M., 'Bemberg's Winks and Camila's Sighs: Melodramatic Encryption in *Camila*', *Revista Canadiense de Estudios Hispánicos*, XXVII.1 (2002), 75–85.

——, 'Mama Coca and the Revolution: Jorge Sanjinés's Double-Take', in *Contemporary Latin American Cultural Studies*, eds Stephen Hart and Richard Young (London: Arnold, 2003), pp. 290–9.

——, 'Luis Buñuel's Box of Subaltern Tricks: Technique in *Los olvidados*', in *Luis Buñuel: New Readings*, ed. Peter Evans (London: BFI, 2004), pp. 65–79.

——, and Richard Young (eds), *Contemporary Latin American Cultural Studies* (London: Arnold, 2003).

Hayward, Susan, *Key Concepts in Cinema Studies* (London: Routledge, 1996).

Hennebelle, Guy, and Alfonso Gumucio-Dagrón, *Les Cinémas de l'Amérique latine* (Paris: Pierre L'Herminier, 1981).

Hershfield, Joanne, and David R. Maciel (eds), *Mexico's Cinema: A Century of Film and Filmmakers* (Wilmington, Delaware: Scholarly Resources, 1999).

Hess, John, 'Neo-Realism, and New Latin American Cinema: *Bicycle Thieves* and *Blood of the Condor*', in *Mediating Two Worlds*, eds John King, Ana López and Manuel Alvarado (London: BFI, 1993), pp. 104–18.

Hintz, Eugenio (ed.), *Historia y filmografía del cine uruguayo* (Montevideo: Ediciones de la Plaza, 1988).

Hojas de cine: testimonios y documentos del nuevo cine latinoamericano (Mexico City: Fundación Mexicana de Cineastas, 1988), 3 volumes.

Ibsen, Kristine, 'On Recipes, Reading and Revolution: Postboom Comedy in *Como agua para chocolate*', *Hispanic Review*, 63 (1995), 133–46.

Irazábal Martín, Concha, *La otra América: directoras de cine de América Latina y el caribe* (Madrid: HORAS, 2002).

Johnson, Randal, *Cinema Novo times 5: Masters of Contemporary Brazilian Film* (Austin: University of Texas Press, 1984).

——, *The Film Industry in Brazil: Culture and the State* (Pittsburgh: University of Pittsburgh Press, 1987).

——, 'The *Romance-Reportagem* and the Cinema: Babenco's *Lúcio Flávio* and *Pixote*', *Luso-Brazilian Review*, 24.2 (1987), 35–48.

——, and Robert Stam, *Brazilian Cinema* (East Brunswick, NJ: Associated University Presses, 1982).

Johnson, Trevor, 'Dog Fights, car crashes, love – that's life down Mexico way', *The Independent on Sunday* (6 May 2001), p. 2.

Kantaris, Geoffrey, 'The Young and the Damned: Street Visions in Latin American Cinema', in *Contemporary Latin American Cultural Studies*, eds Stephen Hart and Richard Young (London: Arnold, 2003), pp. 177–89.

Kaplan, Nina, 'Central Station', *Sight and Sound* (March 1999), 38–9.

King, John, *Magical Reels: A History of Cinema in Latin America* (London: Verso, 1990). Re-issued in 2000.

——, and Nissa Torrents (eds), *The Garden of Forking Paths: Argentine Cinema* (London: BFI, 1988).

——, Ana M. López and Manuel Alvarado (eds), *Mediating Two Worlds: Cinematic Encounters in the Americas* (London: BFI, 1993).

——, Sheila Whitaker, and Rosa Bosch (eds), *An Argentine Passion: María Luisa Bemberg and her Films* (London: Verso, 2000).

Kraniauskas, John, '*Como agua para chocolate*', *Sight and Sound*, 2.10 (1993), 42–3.

Kristal, Efraín, 'The Incest Motif in Narratives of the United States and Spanish America', in *Internationalität nationaler Literaturen: Beiträge zum ersten Symposium des Göttinger Sonderforschungbereichs 529*, ed. Udo Schöning (Berlin: Wallstein, 2002), pp. 390–403.

Lehman, Peter, and William Luhr, *Thinking about Movies: Watching, Questioning, Enjoying* (Oxford: Blackwell, 2003).

Levine, Robert M., 'Fiction and Reality in Brazilian Life', in *Based on a True Story: Latin American History at the Movies*, ed. Donald F. Stevens (Wilmington, Delaware: Scholarly Resources, 1997), pp. 201–14.

Leyda, Jan, *Kino: A History of the Russian and Soviet Cinema*, 3rd ed. (Princeton, NJ: Princeton University Press, 1983).

Lillo, Gaston & Monique Sarfati-Arnaud, '*Como agua para chocolate*: determina-ciones de la lectura en el contexto posmoderno', *Revista Canadiense de Estudios Hispánicos*, XX.1 (1994), 479–90.

Littín, Miguel, 'El cine latinoamericano y su público', in *El Nuevo Cine Latinoamericano en el mundo de hoy* (Mexico City: UNAM, 1988), pp. 41–6.

Mahieu, José Agustín, *Panorama del cine iberoamericano* (Madrid: Ediciones de Cultura Hispánica, 1990).

Manrupe, Raúl, and María Alejandra Portela, *Un diccionario de films argentinos (1930–1995)* (Buenos Aires: Corregidor, 2001).

Martin, Michael T. (ed.), *New Latin American Cinema: Volume One: Theory, Practices and Transcontinental Articulations* (Detroit: Wayne State University, 1997).

——, and Bruce Paddington, 'Restoration or Innovation: An Interview with Humberto Solás: Post-Revolutionary Cuban Cinema', *Film Quarterly*, 54.3 (Spring 2001), 2–13.

Martínez Pardo, Hernando, *Historia del cine colombiano* (Bogotá: América Latina, 1978).

Mesa Gisbert, Carlos D., *La aventura del cine bolivianao 1952–1985* (La Paz: Editorial Gisbert, 1985).

Miller, Denise, 'María Luisa Bemberg's Interpretation of Octavio Paz's *Sor Juana*', in *An Argentine Passion: María Luisa Bemberg and her Films*, eds John King, Sheila Whitaker, Rosa Bosch (London: Verso, 2000), pp. 137–73.

Miller, Toby, and Robert Stam (eds), *A Companion to Film Theory* (Oxford: Blackwell, 2004).

Monsiváis, Carlos, 'Mythologies', in *Mexican Cinema*, ed. Paulo Antonio Paranaguá, trans. Ana M. López (London: BFI, 1995), pp. 117–27.

Mora, Carl J., *Mexican Cinema: Reflections of a Society 1896–1980* (Berkeley: University of California Press, 1982).

Mraz, John, 'Recasting Cuban Slavery: *The Other Francisco* and *The Last Supper*', in *Based on a True Story: Latin American History at the Movies*, ed. Donald F. Stevens (Wilmington, Delaware: SR Books, 1997), pp. 103–22.

Nagib, Lúcia (ed.), *The New Brazilian Cinema* (London: Tauris, 2003).

Neves, David E., *Cinema Novo No Brasil* (Petrópolis: Vozes, 1966).

Noriega, Chon A. (ed.), *Visible Nations: Latin American Cinema and Video* (Minneapolis: University of Minnesota Press, 2000).

Ossa Coo, Carlos, *La historia del cine chileno* (Santiago: Quimantu, 1971).

Paranaguá, Paulo Antonio, *O Cinema na América Latina: longe de Deus e perto de Hollywood* (São Paolo: L&PM Editores, 1984).

——, (ed.), *Mexican Cinema*, trans. Ana M. López (London: BFI, 1995).

Patterson, John, 'Aztec Cameras', *The Guardian* (18 May 2001), p. 11.

Pérez Murillo, María Dolores, and David Fernández Fernández (eds), *La memoria filmada: América Latina a través de su cine* (Madrid: IELPA, 2002).

Pérez Soler, Bernardo, 'Pup Fiction', *Sight and Sound* (May 2001), pp. 29–30.

Pick, Zuzana M., *The New Latin American Cinema: A Continental Project* (Austin: University of Texas Press, 1993).

Podalsky, Laura, 'Affecting Legacies: Historical Memory and Contemporary Structures of Feeling in *Madagascar* and *Amores perros*', *Screen*, 44.3 (Autumn 2003), 277–94.

Potvin, Claude, '*Como agua para chocolate*: ¿parodia o cliché?', *Revista Canadiense de Estudios Hispánicos*, XX.1 (1995), 55–67.

Ramírez, Susan E., '*I, The Worst of All*: The Literary Life of Sor Juana Inés de la Cruz', in *Based on a True Story: Latin American History at the Movies*, ed. Donald F. Stevens (Wilmington, Delaware: Scholarly Resources, 1997), pp. 47–62.

Resik, Magda, 'Interview with Senel Paz', *The South Atlantic Quarterly*, 96.1 (1997), 83–93.

Rist, Peter, 'Orfeu Negro', in *South American Cinema: A Critical Filmography 1915–1994*, eds Timothy Barnard and Peter Rist (Austin: University of Texas Press, 1996), pp. 123–5.

Rix, Bob (ed.), *Changing Reels: Latin American Cinema Against the Odds* (Leeds: Trinity and All Saints' College, 2000).

Rocha, Glauber, *Revisión crítica del cine brasileño* (Madrid: Fundamentos, 1971).

——, 'The Aesthetics of Hunger', in *Twenty-Five Years of the New Latin American Cinema*, ed. Michael Chanan (London: BFI, 1983), pp. 13–14.

Rodríguez, Omar A., 'Poder, institución y género en *Yo, la peor de todas*', *Revista Canadiense de Estudios Hispánicos*, XXVII, 1 (2002), 139–56.

Ruffinelli, Jorge, 'De una *Camila* a otra: historia, literatura y cine', in *Estudios Iberoamérica y el cine*, ed. Francisco Lasarte & Guido Podestá (Amsterdam: Rodopi, 1996), pp. 11–25.

——, *Patricio Guzmán* (Madrid: Cátedra, 2001).

Saez, José Luis, *Historia de un sueño importado* (Santo Domingo: Siboney, 1983).

Sánchez-H., José, *The Art and Politics of Bolivian Cinema* (Lanham: Scarecrow Press, 1999).

Sanjinés, Jorge, 'Problems of Form and Content in Revolutionary Cinema', in *Twenty-Five Years of the New Latin American Cinema*, ed. Michael Chanan (London: BFI, 1983), pp. 34–8.

Santí, Enrico Mario, '*Fresa y chocolate*: The Rhetoric of Cuban Reconciliation', *Modern Language Notes*, 113 (1998), 407–25.

Sarabia, Rosa, 'Sor Juana o las trampas de la restitución', *Revista Canadiense de Estudios Hispánicos*, XXVII, 1 (2002), 119–38.

Schnitman, Jorge A., *Film Industries in Latin America: Dependency and Development* (Norwood, NJ: ABLEX, 1984).

Schroeder, Paul A., *Tomás Gutiérrez Alea: The Dialectics of a Filmmaker* (London: Routledge, 2002).

Segre, Erica, '"La desnacionalización de la pantalla": Mexican Cinema in the 1990s', in *Changing Reels: Latin American Cinema Againsts the Odds*, eds Rob Rix and Roberto Rodríguez-Saona (Leeds: Trinity and All Saints' College, 1997), pp. 33–57.

Seton, Marie, *Sergei M. Eisenstein* (London: Dennis Dobson, 1978).

Shaw, Deborah, *Contemporary Cinema of Latin America: 10 Key Films* (London: Continuum, 2003).

Simens, Dov S-S, 'Two-Day FilmSchool', Raindance, London, 29–30 November 2003.

Smith, Paul Julian, '*Fresa y chocolate*: Cinema as Guided Tour', in *Visions Machines* (London: Verso, 1996), pp. 81–98.

——, *Amores perros* (London: BFI, 2003).

——, 'City of God', *Sight and Sound* (January 2003), 38–9.

Solanas, Fernando and Octavio Getino, 'Towards a Third Cinema', in *Twenty-Five Years of the New Latin American Cinema*, ed. Michael Chanan (London: BFI, 1983), pp. 17–27.

Stam, Robert, *Film Theory: An Introduction* (Oxford: Blackwell, 2003).

Standish, Peter (ed.), *Dictionary of Twentieth-Century Culture: Hispanic Culture of South America* (Detroit, MI: Gale Research Inc., 1995).

——, (ed.), *Dictionary of Twentieth-Century Culture: Hispanic Culture of Mexico, Central America, and the Caribbean* (Detroit, MI: Gale Research Inc., 1996).

Stevens, Donald F. (ed.), *Based on a True Story: Latin American History at the Movies* (Wilmington, Delaware: Scholarly Resources, 1997).

Strick, Philip, 'El viaje', *Sight and Sound* (September 1993), 54–5.

Szuchman, Mark D., 'Depicting the Past in Argentine Films: Family Drama and Historical debate in *Miss Mary* and *The Official Story*', in *Based on a True Story: Latin American History at the Movies*, ed. Donald F. Stevens (Wilmington, Delaware: Scholarly Resources, 1997), pp. 173–200.

Tenenbaum, Barbara A., 'Why Tita Didn't Marry the Doctor, or Mexican History in *Like Water for Chocolate*', in *Based on a True Story: Latin American History at the Movies*, ed. Donald F. Stevens (Wilmington, Delaware: Scholarly Resources, 1997), pp. 157–72.

Tiemey, Dolores, 'The 24th International New Latin American Film Festival', *Screen*, 44.3 (Autumn 2003), 333–6.

Torres, Augusto Martínez, and Manuel Pérez Estremera, *Nuevo cine latinoamericano* (Madrid: Anagrama, 1973).

Vega, Alicia, *Re-visión del cine chileno* (Santiago: CENECA, 1979).

Villagra, Nelson, 'The Actor at Home and in Exile', in *Cinema and Social Change in Latin America: Conversation with Filmmakers*, ed. Julianne Burton (Austin: University of Texas Press, 1986), pp. 211–19.

West, Dennis, 'Strawberry and Chocolate, Ice Cream and Tolerance: Interviews with Tomás Gutiérrez Alea and Juan Carlos Tabío', *Cineaste*, 21.1–2 (1995), 16–20.

——, 'Filming the Chicano Family Saga: Interview with Director Gregory Nava', *Cineaste*, 21.4 (1995), 26–9.

Wilkinson, Stephen, 'Homosexuality and the Repression of Intellectuals in *Fresa y chocolate* and *Máscaras*', *Bulletin of Latin American Research*, 18.1 (1999), 17–33.

Wu, Harmony W., 'Consuming Tacos and Enchiladas: Gender and the Nation in *Como agua para chocolate*', in *Visible Nations: Latin American Cinema and Video*, ed. Chon A. Noriega (Minneapolis: University of Minnesota Press, 2000), pp. 174–92.

Xavier, Ismail, 'Historical Allegory', in *A Companion to Film Theory*, eds Toby Miller and Robert Stam (Oxford: Blackwell, 2004), pp. 333–62.

——, 'Angels with Dirty Faces', *Sight and Sound* (January 2003), 28–30.

Young, Robert J.C., *Postcolonialism: An Historical Introduction* (Oxford: Blackwell, 2003).

Index

Lightning Source UK Ltd.
Milton Keynes UK
UKOW06f2156150816

280758UK00001B/29/P